American
Pilgrim

Roosh Valizadeh

Contents

Introduction 1

1: Icons 5

2: Birds 27

3: Garden 47

4: Christians.. 63

5: Guidance... 79

6: Miracle 95

7: Lust... 109

8: Demons 125

9: Mountains 143

10: Photographs.. 157

11: Homestead 171

12: Temptation 191

13: Decline.. 209

14: Immigrants... 223

15: Pride... 233

16: Prison.. 245

17: Signs... 259

18: Megachurch 267

19: Race.. 277

20: Exorcism... 285

21: Country... 297

22: Apostasy 309

23: Home 321

Epilogue 337

Appendix.. 349

Introduction

I wasted my life. My achievements and accomplishments were all for nothing. Why did my younger sister die and not me? I wanted to go to sleep and not wake up again, to stop the pain.

I didn't start going through puberty until I was 18. I looked like a child when all my male peers looked like young men. Girls were not interested in me, and even if they had been, I lacked the confidence or masculinity to pursue them. When I entered college, I was 5'6", and within a couple of years I grew eight inches, yet I still had the mentality of a naïve boy. I strongly desired to be intimate with women, but I did not know how to go about it, and attempting to be friends with them first, as a way to ease into a sexual relationship, wasn't working. My frustration and anger increased steadily alongside my desires.

My Armenian mother and Iranian father immigrated to the United States in the early 1970s. They quickly discarded their respective cultures so that their children could be filled with the American dream, untainted by the obsolete traditions of the old world. Television and movies were my guides. Public school teachers were my elders. Men's lifestyle magazines were my scriptures. My parents allowed the culture to take me. It taught me that this world is all there is, and the key to happiness is to gain delights from the world, particularly sex, money, and status. I wanted all three, and when I graduated from university with a degree in microbiology in 2001, I dedicated my life to the things which I could attain through my own power and will.

Sex was first. I stumbled upon the internet pickup artist community, which taught that a man could walk up to any woman he wanted, build attraction through his social skills or appearance, and take her to bed. Without the need for existing social connections or even good intentions, this "game" seemed almost like magic, allowing me to conjure sexual pleasure from nothing. Once I started applying game and getting it to work, the high it gave me surpassed all other joys I had experienced in life, and I'm not sure whether that was due to the physical pleasure from sex or the ego gratification from conquering a different woman's body through the artificial interaction I had with her. I ignored the fact that I was pretending to be a masculine man and lying during every pickup, at the very least through omission, but who cared? I was winning at life and gaining sexual pleasure. I was achieving the prize I had always wanted. After six years, I quit my job as a microbiologist to feed my disordered passions full time.

I got better at pickup and started writing about my techniques online. As they say, sex sells, and it was no surprise that I built up a large following of men who were eager to try out my teachings so that they could "win at life" just like I was. In 2007, I codified my game into a book called *Bang*. To teach by example, I wrote numerous "field reports" of how I bedded this woman or that while including all the pornographic details. Now that I was no longer tethered to a physical place of work, I hit the road, traveling from one country to the next to write many more books about foreign women which invariably had "bang" in the title so that no one would be confused as to what my life's work was about. My fornication was a career and a brand that exalted me among men.

My skills increased and my reputation continued to grow as I started to dissect not just American women but women from all over the world. I built a network of websites that—at its peak— were receiving over one million unique visitors a month. Tens of thousands of men used my books, newsletters, and online resources to satisfy their lusts, and since my *Bang* books were among the first sex guides published on the Amazon Kindle platform, I reaped lofty monetary rewards, much more than I had earned as a microbiologist. Then the media came knocking, producing articles and video segments. I relished in the notoriety of being a "sexist" and "misogynist" who used contrived techniques to get women into bed. I took advantage of every hit piece against me to drive more traffic to my websites and increase sales of my books. My sex life was active, I was recognized on the streets by men who admired me, and my bank account was full of money. I had fulfilled my dream and even surpassed it, but I noticed the highs were becoming less intense and lasting for shorter amounts of time. My early sexual conquests would give me a buzz for days, but now they lasted for mere minutes. Trying to increase the high through traveling to another country or doing a pickup in a foreign language did the trick for a while until it no longer did. My dissatisfaction grew, and even though I was supposedly an expert with women, I was becoming angry at them. The shallower the sex I got, the angrier I became. I had done all this work, upended my entire life, and left my job and family to dedicate myself to pleasure from women, but all I received in return was loveless sex. I wrote essay after essay complaining about women, admonishing them for not satisfying me and other men in heat, and yet it totally escaped me that I was receiving from women merely what I gave them.

No matter what I had achieved, and how great in stature I saw myself, I never escaped being a young man out of college who felt inadequate, inferior, and engorged with lust. All my accomplishments could provide only temporary happiness until I was mentally right back where I started. I wanted to feel complete and whole yet I felt empty and alone. I began to see my lifestyle as a dead end, but I didn't know where else to turn. If extracting and gaining from the world wasn't the answer, what was?

The world started to fight against me in 2015. I experienced attacks from the establishment: false allegations about my sexual behavior, deplatformings, and threats to my family. My sister was diagnosed with cancer. A relationship with a Polish woman I had thought would lead to marriage failed suddenly. I was living in Eastern Europe for no reason but to save money and have easier sexual access to women I deceived with my lies and fake machismo. Then my sister died in the spring of 2018. At that point, it was revealed to me that I had ruined my life. I had accomplished nothing; I was a zero. I entered a state of nihilistic despair, believing that all was hopeless. I felt uneasy standing near open windows for fear I'd jump.

For one year after my sister's death, I probed the abyss until March 2019 when I kneeled before Almighty God and begged Him to help me. He answered immediately. The grace that He went on to give me was so full and powerful that I instantly began making miraculous strides away from lust and anger and pride. No more game or fornication. No more pornography or masturbation. No more attacking others to feel a deluded sense of superiority. In a state of spiritual bliss from my new conscience and life, I desired to climb the mountain tops and tell the world what God had done for me, so I planned a nationwide speaking tour where I would drive around the country and deliver my life story and testimony in 23 American cities. While still a very new Christian, on June 17, 2019, on the heels of turning 40, I packed my Dodge Challenger with clothes, electronics, and books, said goodbye to my mother, and left Washington, DC to share my path to Jesus Christ. This book is a story of that journey.

Northern Virginia
January 2021

1

Icons

"A road trip is hard," people warned me. But why? You're just sitting down and driving. You stop for lunch and then continue driving. It should be almost the same as being a passenger on a train or bus, but only three hours into the first day of my journey, driving north through Pennsylvania, my eyelids were getting heavy.

I arrived at Jim Thorpe, Pennsylvania, a picturesque town named after an American football player. It was the first time I had traveled to a small American town as an adult. I had spent years visiting the towns of foreign countries, but none in my own. Walking around, I heard only English spoken and didn't see a single gay pride flag. There was a steam engine ride and scenic, mountain views all around. It would be hard to get ground into dust here, unlike in the big city.

I drove further north and crossed into the state of New York. I got on another country road. For over an hour, I had to come to a stop only three times. No traffic lights and few cars. I saw cows crossing the road and a deer and a turtle. Actual animals! This was amazing stuff, really. And look at all the American flags on the houses. Now I knew why people always told me that I had to "get out of DC." I did get out of DC—to South America and Europe. I thought that the further from home I ran, the more answers I would find, and yet the only answer I found was that you never leave home.

After seven hours on the road, I made it to the Holy Trinity Russian Monastery in Jordanville, New York. I had a reservation for two nights, but when I arrived, the office was closed. I asked a monk for help, but he looked at me with annoyance, as if I was interrupting his prayer. He said in broken English that he would find a priest. I walked up to the church and dared not to approach an anguished monk sitting on a bench. I went inside and saw an open casket containing an elderly woman. Someone was wailing beside it. I had arrived during a funeral service. Mourners were lighting candles and venerating icons. Everyone was speaking in Russian. This wasn't a hotel with a reception desk where I could check in. Would it be appropriate to ask someone for the internet password? Then a monk came up to me. He pointed to my t-shirt and said, "Long sleeves are better." I had already brought disrespect to the monastery.

I went back outside the church and stood on the grass. Monks with stony faces, dressed in black cassocks, walked by me without making eye contact. Would the monks know how I could check in to my room?

I stood by the side of the church for some time, fatigued from the seven-hour drive, thinking about what to do. Was this a test from God? Should I just stand here for as long as it took until someone helped me? Probably not. I didn't want to disturb the monks, so I left and found a motel in the nearest town. I doubted they had dedicated their lives to God to deal with my trifling concerns.

The next morning, I drove back to the monastery to attend the Divine Liturgy. In Orthodox Christianity, the Liturgy is a roughly two-hour worship service that culminates in the taking of wine and bread that is Jesus' blood and body, His *literal* blood and body. It is not a metaphor or a symbol, but through a mysterious process that we humans cannot possibly understand, the energy of God becomes one with us.

When I walked into the church, I saw 15 women with a handful of children standing on the left. Six or so men were on the right. There were no pews, only a few benches pushed up against a wall. I found a spot behind a young man midway into the church. The walls were covered with countless icons of saints framed in gold. There was a central stand with two large icons that most parishioners kissed and several little nooks that seemed to act as miniature shrines. At the very front were three separate doors that led to the altar, which only the priests, deacons, and monks could access. The bishop sat on a chair facing the altar. Ten monks and deacons, in green or black robes, flanked him, holding scepters, candles, Gospel books, cloths, and various other objects I didn't recognize. They kissed his hand when handing him things or taking them away. There were more men serving at the altar, approximately 25 in total, than parishioners in the church.

During the Liturgy, English was spoken about 5% of the time; the rest was Old Slavonic, which I did not understand. The sign of the cross was made almost non-stop. My Armenian church does the sign by going up, down, left, right, like the Catholics. The Eastern Orthodox goes up, down, right, left. I adapted out of respect, to redeem myself from the previous day when I entered the House of God with a short-sleeved shirt. Each of the 25 men conducting the Liturgy had a specific role and, to my eyes, performed as if it were a spiritual ballet. This was the major leagues of liturgical worship.

The aesthetic of the Liturgy was as close to heaven as we'll get here on earth. The holy singing (auditory), the aroma of the incense (olfactory), the elaborately decorated robes, golden colors, and icons (visual) alongside the presence of the Holy Spirit may be the height of material beauty. I have no doubt that the service is but a shade of what goes on in heaven with God and the angels. As the monks kiss the priest's hands, so the angels kiss the hand of God.

After leaving the monastery, I called my mother. She told me that she had a dream where I appeared to her as an angel, telling her, "Don't worry, everything will be all right."

†

I headed east through Westborough, Massachusetts, on my way to Walden Pond. When I began working as a microbiologist in my early twenties, I would use my lunch break to visit the nearest bookstore to read before taking a short nap on one of their comfortable armchairs. I was just beginning my materialistic journey of accumulating stuff, and at the time was debating whether I should buy a BMW. I wanted to be happy, and I believed that things were capable of making me happy. One day at the bookstore, I saw *Walden* by Henry David Thoreau in the classics section.

Thoreau was a non-religious monk for the two years he went into the Massachusetts woods to "live deliberately" by the pond named after him. His intelligent hatred of worldly things convinced me that materialism was a false road. I would not buy that BMW. Thoreau hadn't had the same commitment as the monks I encountered in upstate New York, since he returned to Concord to manage a factory, but his message spread far and wide to an increasingly secular nation that desperately sought purpose. Upon re-reading *Walden* over ten years later in my thirties, I found his message less meaty than before. His "worship nature" thesis, while better than the worship of material possessions, merely substituted one false god for another. Nature is great, but worshipping it does not sate spiritual thirst.

From my base in Westborough, I drove to the pond, now a Massachusetts state reserve. The parking fee was $15. The pond itself was quite large, more the size of a lake. In the name of conservation, most of the shoreline and wooded hills were fenced off. A consequence was that everyone walked on the same narrow path, and I had to adjust my gait to accommodate them.

Even for a weekday, the park was crowded. A group of children near me wouldn't stop yelling "Whoa!" Two older ladies talked about the effects of systemic racism. At the site where Thoreau built his humble cabin, I had to wait some time before I could take a photo that didn't have anyone else in the background.

It took me only an hour to walk around the lake. I sat by a little sandy beach, watching the families and children play. I felt I had paid $15 for a short stroll. Maybe the spirit of Thoreau was present, but I couldn't hear him above the noise of the world. Before I was ready to give up and head back to the car, I got the urge to look at the trail map. I saw that there was a large wooded area beside the pond.

I walked into the woods up a small hill and encountered a large frog. I grabbed a stick and started poking it. He jumped away. I sat on the edge of a cliff and listened to the wind blowing through the leaves. No other people were around. I walked down to a meadow and threw sticks and rocks in the water. I watched the birds, including one that seemed to prefer running to flying. There were dragonflies and crawling things, all living in a self-contained ecosystem not far from humanity, and I was able to enjoy it alone.

I drove to the nearest town, Concord, and walked on Main Street. The peak of American urban beauty is the main street, a two-lane road in the center of town flanked by little shops advertised with hand-painted rectangular signs. It's better than the fake "city centers" the suburbs offer, though a far cry from the European town square encircled by centuries-old buildings and ground-level cafés where you can people-watch the afternoon away. America is too efficient for that. Work must be done and wealth must be made, so purchase your commercial product and get back in your truck and go do something productive.

I walked to the Concord Free Public Library. The name offered a clue that libraries weren't always a public service. It had balconies of books, something I'd seen only in the movies, and high ceilings, real wooden tables (instead of pressed wood), lamps (instead of fluorescent or LED lighting), and ottoman chairs. It was more comfortable than many homes I'd been to, so I stayed for a couple of hours.

While I was reading the Bible, an elderly lady with thinning hair walked up to me. "What are you reading?"

"A study Bible," I replied.

"Not many people read the Bible these days."

I pointed to my smartphone. "Because they have this. People get addicted to entertainment and other sources of fun and feel like they don't need anything spiritual."

"It's getting very pagan here," she said.

In Concord, I saw only one gay pride flag. In Westborough, I saw a single "Hate Doesn't Live Here" sign. In DC, you can't turn your head without seeing multiple gay pride flags, Black Lives Matter placards, and gun control signs. At least Westborough and Concord had multiple churches in the same street, some even right next to each other.

"Then don't go to Washington, DC," I said. "They tear down churches to build luxury apartments."

"Oh my God, really?"

"Yes, down the street from where my father lives was a huge church. They demolished it and built rental apartments, right across from the new mega gym. Rent starts at $1,400 a month."

"And I thought things were bad here. I just got fired from my job because I said something that wasn't politically correct."

When I get banned from internet platforms, the news is shared online, but there are many silent victims of political correctness. They lose their jobs or are falsely accused of a crime, and it never goes viral. For every time I'm deplatformed, I imagine hundreds of normal people are attacked with no ability to get the word out. At what point do those who are silenced decide that they no longer want to suffer silently?

The old lady gave me a few tracts concerning her Baptist

faith. I had begun research of both Protestantism and Catholicism, not because I wanted to convert from Orthodoxy, but because most of the people I meet are not Orthodox. I want to build off the common ground we share.

†

A couple of weeks before my trip, I decided to start the Orthodox fast. In the Armenian Orthodox Church (also known as the Armenian Apostolic Church), it entails 160 fasting days a year and abstaining from dairy, eggs, and animal fats like butter and meat. (The Eastern Orthodox Churches are stricter in that they usually abstain from oil.) The Armenians fast during Lent, every Wednesday and Friday, and during ten special fasting weeks. The point of the fast is not to absolve one's sins or feel pain, but to reduce material excess in the form of rich or—what were once—luxury foods such as meat in order to rely more on God, because when we seek pleasure from eating or other activities, we count on those objects to give us happiness, eventually arriving at a state where we feel as if we don't need God. Although fasting is ascetic in nature, it is not a sacrifice, because there is no sacrifice we can make that is just in the eyes of God. While many Christians are eager to sacrifice for God, and even be martyred for Him, I do not possess the righteousness to pick and choose how to suffer to gain God's glory. I learned this lesson right before I started the trip when I decided to unpublish 11 of my books.

Within a month of seeking God, I became troubled by what I had previously authored. While some of my books could be seen as merely entertaining or at least morally ambiguous, most of them were explicitly written to help men fornicate. They enabled men to sin, and if a man sinned because of me and I was a stumbling block for him, I wonder whether it was the same as me committing the sin myself. At first, I wanted to unpublish all of my books that promoted casual sex, which would have wiped out my entire income. I worried about how I would make a living, and then out of the blue, I received two messages from men who said that my newest game book, *Game*, had helped them to find a wife. I believed it was a sign from God to keep selling *Game* for the time being, so I unpublished only my ten travel sex guides and my older book, *Bang*. I estimated that unpublishing those books would cost me 20% to 25% of my monthly income. I took this action so that men wouldn't be led astray by my work, but I also wanted to punish myself for my past misdeeds.

I had hoped that my sacrifice would be pleasing to the Lord, but in the days following the unpublishing, as the news spread on the internet, sales of my existing books went through the roof. I was making far more money than before. I believed that God was telling me, in so many ways, that I did not know how to punish myself. I started to believe that God didn't need me to help Him remove evil from the world, and that He would use whatever I do, whether good or bad, to achieve His plan. Of course I should remove myself from sin, but this should be done for the sake of my salvation and because I love God, not to do Him a favor or get an immediate reward for committing a deed that I perceive as good.

On a scale of one to ten, with one being an action that pleases the Lord only because it's not evil and ten being so pleasing that it can be performed only by His Son, I believe my public display of righteousness was a one. I'm glad I did it, as it was an important step in my sanctification, but in terms of being a genuine sacrifice, it was feeble. I kept this lesson in mind when I started fasting, knowing that it's meant to strengthen my relationship with God instead of appearing to the world as a good Christian. For each of my events, I planned an intimate dinner to take place on Friday, a fasting day. I would learn how to fast while on the road.

†

I came across a pamphlet for the Museum of Russian Icons, located half an hour away in Clinton, Massachusetts. The notion of viewing icons on a purely intellectual or historical basis, disconnected from the Church, seemed rather agnostic, but curiosity got the better of me.

The museum was started by an American man who began collecting icons after the fall of the Soviet Union. As Russia's economy began to open up, his company sent him there to help improve various factories. As a tourist, he encountered markets of desperate Russians selling their treasures, including icons that had been in their families for generations. He bought them for practically nothing. His story did have a ring of taking advantage of the poor, but to his credit, he restored the icons and presented them to the public. This included many large icons that came from closed churches that had no means to use them.

To a layperson, it may seem that the Orthodox pray directly to icons, but the correct notion is that they pray alongside the icons, using them as a visual aid. The icons are not actually Jesus Christ or the Blessed Mother but a representation of how they appeared to the faithful when they walked on earth and were seen by the multitude.

The museum showed the craftsmanship, process, and labor that goes into icon production, such as the laying of delicate gold leaf and adding egg yolk to prevent bright colors from fading. (Nowadays, if you buy an icon from the internet or a monastery gift shop, you are getting a computer printout that is placed on top of a piece of wood.) The museum taught me standard themes that have been used by icon-makers for centuries: black represents hell, red robes represent martyrdom, a huge forehead represents wisdom, an open book represents the Word of God (the Logos), an almond backdrop around Jesus represents his divinity, and a halo represents one's acceptance into the Holy Kingdom.

For 1,500 years after Christ, the vast majority of believers did not have Bibles, so they would learn the Gospel through icons and the Liturgy. Many Christians today have memorized large passages of the Bible by heart, but for most of Christendom, this feat was reserved for clergy. Ironically, even though anyone today can go to a bookstore and buy a Bible for a few dollars, faith is not stronger than it was in the Byzantine era, where, according to Timothy Ware in *The Orthodox Church*, theological debates were commonplace in the outdoor markets of Constantinople.

As I toured the icon museum, I considered it mildly blasphemous that all of these holy relics were in a secular building managed by nice old ladies discussing the day's weather and what they will eat for lunch. The icons were reduced to trivia, a source of entertainment for people to feel more learned or intelligent. Removed from the context of church, the urge to pray or even do the sign of the cross never occurred to me, and after viewing the thirtieth or so icon, there was nothing more to appreciate. I might as well have been in an art museum.

One icon that did stand out was a Russian monk who constructed a pair of special crutches to allow him to pray throughout the night and into the early morning while staying awake. The crutches also made it easier for him to resume praying immediately upon waking. I stared at this icon for some time and realized that I'm not devoted enough. When I reach the Judgment Seat of Christ, will He ask me why I prayed for only 20 minutes each day? Could I dare answer Him with, "But I prayed more than other people!" Then He will point out the monks I saw in New York, all the Orthodox saints I should be studying, or the monk who sleeps on crutches.

I left the museum after a two-hour tour and stopped for lunch in Framingham, a Boston suburb. It didn't take long to notice numerous attractive young women. A university must be nearby, a place where American parents send their daughters to wear yoga pants every day and learn how to perform various carnal acts while under the influence of alcohol. Such a sight would have gotten me excited in the past, and I would have conjured up all sorts of filthy fantasies, but now it becomes a trial of the will. Men who want to resist the flesh are somewhat lucky that not many women will walk up to them and make a proposition for sex. Most of the battle takes place in the mind. But how I hate my peripheral vision! I diligently maintain custody of my eyes, and look at women only from the neck up to block the visage of their sexualized bodies, but I can still see much more without trying. Do I need to buy a pair of horse blinders? Maybe I can invent a human-sized version for Christians living in pornographic societies.

I will have to accept that the sight of butts and breasts will enter my vision without my consent, and lean on God to help me defeat the urge to crave a woman in a sexual manner, even if that's what she wants me to do. All the women of the world can line up to show me their naked bodies, and I must resist them all.

†

I checked in to a shared apartment on the outskirts of Boston and met up with Mark, whom I first met during my 2015 tour. He was then a new believer, in similar shoes as I was currently. I remembered one thing he told me: "All truth is God's truth." If you accept the truth unequivocally, you will inevitably reach God. The only problem is that we can easily deceive ourselves into thinking we are pursuing the truth when we are not, or in my case, using truth—such as the truth about female nature—not for good (family) but for evil (fornication). Most people need help not only to stay on the path to truth, but also to apply it in a moral way.

Mark took me for a walk around the Boston Harbor. I looked into the bars and restaurants and noticed that nearly everyone was white. The women were prettier than the ones in Washington, DC.

"It's strange that not many men told me about Boston," I said. "Maybe they're trying to keep it a secret."

"It's like the Europe of America," Mark replied. "The best of the Northeast come here, and the cold weather keeps out a lot of the homeless that you see in warmer cities."

"Are there black people?"

"Yes, but the ones who can endure the cold essentially become white. The blacks here are different than what you see if you go south."

"And people here still vote Democrat?"

"They do. They have been given everything, have no idea what 'racism' or civil strife is, but they insist on putting their heads in the sand. They ignore the problems of the rest of the country, thinking that it won't come here, but it will."

We found a good view from the harbor and I took a handful of photos. Mark talked about an argument he had with his girlfriend. She had gone to a career function and met a friendly man who wanted her contact information under the guise of networking. Of course he ended up asking her out on a date, but Mark's girlfriend didn't see anything wrong with it because it wasn't like she would "cheat" or anything. He was "just a friend"—one who was obviously interested in her sexually, which meant he wasn't "a friend" but a man in hot pursuit.

I said, "The problem is that women subconsciously want to keep their options open and will invent all manner of rationalizations to do so. My most recent ex-girlfriend did the same thing. Technically, she wasn't cheating, but she opened the door to cheating."

"Exactly. So I told her she can't communicate with him anymore."

A girlfriend is in active rebellion. The man lays down the rules and observes her carefully, as if he were a private detective, maybe even spying on her smartphone. She transgresses and gets caught. There is a big fight, a period of tension, and then a reconciliation. Back to the comfort of the relationship, especially the regular sex. Every other month will be a short conversation about marriage, yet the prospect of it seems so far into the future. I know enough about women that I can keep them in a box of honor and respectability, but the box is made of cardboard. She only needs to throw a punch to break through. Unless a woman has completely submitted to God and willingly carries her cross like I carry mine, I do not want her. I can barely save myself, so there's no way I can save a woman who is quite content with not being saved.

We grabbed a burger and went into a beer garden at last call. We stood at the far end of the bar. Beside us was a young woman playing a game where she slid pucks across a long wooden surface. She was wearing tight jeans and a top that revealed her midriff. The empty expression on her face suggested she had started drinking while the sun was still out. There was another woman in yoga pants and a tight shirt bending over a bar table. Relics of my past flooded my mind. I instinctually thought of opening lines I could deliver to either women with the goal of having sex, but my feet remained still.

"I don't think it's a sin to have sex before marriage," Mark said. "When the Bible was written there really was no such thing as premarital sex, since everyone got married. Adultery was the problem."

"If Jesus Christ was here right now, and you asked Him if it's okay to have premarital sex, do you think He would say it's okay?"

"But that's whoring around, of just sleeping with someone with no intention of a relationship. I'm talking about premarital sex within the confines of a monogamous relationship, someone you will eventually marry and start a family with."

"And what if you end up not marrying that person?"

"What else can I do? Girls don't want to wait until marriage to have sex."

"Then you don't have sex. Just because girls have fallen and are in active rebellion, doesn't mean that you should follow them like Adam followed Eve."

"But even if most men say no to premarital sex, it just takes one man to refuse and spoil dozens of women."

"And that man is doing you a favor! He's marking all the women who defy God."

"I don't know. There has to be a solution."

I understood Mark's doubt. It's hard not to come up with plots that mitigate the fallen world, but unless that plot puts God at the top of your list of priorities, it will fail.

"Lots of men see game as the solution," I replied. "While it's an important tool, since it is based on the truth of the sexes, most men use it to engage with fallen women in the hopes of a good result. They're using game to allow a woman like these here into their lives to cause all sorts of troubles. You're essentially opening the door for a follower of Satan to enter, whether she knows it or not, because a woman in rebellion is on the side of Satan, and it's just a matter of time until she ruins you. If she doesn't care about her own Creator, why should she care about you? Her caring stops until she can find a better deal or until she gets bored. The tree of this society is bad, and it's yielding bad apples."

"There has to be a good apple on that tree. Game can be used by men to find that apple."

"If game worked on her, how could she be a good apple?"

A man in his prime, with his sexual hormones flowing, and who is desired by women, won't want to hear what I have to say. He wants to believe that he can find the good woman, mold her, train her, and instill values into her, even belief in God. Maybe this is possible, but as a man who has had more experience with women than most men, I don't think I can do it. I don't think I can win at that game. She has to be a good apple before me and without me, and if the monks can take a vow of chastity and sleep on crutches to maintain their faith, surely I can take the sexual experiences I've had, put them on a little boat, and kick that boat out into the ocean. Besides, I'm already halfway towards death, if not closer. How hard can it really be not to have sex again?

†

I was feeling anxious about my car. If it broke down, my events could be delayed or canceled. I wanted to maintain perfect control over an ambitious five-month road trip with innumerable variables. Five days into the trip, after driving on Boston's awful roads for only a couple of hours, I heard a crunching noise coming from the front of my car. I looked underneath. A metal cover hung precariously, a lone screw holding it in place. I took the car to the nearest auto repair shop. They screwed the cover on and charged me $35. If my car has problems during the trip, I will simply take it to a shop, have it repaired, and go on my way. A problem seems far worse in fantasy than in reality. I'm glad I had a car issue so soon into the trip to enlighten me that fixing it would be no big deal.

After the repair, I drove to pick up Mark on the north side of town. The traffic was intense. The estimated time of arrival on my navigation app increased a number of times during the trip, as if I were going back in time. The six-mile drive took 55 minutes. I picked him up and then set the navigation to the center of Boston, only two-and-a-half miles away. Quickly, we encountered a wall of traffic.

"Looks like they shut down the road," I said. "We're barely moving."

"They didn't shut down the road," Mark replied.

"Well, there must be an accident." I examined the navigation app for the car accident icon along the route, but saw nothing.

"There is no accident."

"So what is this?" I said, beginning to lose my composure.

"This is normal. In Boston, it's one chokepoint after the next. A study stated that $2 billion a year in lost time is wasted in this traffic. The city was made for a quarter of the population we have now."

"And people tolerate this?"

"Yes. They stopped counting on politicians to fix the problem."

"So this is why podcasts are so popular. People spend hours a day on the road, and they have to listen to something."

The two-and-a-half-mile ride from Mark's house to a parking garage in the city center took 50 minutes. And now look at the time—we had less than an hour to sightsee before my first event dinner. I got to see a pleasant garden with a pond, several Protestant churches with gay pride flags and Black Lives Matter paraphernalia, the mammoth Boston Public Library with five gay pride flags, and the John Hancock Tower with his signature colored to the gay rainbow. If Hancock had known that his signature would be used to promote sodomy, he would not have signed the Declaration of Independence, or at least signed it with his other hand to make it less aesthetically pleasing to the social engineers of the future.

We did encounter a group of Mennonites handing out literature. They appeared similar to the Amish, a Christian sect that has peculiar beliefs that seem to preserve a godly way of life. A Mennonite man handed us two pamphlets: "Steps to Salvation" and "Jesus is Coming – Perhaps Today." I tried not to stare at the woman I presumed was his wife. She was meek and deferent. She did not play with a smartphone or show off her sexuality. Her reward for living in such a way was being graced with a man of God who provided for her, a life free of the sins of fornication and lust, and, if she was a genuine believer, entry into the Kingdom of Heaven. That seems like a pretty good deal to me.

In a nearby restaurant I met up with the three men who had bought my Platinum-tier ticket. It cost $249 and didn't include food or drinks. I had been hesitant to charge that much for "access" to me, but without it my tour might not turn a profit. Plus, I knew that many successful men followed me, and for them $249 was not a burden. When I met the three men, I told them that I was their humble servant and they could pick my brain in any way they saw fit. I wanted them to get their money's worth.

The three men were at different stages of their lives. One had just been red-pilled and was learning game. The second was deep into the red pill and was extracting sex from random women. And the third was stalled at the bottom of the hill, thinking the journey would be easier than it had been. A problem common to all three was that they lacked a male role model who understood their problems. No one could offer them guidance. Much of the world is hostile to their masculine needs and chooses to forsake them to justify perceived historical wrongs. A psychologist, educated in the same system that pathologizes masculinity, can offer no aid. Parents, unaware that the world has changed since the 1960s, can serve up only useless platitudes. Hollywood, the universities, and the media hate their guts. So all they have is me and a handful of dissidents and dubious gurus on the internet. While I don't see myself as a role model, and should be looked upon more as a warning, who else understands what these men are going through? Who else sympathizes with them? If John Hancock were alive, maybe he'd sympathize with them, but even he was forced from the grave into the cult of homosexuality. In some cases, a three-line email reply I write to a man is all the guidance he'll get from the world.

After the dinner, we walked through Boston Common. The man who was deepest in the red pill journey asked me whether I believed men should be "the best version of themselves."

"Who gets to judge when you have arrived at the best version of yourself?" I asked.

"I do."

"But by what standard are you judging yourself? Who makes the criteria? At some point, you will need the judgments of other people to confirm you really are the best. I want hot women, so I am the best version of myself when hot women want to go to bed with me. I am not the judge of myself—the women are. I want to be rich, so I am the best version of myself when people decide to give me a lot of money for my labor, product, or service. They are my judge. So the best version of yourself will happen to be what pleases other people, but only for the short term, for what the mob likes today will change tomorrow. You will be going from trend to trend to stay on top of what the culture dictates is best."

"But don't you think that you should work towards becoming better?"

"I think you should work hardest in your relationship with God. Everything else is seeking approval from other people. You allow them to define what success is. They're also applying that flawed standard to themselves, so in the end you have pigs in a pigpen showing off their mud to each other. For example, say you want to get attractive girls. You know that girls care about looks and charm. You go to the gym, upgrade your wardrobe, and learn some witty one-liners. You coat yourself with the mud to get a mud-soaked woman. You made it! You're the best version of yourself! But you're more likely the worst version of yourself, one that is purely material, totally disconnected from God, to please those who are far from God themselves."

"I didn't think of it that way."

"It only took me 40 years to learn that. Today my only judge is God. I aim to only care about what He thinks of me. You see my hairstyle now. It's unkempt and unattractive. My beard is not properly trimmed. When I look in the mirror, I know for certain that this is not the best I can look, but I proceed because I don't want to subconsciously seek approval from fallen women."

Two men left and I gave the third a ride home since he lived near my lodging. He was looking for answers about what to do with his life. Like many, he was skeptical about my re-conversion to Christianity. He didn't state that he was an atheist, but I was certain that was the case.

"Now I totally respect you and your work," he started, "and see you as possessing a sharp mind, but do you think your spiritual turn is a midlife crisis?"

"I see this more as a midlife miracle than a crisis, an opportunity to withdraw from the world and seek my eternal salvation instead of playing meaningless games that lead to condemnation. In a genuine crisis, people often look for pleasure to soothe the pain. A woman finds yoga and that is her lifestyle. Or she becomes a vegan. A man buys an expensive sports car or pursues women half his age in the Third World. These things will be pleasing for a while until the crisis returns, but when you find God, there is nothing to achieve and nowhere to go. There is no pleasure to receive but divine pleasure. I believe I've reached the last stop on my earthly trip before I die."

He paused for some time, thinking of his next objection. "But you're a man of science and logic. How can you just come to believe?"

"Through the heart. It's hard to come to God through the mind. If what you believe as 'logic' leads to evil acts then it can't be logical at all—it's the logic of Satan. You're still looking at the material world to make you happy. You believe that if you get a new job, or a woman, things will be fine, but they won't because you have separated those pursuits from God. You will try anyway, and I hope you 'succeed' as quickly as possible so that you can see the truth behind what I'm saying at a younger age, but from what I can perceive about your current frame of mind, there's nothing I can say to convince you there is a God. There's no argument I can give you, because your heart doesn't want to believe. It isn't ready for God, but I pray one day it will."

I dropped him off and returned to my rental. I opened the pamphlets that the Mennonites had given me. They contained brief teachings of scripture, but I couldn't see them converting an atheist like the one I had just talked to. Only a Christian would find value in them. I wondered whether the Mennonites went home and thought that someone had been reached by their day's work, but I doubted that even one person had. An atheist cannot be converted by an article. An article can barely help a man with his sex life, and that concerns matters of the world. Coming to God is not a problem of information or knowledge. The question I must ask myself is how to speak to people's hearts instead of their minds. The best I can do is identify where a man is on his spiritual journey and give him one seed of nourishment that I think he needs. God will then decide whether that seed takes root or not.

†

The day of the speech arrived. I had sent the venue details to ticket holders the night before. Since the speech didn't start until 6pm, I figured I could go out and sightsee for a few hours, although I had hours of work to do preparing for the next week's speech. I left for the hotel venue at 4pm to set up the room and greet the guests. I used a portable hand-truck to haul all my equipment, which included a large speaker, wireless microphones, portable audio mixer, camcorder, tripods, multiple power supplies, and a dozen cables. Hotels will charge hundreds of dollars for you to rent their audio equipment so I bought my own.

I arrived at the hotel and prepared the meeting room. Since I had done a lecture tour before, there wasn't much in the way of nervousness around conducting an event and delivering a speech, but I was tense about making sure everything went off without disruption. I figured that as long as the media didn't broadcast details of my event, I wouldn't have to worry about any leftist activists, who tend to be actuated only when the media shines a spotlight on me: "Bad man is coming to town with bad ideas… at 6pm in this specific hotel!"

Out of the 50 guests who came, five were women, including a mother-daughter pair. One attractive woman wore a low-cut dress that revealed her cleavage. Even when I made an effort to stare directly into her eyes, I could see her breasts in the bottom of my vision, and it distracted me from her words, which I forgot almost immediately.

I delivered a 90-minute speech about the stories of my life, culminating in my testimony to Christ. Thankfully, I seemed to hold everyone's attention, and not until the Q&A session did the guests start squirming in their seats.

In my previous lecture series, most of the men asked questions that had a focus on getting laid, but this time around the audience had more diverse concerns. Many asked me about God, and I used that as an opportunity to dive into my rudimentary faith. I was careful not to teach, since I was only a spiritual baby, and made the effort to share only what I had experienced personally. After all, I had been a Christian for only a few months.

By the time the evening was done, my feet were hurting, my legs and back were sore, and my mind was fried. And the events of the weekend weren't done: the next day at 1pm I had to meet with guests for a four-hour happy hour. When scheduling the tour, I had hoped that I could attend a Liturgy on Sunday morning before the happy hour, but logistics made that impossible. It appeared that the weekends would be full of work, leaving me no time for liturgical worship, Bible reading, or even sightseeing. With so many cares and moving parts, my mind was too scattered for even light reading, although I was maintaining my twice-daily prayers.

I was learning firsthand how keeping busy in the world pulled me away from spiritual life, and for the next five months it would be a constant battle to strengthen the latter. If the tour was permanent, and I was busy every day for the long term, like many people in the city are, God would gradually be squeezed out. He would become a secondary character in my life, getting further and further away, watching me as my life became increasingly dominated by worldly pursuits.

Sunday came. Twenty men and one woman showed up at the meeting spot in Boston Public Garden, a beautiful park with a miniature suspension bridge. We sat on the grass and proceeded to chat for several hours. Most of the men were secular. I could tell that they saw God as a backup plan. They would turn to Him *after* they had achieved their worldly goals. They wanted to dance with Satan for a little while without getting burned, but if Satan knows that you becoming rich or a successful fornicator will keep you away from God, he will happily send you money and women. If making you depressed and angry will keep you away from God, he will send you sadness and daily outrage. Could I now say to God, "I really don't want to go to hell, but can I try dating and casual sex just a little bit longer? I don't trust in You to give me all that I need in this life, and I want to feel pleasure, fun, and a sense of prideful masculinity in the present moment." He would turn away from me. I'd find myself back in the embrace of the devil.

2

Birds

Boston gave me one gift before leaving: a $90 parking ticket when I failed to see a sign for street cleaning. I had driven an hour south to Dartmouth, Massachusetts, for lunch when I received a message from my Boston host saying that I had left my toiletry bag in the bathroom. I drove back to retrieve it and then back down again, eventually stopping in New Bedford, Massachusetts.

New Bedford was once a textile boomtown, but those jobs were long gone. Walking through the downtown, I saw many disheveled individuals with blank stares on their faces. Just three years prior, the New Bedford City Council declared an opioid state of emergency because so many residents were overdosing. I walked by City Hall and saw a gay pride flag flying high. I figured that homosexual rights were the least of their concerns when people were dying on the streets from drug use, but putting up a flag to virtue signal is easy—solving real problems is hard. The more absurd the concerns of a city, such as the banning of plastic straws, the more serious its problems.

There were no addicts at my next stop, Newport, Rhode Island, where the robber barons of old built huge summer "cottages" starting in the mid-nineteenth century. I drove by many stone mansions with turrets, an architectural feature I had seen only in photographs. While there are many rich people left in the city, where a modest house starts at half-a-million dollars, I suspect the super-elite have long since left the area to get away from the hordes of tourists who want to take a ride on Ocean Drive or a stroll on Cliff Walk to experience what the richest men of their time experienced—beautiful seaside views and near-total tranquility.

The upper-middle class I saw dressed respectably, were thin, and displayed no tattoos. I'm quite sensitive to the visage of gay pride flags, but I saw not one, not even on the downtown churches. The rich don't live the same lifestyles as the plebes, who can't stop virtue signaling for degenerate causes. It's almost as if certain causes are targeted to specific socio-economic brackets to keep them weak and fighting among themselves, to keep their eyes off Ocean Drive.

I attempted to explore one of the city's most famous mansions, The Breakers, but balked at the $26 entry charge. The rich ding you the first time when they suck up the world's wealth to build their palaces and then they get you a second time by charging you to view the palaces. I decided to have lunch in town instead, but was faced with $8-an-hour parking fees. I guess I am a plebe, because I can't justify paying that amount. I left town and drove to New Haven, Connecticut.

New Haven pizza is often hailed as the best in the country. The first thing I did was go to the most famous pizza joint in town: Frank Pepe's. The line outside was long. I was more than happy to wait for the best pizza, but I noticed that most people were from out of town, suggesting that I might be entering a tourist trap.

After waiting for half an hour, I was ushered to my seat and checked out other people's pizzas. I couldn't help but notice that the crust appeared burnt, with spots of black char. I ordered a pepperoni and mushroom pizza. Sure enough, the crust was burnt. The flavor of burnt toast overwhelmed my palate. How could all the people in line be wrong? How could all those plaques at the entrance that heralded Frank Pepe's as the best pizza on the East Coast endorse an inferior product? Like most things in America, hype supersedes quality.

To judge the health of a city, I had learned to pop into its central public library. If the library is clean (especially the bathrooms), with families, students, and adults furthering their education under one space, it's safe to assume that the city is healthy. A wide cross-section of the community should be present, as was the case in Concord, Massachusetts. If the library is visibly dirty with countless homeless people loitering around, fouling up the bathroom, the city is not healthy. This was the case in New Haven. While washing my hands in the bathroom, I witnessed a homeless man come out of a stall after defecating and rinse without using soap. He tightly gripped the door handle to exit. I use my right pinky finger to open bathroom doors (it has become the strongest of my fingers), but even that was too risky in New Haven. Despite the presence of Yale University, it felt no different than New Bedford.

I began to dread visiting the big cities on the West Coast, where the homeless defecate not in library toilets but on the streets, and I was fatigued after only one event. I decided to cut out the Sunday happy hour and hold it directly after the Saturday lecture starting with my Denver talk. I would have to pace myself if I was going to last all 23 weeks.

†

When I had been able to study the Bible daily while confined to a more peaceful home setting, my lust had been relatively easy to tame, but now that I was living on the road, traveling from one city to the next, my defense against sexual thoughts had weakened. I was slower to stop dangerous fantasies and did so only after getting physically aroused. I'd even started to have more dreams about sex. Previously, I'd have enough will in a dream to refuse the pleasure that was offered to me, but now I was succumbing. Did this mean that succumbing in real life was not far away? It would take only one attractive female who came to my events and stayed afterwards to seduce me for a crisis to occur. I told myself not to enter a private house or bedroom with a female, no matter how innocent the reasoning might appear at the time, but I knew that when the temptation came, I wouldn't remember anything, maybe not even God.

The woman in Boston who wore the low-cut dress sent me an email saying that she was thwarted twice from talking to me. In the first instance, she went to the bathroom after my lecture and came back to find the door locked. She looked through the door window and saw me surrounded by a group of men. She felt too shy to intrude and decided to leave. The next day, she could not come to the happy hour because of a birthday party that went on for much longer than she expected. I wondered whether God locked the door and whether He extended the birthday party. He knew that I wasn't ready to be tested. I'm certainly not saying that the woman wanted to have sex with me, but she could unwillingly have created an opportunity for me to "game" her and make it happen.

I couldn't believe that I was this weak and had to take such measures to not accidentally have sex with a woman, but when I look back on my life, I had been even weaker, all the while thinking I was "strong" and "masculine." I had been a slave to sex when I had thought I was its conqueror. I had been a fool when I had thought I was wise. I didn't even want to think of the grace that God would remove from me if I backslid and fornicated.

†

I stayed overnight in Hamden, a suburb not far from New Haven. While New Haven was full of derelicts, Hamden was pleasant. The library was full of children, young adults, and seniors, all co-existing in one clean space, with not one homeless person present. I must therefore conclude that Hamden is healthy, and yet beside me in the library a man was having a loud conversation about how he hated Donald Trump. It's easy to complain about the big bad conservative President when you live in a safe and clean city that is predominately white, with only a small presence of Third World immigrants whom Trump has half-heartedly tried to stop. I highly doubt the man goes to the public library in New Haven, because if he did, he would not find a clean place to sit and enjoy his book without being bombarded with sour odors from the homeless men watching action movies on their smartphones. Maybe he wouldn't hate Donald Trump then.

I stepped out of the library for lunch and found a nearby bench next to the welfare housing office. I watched several Africans pull up in cars, go inside, and come back out. So the Federal government is relocating Africans to Connecticut. If I hadn't sat outside this office, I wouldn't have even known there were Africans in Hamden, since I didn't see them in other parts of town, but give it a few years and it will be impossible not to see them. Locals will notice the growing number of ethnic shops in the strip malls and the aroma of goat-head stew coming from their neighbor's window. Then someone will ask, "Where did all the white kids go?" Their parents felt chafed at having to live next to Africans, so they moved further out, but refused to tell their friends exactly why for fear of being labeled a racist. Real estate investors buy up their homes and sign up for Section 8 to place welfare recipients in the suburbs. The African family has a big home now, and invites its relatives to America. The city begins to look more like an international airport. Trash and homeless people suddenly appear on the side of the road. The library is filled with defecators.

My father's neighborhood in the DC suburbs used to be half white when he moved in during the early 1990s, but now it's mostly African, courtesy of the Federal and state governments. When I studied American history in high school, I read about several armed revolts against the government, but there are no revolts these days. Americans are too weak from relentless divide-and-conquer tactics, too scared of losing their jobs and health care. A weakened people in fear don't revolt. They are simply replaced. Maybe goat-head stew won't taste so bad after all.

In spite of the Hamden frog slowly being boiled in a pot of water, I doubt I'll find a more ideal multicultural suburb in America. The housing is reasonably priced and the traffic is light. Many independent shops seem to exist alongside national chains. You do encounter youths blaring hip hop music from their cars, but I see no outward signs of a drug crisis, and the minorities seem law-abiding (for now). If I was forced to live in Hamden, I would accept it. I think my parents would far more enjoy living there than in the DC suburbs, and if they decided to up and relocate to Hamden, I would consider following them, because their current local government accepts kickbacks from developers to turn the suburbs into mini-cities with overcrowding, sprawl, and nonstop traffic congestion. There are already cases of people being shot dead near their neighborhoods. America may be in decline, but each town and city is declining at a different pace. Boston and Hamden haven't yet been impacted by the worst of it, and maybe several more years of calm living can be squeezed out of them.

†

When traveling through the United States, one must go to the parks. Close to Hamden is Sleeping Giants State Park, a wooded mountain with several trails. The temperature was 88° Fahrenheit, and I went in jeans because I didn't want to get bitten by the bugs. Apparently my unusual attire so worried a park ranger that he asked whether I was okay.

I climbed a moderate stony incline and enjoyed the view of two eagles circling overhead. The sweat from my legs remained trapped underneath my jeans. There weren't many people since it was a weekday, but the mountain was close enough to the roads for the sounds of the cars and trucks to drown out the songs of the birds. I knew I was supposed to want to stay in the park all day, relax, meditate, and so forth, but apart from glorifying God for the beauty, my mind couldn't stop wondering how much energy it would take to get back down the mountain. Give me a book and a clean library table and I can sit for hours, but put me on a hiking trail that involves physical effort and it feels too much like exercise. When I lived in Poland, I would rent a city bike and ride around a lake so slowly that joggers would pass me. I grudgingly accept that my constitution is that of a house cat. Give me peace, beauty, and nature, but only if it doesn't elevate my heart rate.

The next day I visited Mianus River Park near Stamford, Connecticut. The park had a flat elevation with wide, smooth trails. I reached the Mianus River after a half-mile hike and sat on a stone to listen to the water. There were young boys riding mountain bikes and adults with their dogs. The park was near a major city but I counted less than 30 people overall. I imagine the numbers swell on the weekends when people stuck with a nine-to-five job search for a bit of peace, only to be surrounded on all sides by others hoping for the same.

Palatial houses encircled the park. I had to travel by car to sit by the river but with enough money it can be right in your backyard. Simply add Adirondack chairs and sit. There are so many rich people in the United States, so many palaces. Where do they get their money? What kind of commitment to the world must one have to own a mansion by the river? If I had one myself, after some time adapting to the wealth and the river view, my mind would be dominated by the fear of losing it. My heart would stop if troubles at work suggested that I might lose my job. I would look at business news and stock prices with anxiety. Perhaps the only time I could relax would be the two hours a week I sit by the river's edge. I admit that I lack many things of this world, but for my spiritual development, I lack nothing.

I drove to the downtown area of Stamford, Connecticut and went straight to the main public library. An army of considerate staff was overseeing a wide cross-section of the Stamford community. There were children and families and senior citizens, nearly all white. There were artistic and historical exhibits. Not a single homeless person could be found. I thought about the public library nearest to my mother's house, composed predominately of minorities, many of whom are Ethiopians studying nursing and computer programming, representing the demographic change that is rapidly happening to the Washington, DC area.

After Stamford, I drove for 90 minutes to the Queens borough of New York City where my long-time friend Max offered me a place to stay for the weekend. He is at the center of my New York City follower-base—or at least what remains of it after my conversion to Christ—thanks to arranging meet-ups in the city for many years. If there is a man in New York City who follows me, chances are that Max knows him. He took me to a Russian restaurant that featured over a dozen types of shish kebab.

"How are the other guys doing?" I asked.

"Ron got married to his Ukrainian girlfriend. And Thomas married his girlfriend."

"They have kids yet?"

"Not yet."

"What happened to Sandip? I remember he was looking for a wife."

"He went to Southeast Asia for a couple of years. He had some girlfriends, but they didn't work out. He said that the culture was just too different for him."

"And how about the others?"

"Still dating. It's all Tinder and Hinge now. Girls here and there, you know how it is."

Max had been married for about a year. Having children was on his mind. If I ever get married, which is not looking likely, I would strive to impregnate my new wife on our wedding night. Otherwise, what is she going to do all day besides stare at my ugly face as I type away on the computer in the spare bedroom? Maybe she will get bored and start pursuing secular hobbies outside the home until she eventually sees me as a roommate she happens to have sex with.

The next afternoon, Max's wife helped me do laundry in a next-door building. "What do you think of New York City?" she asked.

"It smells," I quickly replied. The huge trash piles on the streets continually emitted a stench. Even after the trash was picked up, the stench lingered, impossible to eradicate. She gave me a perplexed look, perhaps expecting me to praise the beauty and vibrancy of the city.

"What are your plans for this weekend?" she asked.

"I have to work for the rest of the afternoon then head out to a dinner."

"You're not going to see anything in the city?"

"Maybe an hour here or there."

Another perplexed look. I knew what she was thinking: "You're in the most exciting city in the world and you don't want to rush out the door to see many of the experiences it has to offer?" That is correct, Mrs. Max, I want to run away from it, from the smells, the entertainments, the crowds, the concrete, the Jews, the feeling of being everywhere and nowhere at once when I hear a new language every 20 paces, the obscene disparity of wealth between the haves and the have-nots. What is there to like for a man who seeks God? I know Max enjoys the city, so I expect him to have a wife who feels the same, but if I meet a woman who likes New York City, I can confidently say that we're incompatible, and if she doesn't like it, she probably lives in a rural area and is therefore inaccessible for me to meet, and she probably married young and already has multiple children. If the family ship had sailed for me, all that was left was hatred of the world, after having sucked at its poisonous bosom for so long, and yet there I was, still in it, dedicating nearly a half-year to its highways, towers, and displays of flesh.

For the New York City dinner, I met with four other men. One was wading into the spiritual, having recently celebrated Lent, speaking well of Jesus Christ. One had achieved his material goals but didn't receive the happiness he thought he would. Another was tired of chasing women and continued to see them only as sexual options, and the fourth was still enjoying fornication, but was able to glimpse his future where that enjoyment was likely to be removed. Most were wondering about their exit plan of finding a good woman. Wouldn't such a woman solve their problems?

"If you marry a secular woman, you will have a secular outcome," I started. "Think of why most men get married today. The first reason is the fear of being alone. They look towards a woman, a flawed creature, for solving their existential problems, and it won't take many years of being with the same person, of living with the same person day after day, until you *wish* you were alone. The second reason is sex. Sex feels good and men want it, but you already know what happens when you have sex with the same person for an extended period of time—you get bored. You will wish to have sex with any woman *but* your wife. I'm sure you know what happened with Arnold Schwarzenegger. He married an attractive woman in the Kennedy family and had all the fame in the world, but he cheated on her with an unattractive Hispanic maid. One woman cannot possibly sate your lust, so you should not marry a woman for that reason. And then there's the third reason to get married: to have children. On the surface, that's a good motive. It's at least better than the previous two, but ask any parent about how fast their kids grew up. Ask them about the rebellion of the teenage years when the culture kidnaps them. Ask them about the silence in their home after they leave the house to become their own persons. They don't remain children that are yours to own. You'll be lucky if as adults they call you once a week and visit over Thanksgiving and Christmas. In the end, any secular reason you can come up with to get married will fail you.

"There's another reason to get married, and that's for the spiritual. In Orthodox teachings, marriage is for a man and woman to work out their salvation together, as a team. Their marriage creates a little church, with the man serving as the priest and the woman as his helper. When you have new children, you create souls—parishioners—that must be saved. Creating life is a wonderful thing, but if you don't guide that life to its salvation, your act of creation will lead to damnation. You become a murderer of souls.

"God created marriage for us to aid in our salvation. When marrying for this reason, you no longer remain in a marriage for the companionship, the sex, or the sake of having children. The entire context changes from serving your needs to serving God through your family. If something bad were to happen, such as divorce, you would see it as a trial from God, part of His plan to preserve your salvation and increase your rewards in Heaven. If your wife cheated on you or harmed the family in some way, how could you not conclude that Satan is corrupting her and drawing her to hell? She exercises her free will to do those things, but don't let her corrupt you. Don't follow her into hell. In good times, maintain the faith, and in bad times, maintain the faith. That's what marriage is for: to save your soul while fulfilling God's plan. You may have to experience extreme sorrow or grief, but with faith, you will not be defeated. You will not be like those men who become suicidal upon divorce. They saw their wives as their salvation, and now that their false god has been taken away from them, they have no meaning in life. Jesus Christ is your savior and the meaning to all. He is above your wife because only He can lead you to salvation."

The men stared at me in silence, pondering my lecture. Yes, they would get bored of sleeping around, but no, they should not just marry any girl. Find one who has repented like they must repent. Otherwise, she is still dancing with Satan, and will spread hellfire to any man she marries.

✝

On the day of the event, my heart was acting up. For years, I've had bouts of heart palpitations, where my heart feels like it is about to pound out of my chest, and also tachycardia, where my heartbeat briefly shoots up to 150 beats per minute before settling back down. While on the road, I experienced palpitations daily and tachycardia episodes that lasted for hours. Besides a weird feeling in my chest, and the anxiety that my heart was about to stop, I didn't experience other physical symptoms such as dizziness or chest pain.

In the past, I thought I had this problem because of coffee, but I had stopped drinking coffee months ago. A few years back, a cardiologist in Poland said that my heart was fine, and it would be best to manage the symptoms without medical intervention. This time around, I thought it was an electrolyte imbalance, but drinking coconut water and hydrating properly weren't helping. While I was on my way to the Manhattan hotel where I would hold the speech, my heart rate was out of control. The best I could do was to conserve as much energy as possible by moving slowly because canceling the event was not an option.

While setting up the room in a Times Square hotel, I checked online and noticed that an Antifa account on Twitter with over 30,000 followers had doxed the venue in the morning, instructing goons to crash the event by 5:30 p.m. I looked at the time: 5:00

p.m. I had checked into the hotel without a problem. I poked my head out of the room and saw no protesters. The tweet with the dox had received less than 100 likes, and the media hadn't picked up on it. Should I tell my guests that there was a possible threat to their safety? A group of thugs could come crashing into the event armed with cameras to film everyone in order to dox them. On the other hand, if I did tell everyone, the event would be ruined. People would be eyeing the door throughout my speech, fearing the worst. This happened with my Canadian events in 2015. No one could relax. I doubt even half the guests heard what I said in my speech. Just the mere threat of something happening would have the same effect as a group of agitators arriving to ruin the event.

I decided not to share the dox with anyone. I was sure no protesters would come, based on the late hour and lack of media involvement, and if protesters did come, I would put myself between them and the guests until hotel security or police arrived. If that didn't work and a guest was harmed, I would take full responsibility. I would absorb the risk on behalf of everyone, which in this case was made more difficult by my heart problem. I had no choice but to stay calm or it would beat even more wildly.

Guests started arriving. One was a large black woman with multiple tattoos. I had met numerous fans from all walks of life since I started writing around 1999, but I didn't recall any overweight black woman with tattoos being one of them. When I tried to engage her in small talk, she quickly excused herself to sit all the way in the back. She made sure not to interact with anyone. When I searched for her name online, I didn't come across anything incriminating, but I did suspect her as the source of the online leak.

After I started the speech, several late guests knocked on the door, but not one was a protester. No one, including the black woman, interrupted the event during its four-hour entirety, though one guest later told me that when he entered the hotel, there were six counter-terrorist police officers posted outside. I assumed that the New York City Police Department read Antifa's Twitter account.

I spoke extra slowly during the speech to conserve my energy, and it had the effect of making my delivery clearer and adding extra suspense during the stories. So the heart condition improved my speech over the previous week while forcing me to block out any source of anxiety. I would rather not feel like I have a fragile heart that is about to stop, but it served a positive purpose, and I prayed to God later that night to advise me how to proceed. I knew the problem was not putting me in immediate danger, but I was troubled by it since I had a long time left on the road.

After the event, I packed up my equipment and left the hotel. I was greeted by hundreds of homosexuals on the streets, all wearing the same uniform of tank top and extra-tight jean shorts. It was June, gay pride month. It seems to me that every month is gay pride month, but June even more so. I ate dinner in a nearby restaurant. Across from me was a table of five homosexuals mesmerized by an MMA match on the bar television set.

The next day was the city's gay pride march, which brings in homosexuals from all over the world in addition to their so-called allies: heterosexual men and women who believe that gays are the civil rights cause of our era. On the subway ride to the Upper East Side for my event's happy hour, the gay rainbow was everywhere—on people's clothes, their faces, on flags sticking out of their pockets and backpacks. Combined with all the storefronts pushing the gay pride rainbow, you'd think that it was the national flag.

I met a group of 30 guests at a fountain in Central Park's Conservatory Garden. The fountain had a metal bowl where birds were taking a swim and cleaning their feathers. I'd never seen birds do that before.

"Hey, guys," I said, "look at these birds taking a bath."

"Yes, Roosh, it's a birdbath," someone said.

"A bird... bath?" I thought that existed only in cartoons. I stared at the birds for some time, enchanted that these creatures not only wanted to take a bath but also seemed to be enjoying it. I decided that if I ever lived in the countryside, I would install a birdbath.

A married couple brought their seven-month-old son. It had been a while since I had seen a baby up close. He vomited on his mother twice though she didn't seem to mind. The baby had practically no control over his faculties, but was taking in the environment with excited eyes. It would be cool to have a baby around, I thought at that moment, but I had wasted too much time doing things opposed to having babies. In an environment where good women are rare, you have to start rather early to find one instead of going on a multi-decade fornication world tour because you value your "sex life" above all else, only to start in earnest when you're middle-aged. While men have more time than women to procreate, that extra time seems irrelevant when fertile young women are more eager to attend a gay pride march than become mothers.

A sudden rainstorm forced us into a bar. I made the rounds, trying to have a one-on-one conversation with everyone.

"I saw you watching the birdbath and I couldn't help but smile," one man said. "When you find God, you regain your innocence again. You are able to appreciate simple beauty as if you were a child."

"You've been through this before?" I asked.

"Yes, several years ago. My family is rich, so I thought the pursuit of money was the answer. I found your books and had success sleeping around. And then I hit a dead end. I looked into all the religions, including the one I was born into, Hinduism, and eventually decided that Christianity was the ultimate truth. I experienced an ego death just like you have."

"A lot of people say ego death is when your consciousness melds into the universe. You become one with infinity. That wasn't something I felt."

"By ego death I mean that you have subverted your will to a higher power. Your ego, your needs, and your desires no longer come first. Within a monastery on Mount Athos, there is written, 'If you die before you die, when you die, you don't die.' If your ego dies before you physically die, when you do physically die, your soul doesn't die."

"Through prayer, I ask God what His will is for me."

"And His will for you fits within His plan. He knows exactly how this story will end, and so it must end in that way. Everything that is happening now, all this gay pride and degeneracy, this globalization—it has to happen for His end to be achieved."

"How far do you think we are from that?" I asked.

"A long way. Obama was the test case for the 'little a' antichrist. Even I bought into him. I thought he would change the world and save us all."

"I voted for him the first time around, too."

"There will be another 'little a' antichrist that even more people get tricked by. Satan is testing his methods until he finally reveals the 'big A' Antichrist, and then the end of human history follows. It is far away. I don't think we'll experience it in our lifetimes."

"It's obvious that evil is increasing. I see it all around me, and my instinct is to fight against it and…"

"You can't!" he interrupted. "The script is written! This evil must happen, and it must get worse. God is testing our souls. He wants to see if we're worthy for heaven, and He will allow Satan to degrade this world in horrifying ways. There's nothing we can do about it except be concerned for our salvation. With faith and humility, we'll get through."

I used to think of God as a sort of watchmaker. He pushed the start button on creation and let things run their course while lounging somewhere on a heavenly beach. Now I see Him not as a micro-manager but as a nano-manager. Not only are the very hairs of your head all numbered, but I doubt it would be a stretch to say that He can account for every atom in the universe. We have free will, but He accounts for all of our choices, and knows how our choices will impact other choices, and on and on it goes into the most impossible of calculations, but for Him it is no effort. Evil will proceed for a while, and then it will turn into good, and those who want to be saved will be saved.

†

I had a dream. I'm driving a yellow school bus. Five men are inside. I stop the bus to pick up two men, but I want to know where I'm going. I put the bus in park and walk outside. I look at the front of the bus. It says "Heaven." A bus is not that big; it contains maybe 50 or 60 seats. Is that the number of souls I must help save until my life is over? Is that my mission?

I decided to visit the gay pride parade to film footage for my YouTube video travelogue. I knew I'd be walking into the biggest exhibition of homosexuality in the world, so I prayed on the subway ride over that what I was about to see wouldn't corrupt me further or make me hate others. I got off at the 14th Street subway stop and walked up the stairs into the middle of Sodom.

I was greeted by a group of black women twerking in the middle of the street. Large groups of gays and their supporters walked by, fully decked out in rainbow paraphernalia. Most surprising of all was that most of the attendees were straight women of college age with slim figures and long hair, dressed up as if they were attending a music festival like Coachella, with little ribbons tied around their arms and their skin coated with a shotgun blast of glitter. I walked by one such female on the sidewalk, and she was sticking out her tongue in front of her smartphone to get the perfect selfie, barely able to keep her eyes open from whatever drug she had taken that wanted to close them.

I walked closer to the parade line. Huge groups of gays in skimpy clothing roamed free, unafraid of judgment. I passed by a restaurant named Garden of Eden, reminding me of where I was not. I made it to the parade line and was greeted by an over-weight, shirtless black man wearing a gimp face mask. His leather pants were so low that I could see his curly pubic hair. Then another group of gays arrived in full bondage gear, whooping it up as if they owned the city. Beside me a white man and Asian girl couple was taking a selfie with several transsexu-als in the background. I imagined it would receive an inordinate number of likes on their Instagram accounts. A parade float sponsored by American Airlines came through with multiple gays and transsexuals dressed as flamboyant flight attendants. The crowd was cheering, waving their rainbow flags and yelling, "Happy pride!" An Irish Pride float followed, and then I looked to my left and saw three topless women, significantly overweight, with random words scrawled across their bodies.

It's one thing to see homosexual activists online, but it's another to see them up close. They are not a niche community and they are not small fry. The gays may be small in absolute numbers, but their corporate sponsors and government enablers have elevated them to be one of the most privileged groups of our time. Their straight allies shout down men like me for being "bigots" while elevating the naked obese women and the black man with visible pubic hair as paragons of virtue. Based on the huge presence of heterosexual women, I concluded that all gay propaganda, from the rainbow flag to the empty slogan "Love is love," is not targeted at gays at all but straight women. It is meant to suck them into a degenerate lifestyle of fornication and intoxication, to develop a hatred for the type of man who is most capable of creating a strong family and resisting the evils of homosexuality. The purpose of gay pride is not only to pat gays on the back but to destroy female innocence, to bombard them with a lifestyle of sex and drugs, to render them sterile. And it's working, because I was stunned at how many attractive women were cheering with their gay flags, at how many women were being pulled down by Satan into hell.

I was happy to leave New York City. Apart from the birdbath in Central Park, I had seen nothing good for a soul that was trying to be good. Everything about the city attempts to draw you into the cult of the world. Many who live there are convincing themselves that New York City is the best city in the country, and that they're living the best life possible, when they're actually living like a diseased rat, soaking in filth, excrement, and sulfur. Just trying to eke out a living in New York City requires such an obsession with the material in the name of "making it" that the spiritual life is unlikely to happen. I must conclude that God has forsaken New York City. He abandoned her long ago, and I can only wonder whether He will enact judgment upon the city in my lifetime.

3

Garden

I drove to Princeton, New Jersey, and toured the university that was named after it. Every campus building appeared to be a preserved historical treasure. To my untrained architectural eye, many looked like castles. Vines and other forms of vegetation covered the facades as if the structures had always been there, born with the earth itself. Large groups of rosy-faced high-schoolers received tours from enthusiastic Princeton students. I presumed none of them had a problem with paying $73,000 a year for tuition and lodging. By comparison, my entire four-year education at the University of Maryland while living at home cost $21,000. I graduated in 2001 and started a job with a salary of $30,000, so I suppose it wasn't a bad investment.

The university chapel was open. I walked in, not expecting much, but was greeted by a massive vaulted structure 12 stories high designed in the Gothic style. Two levels of stained glass windows adorned the sides of the church, detailing scenes from the Old Testament and the New. The most magnificent stained glass was in the front of the chapel, depicting Jesus Christ and the Apostles. I sat down on a pew near the back and recited the Jesus Prayer to give glory to God.

Tourists, mostly Asian, would come into the chapel, take a picture, and then leave. Only two others sat down, perhaps to pray. I wouldn't mind worshipping God in a chapel like this. I looked into the church's denomination and learned that it was interfaith, based on what various world councils of churches could agree on. That comes down to (1) there is a God, and (2) Jesus was a very special person who might be the Son of God. This watered-down Gospel takes the focus away from Christ and onto concepts like "love" and "forgiveness," which do nothing to increase a person's faith and prevent them from sinning. Instead, it leads to the scenes I had just witnessed in New York City. In the name of love and forgiveness, you end up promoting the most vulgar of evils.

I looked at the service calendar and noticed that the head of the church was a woman, and the pastor was a woman, and the visiting pastors were also women. Sadly, the holiest you will feel in the Princeton chapel is when there is no service, because when those women get up to speak in front of the faithful, I must presume that it is not the Holy Spirit who is moving their lips.

Once I stepped out of the chapel and began walking around the town, I expected a situation similar to the one at Yale, where the university was beautiful but the surrounding city was down and out, but Princeton was no Yale. There were no homeless people, and the mostly young adults milling around were polite and respectful. I walked into the brand-new public library and marveled at the three floors stocked with completely new furnishings, the private conference rooms encased in thick glass, the "newsroom" and the "tech room," and the sleek meeting spaces where Princeton University professors came by to give free educational talks. The library must have cost many millions of dollars to build.

There were no homeless people in the library. Because of my long hair and bushy beard, people started looking at me like *I* was the homeless person. Even the university-aged males were dressed in polo shirts and boat shoes. While I was taking a couple of pictures of the library, a security guard came to observe me closely, ready to put his combat training to use. I was the homeless man in Princeton, the one who caused people to go online and complain that the neighborhood was going downhill.

Most everyone in Princeton, at least those connected to the university, preaches about "equality" and thinks refuge should be given to the poor, unwashed masses. Well, I'm poor and unwashed! I'm a person of brownish color! Give me your library! Give me your safe and clean streets! Lift me out of the suburban ghetto of Washington, DC! Give it all to me for free! Would they grant me that wish in the name of equality?

†

I drove through New Jersey to the small town of New Hope, Pennsylvania. For a town with such a small population, it was exceedingly leftist. Of the four stores on the main intersection, two displayed gay flags. There was also a psychic shop, a witchcraft store next to it, and countless art studios, which I presumed were operated by women.

I was starting to understand how the oligarchs feed a tailor-made propaganda program to each socioeconomic class. The poor blacks get hip hop, Nike shoes, junk food, and fashion brands produced in China. The poor whites get opioids, alcohol, and junk food. The middle-class whites get sodomy, casual sex, "racism," and "equality." The upper-middle-class whites get hyper-materialism in the form of luxury cars, boats, Ivy League universities, leisurewear, and real estate. Every group is given a program that will render it harmless to the state, both politically and demographically. Where is Jesus Christ? He is concealed by the state, and yet faith in Him endures, a testament to the Holy Spirit and the spiritual nature within all of us. Our oligarchs attempt to destroy us, materially, emotionally, and spiritually, for their own sake and the sake of their power, yet people still seek Christ. No one preached the Gospel to me, yet here I am. The oligarchs, by pushing strategies of evil to kill God, may inadvertently be helping people come to the faith, for if there is evil, there must also be good, and we know in our hearts who is behind each one.

In nearby Lambertville, New Jersey, I went to the Howell Living Farm, a project maintained by the county to show the public how farm life used to be in the late nineteenth century before mechanization. I learned that hay is made from dry grass, a fact that had somehow escaped my upbringing. I saw sheep, chickens, horses, and pigs. I had seen all these animals before, but not in the context of possibly wanting my own farm with animals. I heard that the amount of work on a farm increases once you start adding animals, and is not something a hermit bachelor can handle unless there is free labor close by.

While watching the pigs sleep in their excrement, I spotted two birds with a streak of dark orange and white on their wings. I loaded up the Merlin bird-watcher app I had downloaded the day before and went through the prompts to identify the birds as red-winged blackbirds. Exhilaration! I'm a bird-watcher now! Maybe it was simply a matter of asking God to change the channel from women to landscapes, from Twitter to birds, from urban living, entertainment, pleasure, impulsiveness, and dependence to farming, nature, beauty, patience, and independence.

After I toured the farm, where I started fantasizing about having my own chickens, vegetable garden, and pug guard dog to protect the chickens from predators, I had lunch on a picnic table. I could not get an internet connection on my phone to read the news so instead I watched the bees pollinate the wildflowers. I listened to the farm tractors roll on by. If I lived in a place like this, how much would I even need the internet? What was there to stay connected to? More importantly, what was the internet taking away from me while I had it? What propaganda was being delivered to me even while I thought I was aware of all the possible propaganda that could be delivered?

The farmer controls crops and animals while the oligarchs control human beings. A man thinks he is free, perhaps like the sheep grazing in the field thinks it is free, but he is constrained in the cubicle pen and the apartment pen, and is tagged and tracked with a number—a financial score and a social score—and is fleeced of his labor, money, and faith.

†

I drove to King of Prussia in Pennsylvania. The name was the most interesting part of this basic suburban town. I went because of Valley Forge, a national park that preserves a winter encampment used by George Washington's Continental Army at the onset of the American Revolutionary War. After losing Philadelphia to the British, Washington retreated a day's march to Valley Forge for the winter, which was close enough to monitor British activities. Washington commandeered the land, "renting" it from the owners with the nearly worthless Continental scrip currency.

The winter was rough. A lack of food, medicines, and other supplies led to the death of up to 2,000 soldiers and the desertion of many more, but Washington and his men persevered and went on to defeat the British. Valley Forge is a critical story in the founding of the United States, one that started the mythos of it being the greatest country in the world.

I received a pamphlet from a park ranger after buying a pocket-sized edition of the Declaration of Independence and the Constitution. The pamphlet informed me how "diverse" Washington's camp had been and how the people had spoken "several languages" and had practiced "several religions." I put the pamphlet in my back pocket and was ready for the tour to convince me that George Washington had believed in the glorious multiculturalism we have today, just like how John Hancock had supported sodomy. Washington would no doubt have supported the flood of Third World immigrants as an indispensable step towards creating a glorious nation.

The first stop on the tour was a re-creation of the log cabins that the soldiers had lived in. Then the National Memorial Arch, erected to commemorate the arrival of George Washington and his Continental Army. As I walked towards the arch, I noticed the etching of an Illuminati symbol, the all-seeing eye atop a pyramid, which you can see on the back of any dollar bill. Below was the following text:

And here in this place of sacrifice
In this vale of humiliation
In this valley of the shadow of that death out of which the life
of America rose, regenerate and free
Let us believe with an abiding faith that to them, union will
seem as dear and liberty as sweet and progress as glorious as
they were to our fathers
And are to you and me and that the institutions which have
made us happy
Preserved by the virtue of our children shall bless the remot-
est generation of the time to come

It echoed Psalm 23:4...

Yea, though I walk through the valley of the shadow of death,
I will fear no evil;
For You are with me;
Your rod and Your staff, they comfort me.

The inscription attempts to tap into our spiritual inclination to worship, but worship who? Dare I say, not God? It wants us to worship Washington and his army as bringers of "liberty" and "progress." Most Americans at that time were godly, so the trick was to invoke biblical language and vaguely Christian ideas to garner support for their crusade against the British monarchy.

The base of the monument had a plaque with a square and compass, a popular symbol in Freemasonry, and another plaque contained additional symbols of their secret society, including a letter with the number 22. George Washington, Paul Revere, John Hancock, and many of the Boston Tea Party combatants happened to be Freemasons, who, on joining the club, had to take an initiation oath to put its needs above those of God or be punished with death, and those needs—as rumor has it—become increasingly sinister once a member passes the thirty-third-degree ranking. Their lives become subservient to the will of the men in their club, not to God, and such men founded the United States of America, a nation that might have been almost entirely Christian in those early days, but in which today we are starting to see signs of the persecution of Christians.

I toured Valley Forge on July 3, one day before Independence Day, when Americans celebrate freedom from the "evil" British who were "oppressing" us. Their taxes were too high, and they constrained our liberty, and so we went to war with them. We threw off the yoke of the British and a king who should have been serving under God to become dominated by homosexuals and anti-racism activists who wheel out drag queens to read to little children.

I opened up my pocket Declaration of Independence.

We hold these truths to be self-evident, that all men are created equal, that they are endowed by their Creator with certain unalienable Rights, that among these are Life, Liberty and the pursuit of Happiness. –That to secure these rights, Governments are instituted among Men, deriving their just powers from the consent of the governed, –That whenever any Form of Government becomes destructive of these ends, it is the Right of the People to alter or to abolish it, and to institute new Government...

The document states that governments derive their power from the consent of the governed, but I have to ask: Is heaven a democracy? Does God take a vote among the angels to see what He should do? No, it's a monarchy. Just rule on earth must also be a monarchy, under a king who exerts God's will and love upon the populace. Democracy depends on the manipulation of feelings, moods, and trends to garner votes for a small group of oligarchical interests. Why should an ungodly man, or one steeped in sin, have the right to steer the direction of society? What kind of good can come from his vote? If you have a community and you want it to fall, simply give everyone a voice, conduct opinion polls, and seek to satisfy their bestial impulses. You will be living in hell before you know it.

The last stop on the tour was Washington Memorial Chapel, something of a misnomer, as it wasn't constructed until the early twentieth century. Like in Princeton, I entered with the intention of praying. The chapel was smaller but beautifully constructed in the Gothic style. I sat down and began reciting the Jesus Prayer while staring at the altar, but a few seconds in I felt the instinct to look down. I paused my prayer and craned my neck to stare at the aisle. There was a black-and-white checkerboard pattern: another symbol of Freemasonry. I stood up and walked to the back of the chapel. Washington's coat of arms was embedded within the checkerboard floor. Elsewhere, I found Latin words below his coat of arms: *Exitus Acta Probat*. The literal translation is "The outcome justifies the deed." In other words, the ends justify the means. But whose means? The means of the Freemasons. And what end? The end of power, for them to be at the very top of an inevitably secular nation.

I looked up at the stained glass windows. I was expecting to see prophets from the Bible, as I had in the Princeton chapel, but I saw soldiers in the act of war. The chapel was not a house of God but a house of the Freemasons, created to worship man instead of God. I immediately left. In hindsight, I'm surprised the chapel even displayed a cross.

It's hard to buy the founding narrative that had been sold to me since childhood. I couldn't see the founders as supernatural men worthy of worship. They were ambitious, intelligent, conniving, and strong, no doubt, but hadn't they been seeking their own glory and power? They overthrew the godly authority of the king—as flawed as that king had been—to establish a secular nation where they would eventually be worshipped on the level of gods. If the National Memorial Arch contained crosses and quotations from the Bible instead of the symbols of Freemasonry, I would sing a different tune, but it's clear that our founders had a level of spiritual belief that was incompatible with what I was learning as an Orthodox Christian. For a tour that was supposed to make me feel like a true American, I felt disappointed, empty, and void of national pride. It made sense to me why America had no resistance to the evil that encroached on its shores, because from the very beginning, the intention might have been to dethrone God.

†

My next stop was Chanticleer Pleasure Garden, a 35-acre garden estate in Wayne, Pennsylvania, built by a family that got rich in pharmaceuticals. The estate was eventually donated to a non-profit foundation that opened the gardens to the public for a reasonable fee.

I started my tour of the estate in the courtyard of the main house, where I was greeted by a gentle fountain surrounded by dozens of species of plants, bush, and flowers. I do not have the writing ability or vocabulary to describe the magnificence of what I saw, but I immediately thought of Adam and Eve and the sublime natural beauty they experienced when God placed them in the Garden of Eden. If man can create such an impressive monument to nature as Chanticleer, I can only wonder what God has prepared for us in Heaven.

The pessimist in me, strongly activated from the visit to Valley Forge, wanted to assume that Chanticleer had not been made to glorify God, but since its substrate was nature itself, a direct creation of God, it glorified God even if that had not been its creators' intention, unlike buildings and monuments made of glass, concrete, and steel, which were wholly formed by the hand of man. You can walk into a dense city and not see God in a single street or alley, but the second you walk into a little forest strewn with branches and foliage, God can be felt even by those without sight.

The previous day, I had bought a pair of binoculars so I could better identify the birds. Next to the courtyard, I saw a hummingbird at a nectar feeder, the first time I had seen one up close. Beyond the courtyard, birds with orange chests were scanning the grass for worms. American robins. Nearby were smaller birds, brown in color, hanging out in pairs. Brown-headed cowbirds. Then a small bird, with white and brown striations. A song sparrow.

The garden's employee told me that it would take an hour to walk the entire path of the garden. I took three hours, stopping often to watch the birds with my binoculars. I meandered along the stream and listened to its constant chatter. I watched the mustached koi fish squabble over food. I stared at the lone lawn chairs and imagined myself sitting in them day after day, reading thick, impossible books, and I lounged on the stone couch, the surface of which retained the day's heat. There was too much beauty for me to handle, and I didn't think I deserved to see it because of all the ugly things I had done.

I found a picnic table to relax from relaxing. It began to rain. Many of the guests hurried for cover, but I let the rain fall on me as it fell on the plants. A gray catbird flew to my table and perched only three feet away. He stared at me intently, unafraid that I could harm him. I wondered whether God was trying to tell me something with His birds.

†

I thought Philadelphia would be like Baltimore, a city in great decline from its peak, but it was more like Cleveland, rough around the edges, its glory days long past, but at least not as dense as New York City. I even picked up on some conservatism in the form of blue-collar white men wearing loose-fitting jeans and old baseball caps, an increasingly rare sight in American cities that are becoming dominated by foreign laborers.

On the day of the event dinner, my stomach was in intense pain. It was so bad that I couldn't stand without crouching. Since becoming infected with giardia and other intestinal bugs when I went to South America ten years ago, my stomach has become extremely sensitive. Sometimes, for no reason at all, I have pain that lasts for days. A doctor once diagnosed me with post-infectious irritable bowel syndrome, which was the same as saying, "I don't know what's wrong with you." At least my heart condition abated when I got the idea to take magnesium citrate supplements, which I vaguely remembered had been recom-mended by my Polish doctor.

I checked my email and discovered that the credit card pro-cessor I was using to sell tour tickets had shut down my account without reason. It was the second processor to do so since I had first offered tickets. I had a backup credit card processor, but the checkout process wasn't working, so for a day I couldn't sell tickets. With my stomach still in great pain, thoughts of canceling the entire tour entered my mind. It was crazy to try to hold events in 23 cities. I prayed to God for guidance.

I arrived at the dinner location and met with four men. Guests at the previous dinners had usually been armed with questions, but this group hardly asked me anything. We had little to talk about. The one man who did ask me questions was most interested in my conversion to God. A part of me felt bad for the secular-minded men who followed me. They just wanted tips on how to get laid, and here they had the pickup guru in the flesh but he no longer picked up girls. They were a few years late in meeting me, for during my 2015 lecture tour, all I would talk about was women.

One of the guests said he was sleeping around to gain the game experience to settle down with the girl he wanted to eventually marry.

"The problem with that," I replied, "is that a girl who needs a lot of game is not a good choice. She desires a man who can emotionally excite her, and while you may be that man today, you certainly won't be that man tomorrow. What you really want is a girl who requires no game. She should be meek, shy, humble, uncomfortable flirting with men, and devoted to God. She is almost impossible to find in the city, since any woman here is likely a pleasure seeker who is hyper-socialized to flirt with numerous men and interact with them. She will have high expectations and require tight game to remain in a permanent state of attraction. You will end up mastering game to use on the woman who you should never choose as a lifelong partner."

"Then do you advise getting no experience with women at all, even remaining a virgin?"

"A promiscuous woman doesn't want a virgin or chaste man, but the woman who is chaste herself wouldn't mind it, and may prefer it, because she knows that would help create a lasting marriage, yet it's so rare to find a chaste woman to marry that if you go the route of chastity, you may never be intimate with a woman again. That's an outcome I'm willing to accept because I have God in my life, but without God, how can you possibly take this route? There would be no immediate material benefit and no guarantee of a future benefit. In that case, having sex with anyone becomes the likely option. It's fun and feels good. It can be done in a 'safe' manner even while drunk. So you will pursue sex and hope that after you bang X amount of girls, there will be one good girl in the bunch to have a fairytale marriage with before you get too old. The more likely outcome is you get only sex, and after a few years you won't even be satisfied with it. The downsides become evident in the form of guilt, regret, or something more material like drama, pregnancy scares, sexually transmitted diseases, and false rape accusations. If you sleep with too many women, you will damage your ability to bond with one, or develop such unreasonable standards that no woman will ever be good enough for you. Every woman you meet will be a 'slut,' because that's all you have experience with. When deciding to avoid fornication, there is no immediate benefit. There may not ever be a benefit in this world, but at least for your soul, the benefit is eternal."

I looked at the faces of the men. One wasn't paying attention. The man who asked the original question stared at me vacantly. Another raised his eyebrows. The last took out a piece of paper and a pen to take notes. In the previous week in New York City, I saw a man with tears in his eyes when I arrived at the most emotional part of my speech, while at the same time two guests in the back were goofing off and laughing. I can never guess how my words will be received.

†

Within a day of asking God whether I should continue my tour, I received two emails. The first email:

You pulled me back from the brink. The story of you, your past, your present, and your plans for your future saved me. I know you said you feel ashamed of your past now, but I don't think any other story would have connected with me and made me see the right path.

And the second:

> *I just wanted to say that I really enjoyed your event. It's really inspiring me to come to God and rid myself of addictions to sensuality, etc.*

I don't look for signs, and it's possible that God didn't enlighten these men to praise my current work so soon after I asked Him for help, but if you do believe in God, how can you also believe in coincidences? I don't believe we live in a purely Newtonian world where everything that happens is based on mathematics and probability. If I pray for help and don't tell another soul what I asked for, yet I start receiving answers that aid me in my decision, it must either be guidance from God or deception from the demons, though if what I'm being steered toward brings me or others closer to God without involving sin, especially pride, I want to believe it's coming from God.

I couldn't help but wonder how God works. I prayed for answers to a specific question, and then men contacted me with a message that was specific to that answer. Why did those men decide to email me at the time they did? Did God present them with a mental impulse to perform an action and allow them to use their own free will to decide whether or not to follow through? If two men contacted me, could that mean that God put the impulse in five or more men, and most chose not to send an email? Then I started to feel uneasy trying to understand God's ways, that by doing so I would be going down the road of pride.

The Philadelphia lecture and happy hour were successful. Three down, 20 to go. After the lecture, I wanted to feel pleasure, so I rewarded myself with a burger, fries, and chocolate pie despite my stomach's condition. Seated near me was a black man trying to seduce a black woman. She admitted that she was married but did very little to fend off the man's advances, even encouraging him to contact her the next day. I couldn't help but think of my past when I had pursued women who I knew were in relationships. Many gave in and slept with me. What the black couple was doing was none of my business, but I hated being reminded of what I used to do.

4

Christians

After Philadelphia, I drove to a Mennonite bed and breakfast near Lancaster, Pennsylvania, the home of a large Amish population. I was greeted by a young woman in modest dress holding a toddler. She appeared to be no older than 25. She checked me in and then I went for a walk on their dairy farm. The cows stared at me intently as I moved around. I encountered the milking area where her husband, who couldn't have been over 30, was finishing his day.

"It's okay, you can come in and see the cows," he said.

"I haven't seen a cow since I was a child," I noted. "They look a lot bigger in person than on the television."

He attached an apparatus to the udder of a cow, which I knew meant it was female, and turned on a machine that pumped her milk through a filter into a glass tank and then into a stainless steel tank.

"This is the milk I drink," the farmer said.

"I'm embarrassed to say that I'm lactose intolerant."

"You know, we had a guest who was the same, but he drank raw milk and didn't have any problems. The pasteurization process destroys a lot of enzymes. I can't drink pasteurized milk myself."

The farmer eventually asked me where I was from. "The Washington, DC suburbs," I replied. "Apartments and strip malls were built over the farms a long time ago."

"Well, farming still goes on," he smiled. "What kind of food trends are popular there?"

"Organic. People think that if they eat organic, they have a lower chance of getting cancer and other diseases. There is a real fear of dying, so people don't mind spending more to supposedly live longer. Do you eat organic?"

"Never. I think it's a scam."

"People are scared of Roundup weed killer."

He thought for a moment. "If you open a bottle of Roundup and drink it, you'd definitely get sick, but in the amounts we use, I believe it's safe. Pesticides and herbicides are expensive, so there is an incentive to use the smallest amount possible. The crops aren't soaking in them."

He may be right, but if I'm able to buy food grown in a natural environment without chemicals, why shouldn't I? My problem as a suburban consumer is that I don't know whether the organic product I buy is truly organic since I never visited the farm that the food came from. I must assume cheating is rampant, since the financial incentive to do so is substantial. In theory, organic sounds natural and healthy, but in practice it does seem like a scam for city folk who are scared of dying.

"Walking on your farm makes me realize I missed out on a whole way of life," I said. "I'm really good at sitting down on a chair in an air-conditioned room and typing away on a laptop, but not much more. Even if I move to a rural area and start a farm, I would have to begin with the basics as if I were a child."

"This farm has been in my family for three generations. If you want to make the move, you have to start with something."

"The cities are getting bad now. The homeless problem is growing. And the gay and transsexual propaganda is getting more intense. Are you aware of the things going on?"

"Oh yes, I hear about it. They were forcing that Christian baker to bake the gays a cake. Now they're suing him for a second or third time?"

"I think they're on the third. They're not doing it because they want the cake but to make an example out of people, to scare others from speaking out against immorality. They want everyone to be silent and allow evil to happen."

The farmer nodded his head and began spraying down the floor.

"I was living the immoral city life for a long time, drinking alcohol and chasing women, until I couldn't do it anymore," I said, perhaps offering too much information.

"You got tired of it?"

I assumed that his wife was the first woman he'd been with.

"You adapt to it. Your body gets used to the pleasure, and then you need to increase the dose to experience the same pleasure, but you soon hit a ceiling and then you're stuck, so you have to look for new ways of experiencing pleasure that are even more self-destructive. In the end, you lose yourself."

In the media, Christian farmers are portrayed as simple-minded and aw-shucks dumb. The Mennonite knew his way around a farm that allowed him to provide for his family. He was aware of what was happening in the secular world, and while he didn't have first-hand knowledge of the nature of carnal sin, he was better off for it. He had a healthy child and a devoted wife who didn't take selfies or wear sexy clothing. He lived connected to God, nature, and family. His life wasn't easy, for he woke up at 4:30 in the morning every day to milk the cows, but what did he lack? He toiled on the farm and for that he was rewarded as much as he could be in this life.

I thought about my life in contrast. I had satisfied every pleasure under the sun—girls, travel, fame, money—and yet what fruits did I have to show the farmer? The books I wrote to help men in the city get laid? My live streams where I outraged my audience with news stories about homosexuals doing disgusting things? What creation of mine could he even pretend to show an interest in out of politeness? My life's work was useless to him. It was godless and sterile. I had been presented with temptations and had accepted all of them without a fight. If I had been born a Mennonite on Pennsylvania farmland, I might have my own farm and family. Sure, I would be curious about sin, and wonder what it would be like to sleep around, but those thoughts would dim when gazing upon my humble wife who took care of the household chores while I took care of the farm. Instead, I was born into a loving but secular family in the dense Washington, DC suburbs. I was approaching 40 not sure which hole chicken eggs came out of, or whether or not cows were dangerous. I was still a little child when it came to things of the natural world and of God.

I usually don't eat before noon, but I decided to try the wife's cooking for breakfast at 9 a.m. She first served me a basket of homemade biscuits and farm butter, along with a big glass of raw milk, which lacked the sour aftertaste of store-bought milk. I would soon find out whether or not I was lactose intolerant. Beside a kitchen window, I noticed a small shrine that contained a pair of blue baby shoes but no picture. Bible quotes were displayed throughout the house.

"Do you lock your doors at night?" I asked. The bed-and-breakfast section of the house was protected by only a screen door.

"We don't. Even if we wanted to, the house is so old that we can't fully secure it."

She brought me a bowl of scrambled eggs and an iron skillet of apple pancakes baked in the oven.

"So the Mennonites are not as strict as the Amish when it comes to technology?"

"We don't have a television or internet access, but most other things we have." I noticed she didn't have a dishwasher. "But the Amish are starting to modernize. They have milk units now on dairy farms and some use technology for businesses that are not on the farm."

"Do the Amish look down on you for using technology?"

"No, I don't think so. We get along, though we don't interact too much. There is a large Mennonite community here."

The long pauses in our conversation about farm life and how it compared to the city encouraged me to pre-edit my speech instead of babbling on. People usually wait for their turn to speak without paying attention to what the other person is saying. Just two days prior, I had been in a café seated next to two women who did not take a single audible break for an hour. One of them had gone on about how angry she was over a man who didn't want to be her friend after she rejected his romantic overtures, and what emotions he could be experiencing for coming to such a bad decision. Somehow, just being able to hear them had left me feeling exhausted.

As I finished breakfast, the Mennonite woman cleaned the kitchen. If you asked me to rate her beauty on a scale of one to ten, I would not be able to do so. I could not see this devoted wife and mother as a sexual object to be evaluated, because when someone has great inner beauty, it radiates through their outer beauty. The reason for her devotion was her faith in God, which means that inner beauty *is* faith. When a woman has no faith, outer beauty is all she has, and she will obsess over it to ensure she looks perfect for men who also have no faith. The faithless woman's outer beauty, the first thing you see, is her most important asset, but outer beauty is the least significant aspect of the woman who has faith. All the outer flaws of someone with faith are beautiful, while all the outer flaws of someone without faith are ugly, because the further you venture into the soul of the latter, the uglier they become. If I can look at a woman and easily quantify her outer beauty, without perceiving anything of beauty coming from within, I must lean to the conclusion that she does not have God in her life.

I finished all the food she served me, which was enough for two men, and proceeded to enter a four-hour food coma where I wanted to sleep but couldn't. Thankfully, I did not have to run to the toilet, suggesting that the farmer was right about pasteurized milk causing symptoms of lactose intolerance.

Later, I drove to downtown Lancaster, expecting to find a holy city due to the presence of the Amish. I was disappointed to find a secular one. Having a church located on every other block did not seem to make a difference to the man I saw sashaying down the street in woman's clothing or the churches promoting sodomy through their female pastors. The Amish and Mennonites may be faithful, but living beside them won't passively give you faith through osmosis.

While I was walking in the city center, a man with a woman and two children approached me with his hand outstretched. "I really admire what you do," he said. "You're reaching so many men. Can I pray for you?"

"Yes," I replied.

He put his hands on my shoulders and said a brief prayer, asking God to give me the strength to bring more men closer to Him. His wife and children didn't at all seem surprised at what was happening, so I presumed this was a somewhat common occurrence. After he had completed the prayer, I was ready to have a chat, but he thanked me and walked off.

Inside the Lancaster Free Public Library, half of the men were homeless or newly homeless, using the free internet to watch movies on their phones. I attempted to use the bathroom but was stymied three separate times by men who were defecating. I went upstairs and tried to use the restroom on the children's level but the staff said I was not allowed because I didn't have a child with me. I had to leave the library early so I could find a place to urinate.

As part of my farm stay, I signed up for an Amish dinner for a suggested donation of $20. Still sated from breakfast, I drove to another dairy farm in the early evening. I was joined by seven other tourists—an older Australian couple, a younger couple from the Netherlands, and a married Spanish couple with one child. Since my hometown was only two hours away from Lancaster, I was considered a local.

The Amish wife introduced us to her family. She had eight children, most of them girls, all wearing modest garb. Two of the older girls were helping their mother with the meal. The youngest child, a boy of four, brought out a toy John Deere sprayer that he had just received for his birthday. None of the children had seen a movie or a cartoon. The family did not follow the news beyond what happened locally, so outside of major wars, they had no idea what was going on in the world. Based on the traditional home they were maintaining, I could not imagine how following the news would aid their family life in any way.

The dinner was something out of a 1950s American family movie: potatoes, green beans, zucchini casserole, chicken casserole, meatloaf, freshly baked bread, and apple pie. This was the kind of meal you needed to eat if you worked on a farm all day, but if you were like me and mostly sat, nap time would have to follow immediately after.

The man from the Netherlands stressed multiple times that he could not eat any dairy products. The Amish wife went to great pains to meet his dietary requirements, though I wondered why anyone would pay to have dinner on a dairy farm when they couldn't eat any dairy. To add some fun to the dinner, I asked the Dutch couple what they disliked most about America.

The woman answered first. "There's too much talk about God. I was asked by a Mennonite man if I believed, and when he found out I was an atheist, he wanted to have a conversation with me to save my soul."

"About 65% of people in the United States identify as Christians," I replied.

"We believe that you just have to be a good person. We don't need a religious belief for that."

"What is good?" I asked.

"It's doing the right thing," she said.

"But what is right? Pretend I haven't been a part of society for the first 20 years of my life. Now tell me what is good."

"Well, the problem is that the definition of good changes with the times. What is good now is different than in the past."

"So there is no good!" I exclaimed. "Just do whatever you feel is right according to the trends of the day."

"But don't hurt other people's feelings."

"How about if the person is a murderer who killed a lot of people? Can I hurt his feelings?"

"Hmmm," she pondered. "The problem with religion can be seen in the following scenario." She was gearing up to destroy my Christian morality—I was in trouble now! "Imagine you are the conductor of a train, and on the track is ten people tied up. You can change direction to another track, but on it is a little girl. Either you have to kill the ten people or the little girl. What do you do?"

"I pray to God at that moment and ask Him to tell me what to do."

"But how about if God doesn't respond?"

"He will. He responds even when I ask him dumb stuff."

"But how about if there is no God?"

"But there is!"

"Okay, but if there wasn't?"

"Minimizing harm would make sense in this case, so the little girl would be the sacrifice."

"So you would *kill* the little girl?!"

"No, I'm just playing along in your scenario. God would tell me what to do. He knows more than me."

She wanted a philosophical answer that could be justified in a secular way, but I didn't live in a secular way, so it wasn't necessary for me to play along.

Her dairy-free life partner chimed in. "It's about treating others as you would want to be treated."

The atheist was preaching the teachings of Jesus Christ to me! Amen! When you're born in a Christian nation, and the society has normalized many Christian beliefs through various cultural habits and sayings, such as the Golden Rule, it's easy to say you're proud to be an atheist, but they were more Christian than they wanted to believe.

One of the daughters came by to turn on the fan by attaching it to a car battery. I looked at the walls of the house and could not identify any power outlets.

"Is it okay if I put the fan here?" she asked me.

I nodded and she turned on the contraption. The fan blew air directly onto my face.

"It's ruining my perfect hair, but that's fine," I said.

She let out a big laugh, much larger than I expected from such a simple joke, but for someone who had never seen a comedy movie or stand-up program, I may have been the funniest man she ever met.

She and her siblings were sheltered but mature. They possessed practical skills and performed them with confidence. Their health and vigor were superb. Sure, they didn't know about various acts of violence and sex, and they weren't over-socialized to come up with jokes on the spur of the moment, but those things were more useful for city slickers who needed to impress a date. They had all that they needed to serve their family and God.

After the dinner was completed, there was a period where we could ask the Amish wife about her way of life. Most of the questions were about not using technology. The Spanish wife asked whether she did "all" of the household chores, a hint that her husband didn't mind washing the dishes.

It was my turn to ask a question. "Do you feel that the modern way of life is encroaching upon yours?"

She paused for some time and said, "Not as much as the decreasing income we make from farming. A lot of Amish are leaving the farm and moving into businesses closer to the city, and that changes them. You need a lot of conviction to stay a farmer these days when agricultural companies are maintaining huge farms and pushing prices down. It's hard to compete, and when our growing boys see how much more they can make with other jobs, they don't want to stay on the farm like with the previous generations."

Their farm life may be in danger, but the Amish are flourishing. Their population was 325,000 as of 2018, nearly doubling in the past 20 years. If they maintain the same growth rate, their population will reach close to three million within a hundred years. What a surprise that refusing secular technology, living in rural areas, and committing to family and God will cause their population to grow at a much faster rate than all other demographic groups.

Once you get past their peculiar outfits and way of living, the Amish and Mennonites are simply devout Christians. They are honest people who work hard. Their communities are strong, their families are growing, and they don't commit crimes at nearly the level of outsiders. The entire country should have their ethos, and yet it's more common for others to make fun of them. They will continue to be seen as fringe and weird by people who stare at their smartphones for six hours a day and live alone in their urban apartment box for which they overpay so that they can have access to the coolest bars and restaurants in the city.

The pieces were starting to come together: get out of the city. It would be nice if I could meet a woman who realized the same thing.

†

I had picked the next city specifically because it was Trump country. Trump received 55% of the vote in Havre de Grace, Maryland, a city of 15,000 built next to the Chesapeake Bay. It didn't take long before I saw a gigantic Trump flag attached to a house, the first time on the trip I had seen public support for him. So far I'd seen hundreds of gay flags and only one Trump flag; not the best ratio, but at least American flags had been rather common, especially at rest stops and car dealerships.

Downtown Havre de Grace was so quiet that the sound of one woman talking on the phone outside a coffee shop carried for a full block. Parking was free and plentiful. Traffic was non-existent. The extent of liberalism were two tattooed millennials and a lonely rainbow flag on a French bakery owned by a rotund woman. I did not hear any hip hop blaring out of cars. There was more action near the water where a youth group was taking sailing lessons. Senior citizens and families walked on the promenade, enjoying views of the bay, while men staked out prime spots for fishing. Many were friendly and said hello as I passed by them.

For a decade, I traveled the world to find the "perfect" town based on my needs at the time (mostly sexual), but my needs kept changing, so a town that was good for me one year was not the next. And all that time, only 75 minutes away from where I used to live in the DC suburbs, was an ideal town to live a peaceful, tranquil life, yet I never saw it because I didn't want a peaceful, tranquil life. I wanted excitement, women, and novelty, and, as they say, be careful what you wish for because you just might get it.

I left Havre de Grace and headed towards my mother's house in a Maryland suburb near Washington, DC. As I got closer, music in different languages from multiple cars violated my ears. After greeting my mother and spending time with her, I went to a nearby café to complete my day's work. From my table, I could see Hispanics from various countries, Africans from various countries, Indians, African-Americans, and a smattering of white boomers. *Where was I?* It was like a fish tank containing multiple species that wouldn't normally comingle in the wild.

After I had been multiculturally enriched in the café, I walked outside and observed a conflict in the parking lot. A North African woman had made a sloppy turn into a parking lane, causing her car to encroach onto the lane of oncoming traffic. A black female was blocked from exiting while the North African didn't have enough space to complete her turn. The North African was in error and should have reversed, but she refused. She yelled at the black woman to reverse her car instead.

"I don't have space!" the black woman yelled.

She did have space but didn't want to yield. They argued for another minute until a Hispanic man in the car behind the black woman's yelled, "Look, let's just be nice people, so we can get out of this parking lot." The women refused to budge. He addressed the North African directly: "Ma'am, just reverse your car and find another spot."

"Who are you to tell me what to do?" the North African woman replied. She got out of her car to trade words with the black woman and the Hispanic man. Then an older white man in an orange shirt, who was behind the Hispanic man's car, got out of his car and yelled at the North African woman to move. Another older white man, this one in a red shirt, entered the fray on foot to film everything with his phone.

When it became clear that the North African woman was not going to budge, the Hispanic man convinced the black woman to reverse her car to let the North African woman in. She did, and the North African woman, very slowly, entered the lane and parked her car. Just when I thought the conflict had ended, the white man in the red shirt blocked the black woman from exiting so that he could record her car plate with his phone. She yelled, "I have a baby in the car!" Then the white man in the orange shirt ran up to the man in the red shirt. "Get the hell out of the way! We're trying to go home!" The man in the red shirt yielded, and cars started moving.

Five adults had battled each other, almost coming to blows. Not only are there many different species of fish in the tank, but the tank is not that large. The fish are starting to fight each other.

†

Two men attended the Washington, DC event dinner along with a couple, of which the woman was Orthodox and the man was atheist. The man told me how he had turned his life around spontaneously, seemingly without the help of God. I listened attentively and then a question popped into my mind. I looked at his girlfriend and asked, "Before he turned his life around, did you ever pray for him?"

"Every day," she replied, solemnly nodding her head.

"There it is," I said, smiling, insinuating that his turnaround had not been born from his own strength but through the grace bestowed on him from his girlfriend's prayers. Needless to say he didn't exactly welcome this idea. He had read the Bible several times, and while he had extracted wisdom from it, his personal "research" had determined that it was rife with error.

In New York City, I had met a man who was following the faith, but then determined through "research" that premarital sex was not actually a sin, and so he deliberately committed it. Another man on my forum was doing "research" and constructing a theory of the nature of God, very proud that he was going to break new spiritual ground. Whenever a man starts by telling me that he has done "research," I know that he has found a way to bend God to his desires instead of bending to God.

The next day was the lecture. I drove to the hotel venue two hours before it was due to start. Sixty-five chairs greeted me in the conference room. I connected my PA speaker and wireless microphone system to a portable audio recorder. I set up a camcorder atop a tripod in the back. I placed my notes on the podium then double-checked with the staff to make sure the banquet order was correct. There was no fee to rent the venue but I had to spend $1,100 on food and drink. To hit the minimum, I ordered over $500 worth of cookies and brownies. I looked at the clock: 4:45 p.m. I had at least half an hour before guests would start to arrive. I sat in the lobby and stared out the window, asking God to help me guide men in the way that He wants.

The crowd in DC was exceedingly calm. In New York, men had participated by shouting out answers as if I were in a rowdy beer hall. In DC, the audience gave me no feedback, even though the speech was identical. Did they not like the speech? I feed off the audience, so when their reaction is muted, I identify two or three men who seem the most interested and focus on them to the exclusion of others. If I catch someone not paying attention, or worse, sleeping, I never look in their direction again. When the speech was done, many of the men said how good it was, even more so than in New York, which taught me that I must always continue the speech in high spirits even if the feedback suggests otherwise.

For several days, I had been consumed with the idea of living in a cabin in the woods. I couldn't stop researching land plots and cabins even though I had just started my nationwide tour. I found many websites that sold cabin kits that included all the materials I needed. I fantasized about buying land with access to a river, of growing my garden and going on walks on my property. These fantasies pleased me, not unlike how I used to fantasize about fornicating with women. Instead of being tempted by women, I was suddenly being tempted by cabins, which had the effect of taking me away from the present and into a world that didn't exist, and which might never exist.

The Sunday happy hour started in Meridian Park, which features a pleasant staircase fountain. For a big city, DC is not ugly. The buildings are on a human scale and there are plenty of trees and greenery. It's clean without any foul odors, and the homeless are few and far between. The problem lies with the people—most are transplants who are using the city as a way station to becoming a somebody. They come to DC to "make it" in the government or a field connected to the government. Their main goal is to achieve power and status. The lens through which they judge and evaluate others is almost entirely based on who you know and what material benefits you can provide. A woman you meet in this town will ask you what you do faster than one in any other city, because before she can consider a relationship with you, she must identify whether you're useful in her journey to becoming a somebody. If a good chunk of these people were conservative, the city wouldn't be half bad, but nearly all are liberal, and many are gay. The result is a city filled with power-hungry homosexuals and their allies who nullify the beauty of the greenery and the relatively clean streets.

I was usually in good cheer during the happy hour when men asked me dozens of questions, but this time around I was in a state of agitation. I was tired and wanted to be alone, but these men had paid for an event. They were depending on me to perform. I didn't want to act happy when I wasn't, but I didn't want to disappoint them either. I held it together for five hours and then had dinner at my father's house. I had nothing left over for him and my brothers, and even less when I went back to my mother's, where I immediately got on my computer to spend hours editing my new travel video.

5

Guidance

My friend Rohil had recently bought a large patch of land near Lexington, Kentucky. He invited me to see the hobby farm he was building. I decided to visit before my next speech in Ohio.

I first stopped in Clifton Forge, Virginia for lunch. The "redneck" stereotype I had in my mind came to life in the form of men in jeans with Southern accents lounging by their pickup trucks. The only loud music I heard was country. Unlike Pennsylvania, there was a considerable number of black people, but they were different from the blacks in Washington, DC. They didn't appear to subscribe to thug culture, and none had their jeans hanging down their butts. One even said "How are you doing?" to me on the sidewalk. In DC, if a black man asked you that, he would follow up by asking for money or a cigarette, often with a menacing aura.

I thought I could make the nine-hour drive to Lexington in one day, but my meandering stop in Clifton Forge killed that notion. I studied the map and figured I could make it as far west as Huntington, West Virginia before it got too late. Then I vaguely remembered that there was an Orthodox monastery in West Virginia. It was in the town of Wayne, only half an hour from Huntington. I decided to visit.

After spending the night in Huntington, I got up early and headed to the Holy Cross Monastery, part of the Russian

Orthodox Church Outside Russia (ROCOR). My expectations were low. When I visited the Holy Trinity Monastery in Jordanville, I didn't have much interaction with the monks. I figured it would be the same in Wayne. I'd check out the gift shop, pray for a bit in the church, and be on my way.

The monastery was up a small mountain, serviced by a one-lane road. I knew I was close when I passed an old mobile home that featured a huge blowup of an Orthodox saint alongside an American flag. The one-lane road eventually turned into a long gravel driveway. I parked my car in the small lot and noted the buildings that lined the top of the hill. I walked into the gift shop and began selecting gifts for Rohil and his family. I found a Jesus car icon and bought it for myself, because you're not a true Orthodox unless you have icons in your car.

I paid for my gifts to one of the monks and he asked me whether I would like to join a tour of the monastery. I said yes and went to join in the church, which was the size of a small house. After I introduced myself to Father David, one of the faithful on the tour looked at me and said, "I know you." He was with his wife and two children, on pilgrimage from Tennessee, and said that my work often came up in the conservative group chat that he was part of.

After the church tour, Father David told us that the monks made candles, soap, and incense in the workshops. This labor was part of their obediences, duties that allowed them to earn their daily bread, both literally and spiritually. The Orthodox life is centered on obedience, first to God and then to your elders. Monks in a monastery cannot simply do what they want, and must ask for permission, called blessings, from an abbot or spiritual elder to undertake most personal actions, even going to bed at night. As a layman, I don't have to seek out daily blessings, but I know that any action I perform outside of God's will is, at best, a waste of time, and, at worst, detrimental to my salvation. In a monastery, the abbot knows what is spiritually profitable for all the monks, and they must follow him without complaint.

Father David told the group that the monks pray over the items they make, so buying a candle from the monastery is not the same as buying one from Walmart. One has been blessed and the other has been made by a factory worker in China. He showed us the candle-making machine they imported from Greece and explained how they used to do everything by hand. I thought of the Amish, who until recently had avoided all mechanization. I asked Father David how the monastery balanced mechanization of this sort with the spiritual life.

"This machine is a tool," he said. "We respect the tool as given by God to aid us here in the monastery. We use this tool but do not allow it to use us."

He told us stories about the monastery's soaps. Sold in faraway retail outlets, they have managed to draw people to the monastery. "Many pilgrims who come here first heard about us through the packaging on our soaps. I remember one woman visited us when she encountered our soap in a gift shop on a cruise ship. She came here and eventually converted to Orthodoxy. Our faith bears fruit in ways we did not expect."

After the tour, Father David invited me to sit with him in the library. I told him my story. I strayed badly from the Church, feeding my lust while enabling other men to feed theirs. My sister's death threw me into a deep pit and made me realize that I had lived immorally. God gave me the gift of faith. I repented. I now wanted to do right, especially among the men whom I had led astray.

"You're in great danger," Father David said.

"Why?" I was expecting a compliment or maybe a "Good job."

"You were doing the will of the evil one for a long time. He's not going to let you go so easily. Many people, when they turn to God, are given a moment's rest. Things appear easy because they are full of God's grace, but there will be a moment where it appears God has left you. Then you could exceed the sins that you committed in the past. I knew a man who experienced one-and-a-half years of incredible grace. He thought the fight was over and his salvation assured. Then the grace was removed. God never left him, but went silent to let him walk on his own. Unfortunately, he went back to his old ways."

"What can I do to prevent this?" I asked.

"Know that you cannot do this on your own. You need spiritual guidance, and you need to participate in the sacraments. Are you close to your priest?"

"Yes, though I'm on the road now. I'm aware of the danger so that's why I no longer trust the thoughts that enter my mind, because I know they can be placed there by evil. When making important decisions, I ask God, and when I'm tempted, I recite the Jesus Prayer."

He approved of my approach, but stressed the importance of guidance. There are men with more spiritual experience than I have who can identify potential temptations. Without a spiritual elder, there is a greater chance I can fall for a trap.

The church bells rang. It was time for the afternoon prayer. I walked with Father David to the church and stood in the visitor section at the back. The service was performed in English. I recognized most of the prayers. In front of me was a short man wearing suspenders stained with mud. He venerated the icons and made prostrations like the monks. Beside me was the man from Tennessee with his family. There was also a black man with an Afro. We were all praying to the same God as one body, united in love for Him. Within the small church, the monks were closest to the altar, and behind them were the laypeople. The monks are closest to God and so the layman seeks out the monks. Without them, we'd have no living example of holiness as practiced by the earliest Christians.

After the prayer, visitors were invited to lunch. On my table was potato salad, egg salad, bread, and fruit (the monks don't eat meat). The elder said a prayer and we dived in while one monk read stories from the lives of the saints. Once everyone was done eating, the elder rang a bell and made a few brief announcements. The monk who had read to everyone during lunch was then allowed to eat.

Father David invited me to tea. I revealed to him the nature of my speaking tour, how I was testifying to my experience. He displayed concern that I was teaching about God while spiritually immature.

"I'm careful not to preach," I said. "I'm focusing on sharing my testimony. Many men who follow me can go weeks and months without even hearing about God. I'm one of the few exposures they are going to get, but I know not to teach from the Bible or claim I have the answers. A lot of men want to make me a guru. They want to put their full trust in me, but I tell them to seek out a priest. I see myself a bridge for some non-believers to the faith, to get them to make that first prayer or to walk inside a church again."

He was skeptical. "Just know that you don't always need words. One saint, when asked how he strengthened the faith of so many, said that he was merely present with them and only sometimes used words. By leading through example, people will feel your holiness, all without persuasion or convincing."

Father David and his fellow monks weren't preaching the Gospel from street corners, they weren't participating in Twitter arguments with atheists, and they didn't have a mega-church with electronic billboards, but I ended up in their monastery anyway, soaking up their faith along with so many other pilgrims, some of whom got the idea to come because of soap. Holiness is evangelizing on its own. It may even be more effective than direct evangelizing, because you don't put people on a temporary emotional high that they may be deceived into thinking was a spiritual experience.

†

I drove to my friend's farm in Lexington, Kentucky. He's married with children and has no use for game, and although I am unmarried without children, I also have no use for game.

The work he had done on his acreage in the three years since he had bought it was impressive. He built a stone fence on the front of his property and installed an electronic gate. He grew an orchard with all types of fruit, such as figs and apples, and protected them from deer with an electric fence. He built a greenhouse and an open barn. Biggest of all, he built a house for his family (using a general contractor). In three years' time, I could complete two, maybe three books, but he had created a home and farm.

"How did you learn all this?" I asked as we walked through his orchard.

"Mostly Google and YouTube. A lot of people make a living online showing you how to do things on the farm."

"So you learned it online and then bought the stuff you need-ed?"

"I purchased a used trailer and hitched it to my SUV. There's a connector on the trailer that you plug into the SUV so the brake lights are synched. I go to Rural King or Home Depot to buy what I need."

"Can't I buy a pickup truck instead?"

"Yes you can, but a trailer is cheaper if you already have an SUV. I got mine for about $600."

"How fast can you go with a trailer attached?"

"About 70 miles per hour."

"And then you buy the seeds or plant starters and just start planting?"

"Yes, you get the tools you need, and plant them."

"How do you keep the plants safe from pests?"

"You talk to local farmers and see what are the pests in the area and how to combat them. The deer were eating the fruit in the orchard, so I built the electric fence."

"How did you build it?"

"I bought the posts and the wire. Then I connected the electricity to that post over there."

"How long did it take you?"

"About three days. There's a farmhand I hire if I need help."

"I'm only used to solving computer and office problems. So if there's a problem with my website, I know how to troubleshoot. If I need to reserve a conference room on short notice, I know how to do that. But in the farm world, I don't know anything."

"On the farm, you're building and learning at the same time. There's no perfect way to do things so you take the knowledge you've got and give it a go. If you fail, you learn. If you create something imperfect, like that wood storage shed over there that I built, you use it for as long as it works and then build a new one."

"I want to create a log cabin, but I don't have the skills. It definitely won't be perfect."

"And those imperfections in the cabin will be the 'cost' of your learning experience, so that the next home you build will be much better. If you don't try to build anything, you will never learn. You'll always have to depend on other people to build it for you. The general rule is that if you do things yourself, the cost is one-fourth of what others will charge."

It's fascinating how a man can have complete confidence in one area but lack it in another. I can walk up to any girl and start a conversation, something most men can't do, but I start feeling anxious at the prospect of building a woodshed. It was the false confidence I accumulated from doing things I shouldn't have been doing that my ego eagerly pursued to hide my real weaknesses (lack of faith and practical family-building skills). I was essentially a magician who knew only one cheap trick.

I asked Rohil more questions about clearing land, building a home and serving it with utilities, cutting down trees, wildlife, relations with neighbors, mosquito bites, solar electricity, and raising farm animals. He kept stressing that he's still a beginner, but he knew so much more than me that he could serve as a stepping stone to deeper knowledge, just like how many men who lack faith can ask me questions about God, as early in my walk with Christ as I am.

Rohil was the first man to put the idea of buying land into my mind. During my friendship with him I saw how he went from being a suburban homeowner, a standard consumer like myself, to a homesteader with useful skills. I was inspired, and this added to my cabin obsession. I began spending hours at a stretch online doing cabin research, even checking land prices. This coincided with ramping down my use of Twitter, which I mainly used to feed my pride by attacking others whom I felt were inferior to me. Because I couldn't gain pleasure through Twitter, my corrupted flesh tried to receive pleasure from cabins. It felt like a game of whack-a-mole. Living in a cabin was, no doubt, less sinful than fornicating, but how could I extinguish my need for pleasure completely? Worldly desire was still lurking within me, ready to flash to the surface when the opportunity presented itself.

I stayed on Rohil's farm for two nights. During that time, I should have explored the city of Lexington and various sites for my video travelogue, but I didn't want to burn myself out. Besides, how different were the cities? Here's a city with a gay flag on a Protestant church alongside quaint shops in the downtown area, and here's another with the same thing. Here's a city with a bar district where young people go to intoxicate themselves, and here's another city with the same type of area. And here's the same food, banking, and shopping brands.

They're not identical, for sure, but they're not different enough to provide me with a novel experience. If I wasn't creating a video travelogue, which served as a way to promote my tour, I'd have driven right past them.

†

I went to Petersburg, Kentucky to visit the Creation Museum, which was built to display a literal interpretation of the Bible. I hoped to learn counter-arguments to the claim that human history is way older than 6,000 years, which many Protestants believe is the actual age of the earth.

Many Christians have bought the lies of anthropological "science," where a tiny bone fragment that is supposedly 250,000 years old is enough to reconstruct an entire skeleton and provide "evidence" for evolution, but if the "experts" can't even get the news of today right, I don't trust them to know with precision what happened thousands of years ago, let alone millions or billions of years ago. I rather put my faith in the Bible and what it says about creation than in atheist scientists. While I don't want to throw away science completely, if my mind is able to accept a literal interpretation of some aspect of the Bible over modern man's interpretation, I'll take the Bible.

The entry fee to the museum was $35. It was more a theme park than a museum, with a large garden, zip line, petting zoo, and other activities aimed at children. Once inside, I was greeted by an exhibit that explained various dragon myths throughout the ages. Then I passed by a featured exhibit of two cave children petting a little dinosaur. The evangelical group that created the museum wanted to stress that the earth was young, and to bring home that message, they put dinosaurs everywhere. There was a 3D film of Adam hanging out with a dinosaur and an exhibit of a *Tyrannosaurus rex* frolicking in the Garden of Eden. The children visiting the museum loved the dinosaur displays, so I began to wonder how much of what I was seeing was inspired biblical interpretation versus genius marketing.

It's possible that Adam had a T. Rex as a pet, but one problem with Protestantism is that any man can interpret the Bible as he wishes and, thanks to his charm or speaking ability, open a church that draws in a large crowd. If his interpretation is correct, he will save souls, but that presupposes that all of the interpretations that came before his were at least slightly incorrect, or he wouldn't have had to start his own denomination. If his interpretation is incorrect, he may lead people to condemnation. If one man believes that dinosaurs were in the Garden of Eden, and he can convince others that the Bible backs up his claim, he can spread that idea to huge numbers of people. It then has the potential to cause harm to the faith of Christians who can't believe in the presentation and then decide to throw out all of Christianity with it.

As an Orthodox Christian, I cannot use my interpretation to create such a museum and label it "Orthodox." I cannot start my own church or monastery. Only the church hierarchy can approve such measures, and if I go against their wishes and proceed anyway, I will be excommunicated from the Church. This is a great check on false or errant teachings. As a zealous new believer, I want to think that I have been graced by God in a special way, and preach the Gospel as I see it, but the notion of specialness is pride, which opens the door just wide enough for Satan to hurtle me down a road of deception. My preaching would inevitably be full of imprecise doctrines or outright heresies that risk the salvation of those I'm trying to save. I'm aware of this danger, and if any Orthodox Christian hears me spread doctrine that goes against Orthodoxy, I hope they immediately bring it to my attention.

I left the Creation Museum not fully convinced that Adam played with dinosaurs. The specific details of creation are a mystery, and I don't think I'll ever have a complete answer, but even if I did, would it matter? Unless you are trying to arrive at God intellectually, which has a high failure rate, it's okay to have big question marks in your mind as long as God is in your heart. If there is something in the Bible that your mind refuses to accept literally, simply interpret it metaphorically. God created the universe—this is undeniable. The details are trivia. As a lay Christian, I don't need to know the exact details to "prove" them to others. If your heart is hard, even perfect explanations won't lead you to God, so ultimately what the Creation Museum provides is biblical entertainment to the faithful who are tired of the content produced by the secular world. It won't convince non-believers, but it doesn't have to. I want to believe that the museum is doing a net good for Christendom, but ultimately that's for God to decide.

Until my visit to the museum, I had been consuming any worthy spiritual content I could get my hands on, regardless if it was Protestant, Catholic, or Orthodox, mostly in the form of podcasts and videos that I listened to while driving, but now that my general theological foundation had been laid, I was seeing less value in non-Orthodox materials. I was able to quickly identify their doctrinal problems, and for the ones I didn't spot, I ran the risk of letting erroneous beliefs slip into my mind. I respected the work that Protestants had done in analyzing the Bible, especially John MacArthur and Dr. Robert Luginbill, and I appreciated the sermons of Catholic priests Fulton Sheen and Chad Ripperger, but it was time I weaned myself off them. There was more than enough Orthodox materials out there for me to study. I was already seeing value in the book that Father David gifted me before I left the monastery, *Wounded by Love: The Life and the Wisdom of Saint Porphyrios*. Other than a Christological dispute that separates the Armenians from their Eastern Orthodox brethren, I could read it without having to worry whether what Saint Porphyrios states goes against my faith.

✝

My next event was in Columbus, Ohio. For the Friday night dinner, I booked a restaurant that was in the hip area of town, but these days "hip" means "homosexual," so the restaurant had a gay pride sticker on the window. More jarring was being greeted by a hostess who was a male-to-female transsexual. Most of the staff were gay as well.

Two of the men who came to dinner were friends from Canada, and the third was from Ohio. We were all around 40 years of age, and we had many of the same life scars in common, particularly concerning women. We had all been betrayed by a serious girlfriend or wife, but unlike me, the other men had to endure material hardship since children and substantial amounts of money were involved. The relationships I formed had been created on such weak bonds that withdrawing myself from them was only temporarily painful.

At one point during the dinner, we were surrounded by tables of women decked out in sexy summer wear and thick makeup. I like to think that we were looking for honorable women of the faith while they were looking for men who would sexually excite them and treat them as goddesses. If we, as men, failed in our mission to find a suitable wife, a life of chastity awaited us. We'd be monks in the world or monks in a monastery. Maybe if these sexy women didn't find a man, they'd become nuns, though it was more likely than not they'd redirect their nurturing instinct to cats, dogs, gays, minorities, or refugees. One way or another, they would become a "mother"—the only question was to what or to whom, but based on the excessive display of gay pride flags in Columbus, my bet was they would primarily be mothers to the gays. I even saw my first transgender pride flag hanging from a Columbus coffee shop. It consisted of five horizontal stripes: a white stripe in the center surrounded by two pink stripes and then two light blue stripes. Since the transsexuals mix up their sexes, shouldn't there be a lack of delineation between the stripes? I nominate the flag to be purple (a mixture of pink and blue) with a skull and crossbones in the center, since if you stray that far from the natural order to the point of surgically changing your sex, you're firmly on the path of spiritual death.

I was tempted by the women surrounding us during the dinner. One in particular, three tables down, caught my eye. She had an olive skin tone and wore a black cocktail dress that revealed her slender thighs. Her face was exceedingly pleasing. After the fifth or so time I looked at her, I knew I was receiving pleasure from her beauty. I turned away, disappointed with myself. With American cities becoming so ugly and perverted, including the cookie-cutter architecture, the only beauty left is women in their prime, even if they mar that beauty by following popular trends that make them look more like a prostitute than a potential wife.

After dinner, we walked outside and were greeted by a bustling night scene. There were at least five bars within a stone's throw and dozens more in the city proper. I couldn't help but wonder: how many bars do people need? A million bars for a million micro-identities to drink micro-brews with funny-sounding names while on their way to entering micro-sexual relationships with a member of the opposite sex (or same sex). And in order to cater to the needs of your micro-identity, you need to live alongside others in expensive micro-boxes. You become a rat that needs to live with other rats.

Sixteen people came to the Saturday talk, the smallest event yet. There was one young woman who was quiet for most of the event. During the meet and greet, she came up to me and asked how she could get over a man she was grieving over. I asked whether she was praying to God and she said she was not. I told her that her problem was spiritual. Because she was disconnected from God, she was feeling sad and hopeless, hoping to fix things through secular means. What she really needed was to ask God and follow His will as it was laid out for her. I had joked with the guys that my new book would be called *Ask God*. Each page would contain a simple admonition. "Have you asked God yet?" "Only God can help you." "Why are you still reading this book?"

I looked online to find a suitable venue for the Sunday happy hour. Google recommended a bar called The Walrus. It had received great reviews and had an extensive menu. Upon arriving, I was greeted by a gigantic gay flag. The interior had additional homosexual paraphernalia. My bar selection was an amusing topic of discussion with the guys, but for the second day in a row I felt conflicted about giving money to a business that openly supported sodomy.

The bar's ambiance and food were excellent. Of course it was—secular hipsters devote their entire lives to food, alcohol, music, and other forms of worldly pleasure. Their main expertise is serving up entertainment and making you feel good in the moment, and if I did not have God in my life I do not doubt that I would attempt to return to the bar at night to pick up some easy feminist-minded women who have no objections to one-night stands. The gay flag wouldn't even bother me. Either you pay $600 a month to live with five other people or $1,500 to live alone in a box simply to have access to the pleasures that only The Walrus can give, but all of that is not worth even a single dollar because of what it takes away from you—your time, your life energy at the peak of your bodily existence, and your soul. I've paid tens of thousands of dollars for city experiences that I pray to forget.

One man at the happy hour told me that while he had come closer to God, his wife hadn't, though she wasn't actively resisting his strengthening faith. It's easy to lament that the person you love most in life is blocking their salvation, but from another perspective, you are given a gracious opportunity to save a soul, not the white knight definition of saving a woman from a bad material situation, but lifting up a woman you love from the possibility of hell to serve with you beside the right hand of the

Father. Do you evangelize your wife with daily Bible verses, potentially annoying her in the process? Do you drag her to church every Sunday when she would rather sleep in? I look to the monks for the answer. They believe you can impart your holiness to others without direct evangelizing. Since most people really do crave a peaceful and tranquil life, they will be inspired to see you living that very life due to your faith in God. At some point, they will say to themselves, "There must be something to this God stuff if my husband is protecting me and providing for me with strength and calm." This assumes that the wife has a redeemable soul. Otherwise, peace and tranquility will not be sought. She will place no value in her husband's ability to protect and provide, and subconsciously look for ways to destroy the relationship.

The monks place bird feeders throughout the monastery, containing the food of the Gospel, and birds like me come to feed on their holiness, but the monks don't force the birds or catch them with a net. The birds have to come of their own volition, and I believe that a man who is married to a backsliding Christian woman, or even to an atheist, has no choice but to wait for his beautiful bird to come and feed on spiritual food, and be patient during those many months or years until she decides to eat.

6

Miracle

I drove to a suburb of Indianapolis, Indiana, to visit an internet friend with whom I have communicated for several years. Dan and I developed a strong rapport, since we are of a similar age and grew up in the Northeast. On the approach to his home, which he shared with his wife and three children, I thought I was driving through the set of the old television show *The Wonder Years*. The homes were large and the lawns perfectly manicured. White families were walking their dogs and there was no loud music or beat-up automobiles. It seemed like a museum. At the entrance to his subdivision there might as well have been a placard: "This is how America once was." When you're stuck in the cities, and only drive by the overcrowded and overpriced suburbs that still feel like the city, it's hard to imagine that there are pockets of the United States that remain pleasant to live in.

I met Dan. He struck me as an all-American man—tall, outgoing, and intelligent, with a blend of small-town and big-city values. His three children were playing with binoculars and walkie-talkies. I'm supposed to believe that raising children is arduous and expensive. It limits your freedom to pursue entertainment options in the city and will result in failure because of divorce rape and other anti-male laws. I can devise a dozen more reasons why one shouldn't get married and have children, but in Dan's house those reasons were absent, replaced by joy and love. His youngest boy blew bubbles in my face, and I didn't mind. Blow all the bubbles you want! The girl was peering through the binoculars from the wrong end, stating that she's looking for birds. I look for birds too! The oldest made funny faces when I told him I still wear a diaper at night. Like you, I used to be a child! Just as I was in the process of changing the TV channel from the city to nature, I saw there was a family channel that might be even better.

I ate dinner with Dan and his wife. It would be effortless to covet Dan's life, but God has not given us the same plan. Nonetheless, I was encouraged that healthy family life can still be achieved. Not every man has a nagging wife who controls him. Not every marriage is doomed to end in divorce. There are men in this evil age who are making it work, and regardless of whether or not that is my destiny, I cannot advise men to avoid marriage as I have in the past. Each man has to decide on his own whether or not a woman he meets is right for him, and the best way for him to do that is to read my future book *Ask God*.

I met up with Dan again the next afternoon. It was a fast day, so he took me to a local café that had vegan items. I ordered the vegan pancakes and veggie wrap, much to the amusement of Dan, who remembered how I helped to elevate the soy boy meme to popularity online. The topic of women came up and he asked me whether I was a "volcel" (voluntarily celibate).

"I suppose I am. I don't intend to have sex unless I get married. And masturbation never more."

"Wow. Has it been difficult?" he asked.

"Less difficult than I thought. With God's help, things you thought were impossible are relatively easy. Controlling your lustful thoughts is the hard part, but once you do that, behavior follows."

"You don't have a regular job, but for many men who work for corporations, sex is increasingly being used to control them as they ascend the ladder."

"What do you mean?"

"The big-paying jobs are either in managerial or sales. To break through six figures and higher, you have to be a 'team player,' not only while on the job but also outside of work hours, which means going to happy hours and drinking. Soon you'll be invited to strip clubs. Your boss will insist on buying you a lap dance, whether you're married or not. Men accept because they don't want to seem like they're not part of the group, but now they have dirt on you. The next time a situation comes up when they need you to go along with a plan, such as signing off on a deal, it's implied that you have to agree. Otherwise, they remind you of the dirt they have: 'Remember that night in the strip club? Whew, I wonder what happened when you went in that back room!'"

"What happens if you don't go along with the deal?"

"At worse, they make a call to your wife or slip her a note, but usually you just lose out on a promotion or position. They identify you as not being a good 'fit,' and then the opportunity to become a VP is lost. But the stakes can get higher. They may invite you on a cruise, and there will be beautiful girls that are abnormally friendly to you. Things may happen. If you're particularly strong-willed, they'll send two girls at you."

"And the girls are prostitutes?"

"Yes. Every modeling agency has a portion of the girls who are prostitutes that can be hired for 'corporate functions.' It's their job to sleep with the men there—men who have never received attention from such a caliber of women before."

"But how about if I'm single? How would they get me then?"

"Through shame. They make you do things you didn't want to do and then use that to control you. In other cases, if you do production work like an engineer, they simply keep your salary just under $100,000 and you'll never have power within the company. But if you want to make the big bucks, or you want real power, they first want power over you."

"So what's a good Christian man to do?" I asked.

"You have to pick your career carefully. Go out to the happy hours, have one drink and no more. If you go to the strip club, never accept a lap dance, but these days it's getting much harder to refuse. And then you have all the female realtors and pharmaceutical reps sleeping with clients and doctors. Sex is the driver of business in America."

Before it was time for Dan to leave, he told me to wait so that he could get something from his car.

"When your sister was sick, I told my kids that we have to pray for a friend who is going through a hard time. Today, I told them that the man we prayed for was you. My daughter drew this picture today." Dan handed me a piece of construction paper. "It's her, the boys, and you."

The drawing had everyone lined up by age, the youngest boy on the left and then me on the far right with a bushy beard. We were all holding hands and had big happy faces. There was a yellow sun in the upper left corner. If I were a parent, I might get tired of my kid's drawings, but this was the first time a child had drawn something for me. In spite of all the evil I'd done, God was showing me His love in the form of a drawing by a little girl who prayed for me. My eyes began to fill with tears.

"A lot of guys ask me if your conversion is serious or not. Many are skeptical. But I know it's real. Within the dissident movement, you're St. Augustine. A lot of men will follow you."

"I pray they do," I said. "I have to fix the wrongs I've done."

"And you will. Just don't be too hard on yourself."

We hugged each other goodbye and I got in my car. I grabbed a pencil and wrote the date on the back of the drawing. If I see his children when they are grown up, I hope to show it to them.

†

Many months before, a young woman from Indiana had contacted me through my blog. We emailed several times and had two video chats. She was 19 at the time and someone I wanted to fornicate with. Times had changed, but could she possibly have been sent by God for me to marry? I decided to visit her in Fort Wayne, but I was nervous that she could tempt me. Before meeting, I told her *not* to dress sexy, a departure from my old days when I would tell girls to dress sexy so they could arouse me. I determined it was safe to have tea with her. I also wanted to endure a test of my longstanding vice to see whether I was at least making progress, and I figured this date would be a good way to do so without entering danger.

The drive from the Indianapolis suburbs to Fort Wayne was an hour and 45 minutes. I started late. Early into the drive, my eyes felt heavy. My head kept dropping. It didn't help that I was driving through flat farm country on a completely straight road. Thirty minutes into the drive, my eyes closed for a dangerously long time and I had to jerk my head up to open them. I slapped my face hard, but it happened again not long after. I couldn't stay awake and there was nowhere safe to pull over. I looked at the Jesus icon hanging from my rearview mirror and in desperation I yelled, "Please God help me stay awake!" Again I thought of pulling over, but then, just three seconds later, I suddenly felt alert, like I had been splashed with a bucket of cold water. The fatigue had left my body completely, at once without cause. I sat erect in my seat with my eyes the widest they've ever been. I looked at my Jesus icon hanging from the rearview mirror and back to the road. I looked at the icon again. I turned off the radio and began having a conversation with myself.

"You were about to fall asleep and now you're completely alert. How did this happen?"

"Through God."

"But how?"

"He hacked into your body."

"But how exactly did He do this?"

"He's God, you dummy! He can do anything."

"Yes, He is God and did this to help me and show me His power."

God is with me every second of the day, helping me to stay on the path that He has set out for me, all without violating my free will, and as I show increasing faith to Him, He reveals more of Himself to me. He didn't have to wake me in the car, but I believe He wanted to share Himself with me in a way that could build my faith, and it surely did. I finished the drive in silence, remaining completely alert.

✝

I picked up Christina from the motel where she lived. She dressed in a way that was extremely sexy, with high heels and a skirt that was above her knees, displaying her petite body. I gave her a platonic hug and she got in my car. When I saw a large tattoo on her left arm, I instantly felt that she was not sent by God to be my wife.

Most of the cafés in downtown Fort Wayne were closed. All we could find was a Starbucks. She was rather quiet, which I liked. She would often look at me and blush, suggesting she was attracted to me. I asked her about her life and was not surprised to find out that it was rough. Her father died when she was young and she started working a full-time job after high school. She was going on dates but not having much success. The old me would have talked to her for an hour or two and then invited her to "listen to music" in my hotel room so that I could sleep with her. This time, after sizing up her situation, I began preaching to her.

"Are you religious?" I asked her.

"Not really. I used to go to church when I was younger."

"Which church?"

"Baptist."

"Some women think that the man of their dreams can whisk them out of their situation like they were Cinderella. Even if you do meet him and get married, things will be fine for a short period, one year, maybe even five years, but then the unhappiness will return, because no man can save you in this life. Only God can save you. Do you pray?"

"No, I don't."

"Prayer is a good place to start. When you pray, you establish communion with God so that He can start to guide you. But if you don't pray, the things that happen to you will appear random and unfair. You won't be able to make any sense of it."

She offered no response. The look on her face suggested that she didn't care for what I was telling her, but since I had her attention, I figured that I would attempt to sow a seed as best as I could. It might not fall on fertile soil, but if she were to meet another man in the future who delivered a similar message, the seed might take root.

"Let me send you the website that I use for prayer." I pulled out my phone and texted her a link to OrthodoxPrayer.org. "It lays it out for you. You humble yourself and ask God for help, and He will help you."

I asked about her dating life. She said that besides a few dates here or there, she didn't have time to date.

"You live alone?" I asked.

"Yes."

"Why don't you live with your mom?"

"Because I have to be close to work. I work around 50 hours a week."

"So you're working yourself to death to live alone and you don't even have time to properly meet a man. If you move back home, you'd have to work less, right?"

"Yes."

"And then you'd have time to meet the right man, perhaps by joining a church. You may be only 20 years old now, but nothing will change if you work that much a week and tire yourself out."

She took out a can of chewing tobacco and put a wad in her

mouth and stared off into space. I guessed she was mildly disappointed and wanted to do something else more fun.

I drove her home and remembered that I had extra Orthodox prayer books in my trunk. I got out of the car and gave her a copy. Then we hugged and said goodbye.

†

I had been in touch with writer Dr. E Michael Jones since I had interviewed him for my YouTube channel about his excellent book *Libido Dominandi*, which explains how sexual liberation is used as a form of political control. It helped me realize that sleeping around, having no self-control over my passions, and being a slave to my lust were not at all "masculine" as I had thought. His book discussed how the norms of sex were controlled by the state, and since I was a slave to sex, I was a slave to the state. Dr. Jones figured out this truth without making the same mistakes I did (he married at 17).

He invited me to his house in South Bend, Indiana, on the northern edge of the state near Lake Michigan. I was greeted by him and his assistant, Dave Reilly. We talked in the living room for some time while surrounded by pictures of his five children and 18 grandchildren. I updated him on the progress of my tour and shared the details of my testimony, including how his work was the last necessary step before I accepted God.

"When we did the interview a couple months ago," I said to him, "I remember you told me that my actions were 'evil.' It hit me that, yes, how I lived my life was evil. I needed to hear that."

When I arrived back in the United States from Europe to start my tour, I told my mom that I needed to go to church to confess my sins. She replied, "But son, you didn't do anything wrong!" Other people would say that what I had done was just a "stage" and that every man should have his "fun," but unless I know what evil is, to have it defined to me in terms of my actions, how could I successfully turn away from it?

Dr. Jones showed me his book-selling operation. I was astonished at the number of books he had written. "I'm a writer myself," I said, "but I don't think I could maintain this level of output. How many hours a day do you work?"

"I work normal days," he said.

"I'm guessing it's helpful to have a wife. Do you do the cooking or cleaning?"

"I wouldn't be able to write all these books if I did. There's a lot of things I don't have to worry about because of her."

Dave suggested I do another interview with Dr. Jones. I retrieved my equipment from the trunk of my car and set it up in his garden. During the interview, I asked him questions about the state of America, religion, and what he thought of my idea to move to a cabin in the woods to read, write, and pray.

"That sounds like a horror film. You will need a lot of spiritual firepower to do something like that." I suspected that the idea was a trap, since I had been receiving so much pleasure from fantasizing about it. "Don't go from 0 to 60," he added. "Do it in steps."

I have complete trust in Dr. Jones's work, and I consider him both a spiritual and intellectual elder. When it was time to leave, I graciously thanked him for inviting me to his home and having an impact on my life. He's had a powerful influence on men of my generation, and I believe that influence will continue decades into the future.

The next morning I visited the University of Notre Dame, the famed Catholic university that is more known to the layman for its athletics than its religiosity. I walked through the campus and admired its large basilica and monuments dedicated to biblical figures and saints. Even if you attend this university as an atheist, you'd be reminded of God every which way you turn. An atheist wouldn't be able to tolerate a campus that is dedicated to giving glory to God. If only our cities were constructed in such a way. Instead, we get advertisements, glass towers, and gay pride. For cities to succeed as the incubators of degeneracy, Satan had to remove God so sinners would never be reminded of their sins, and for the things he couldn't remove, such as old churches, he had to drape them in rainbow flags and woke statements such as "Black Lives Matters" and "All Refugees Welcome."

Throughout the day, I noticed a growing itchy rash on my body. It started on my stomach, then spread to my thighs, arms, shoulders, and groin. I counted over 50 small red spots that looked almost like pimples. I doubted it was scabies, which can be transmitted from dirty bedsheets, and I also ruled out bed bugs, which look more like mosquito bites, but it sure did look like scabies.

Before my nightly payer, I questioned whether I should ask God for help with the rash. Wasn't I bothering Him with this sort of triviality? But without Him sustaining me, how could I complete my tour? It would take only one or two more mishaps to make things especially difficult. I took the middle ground in my prayer: "God, if You can, please help me with this rash, unless it's Your will for me to have it." That night, I lathered my entire body with *aloe vera* gel.

†

I headed to Chicago. As I got closer to the city, I knew I would hate it. The highway was unsightly and devoid of trees, lined with dozens of billboards advertising solutions to baldness and erectile dysfunction (in Indiana, billboards implored women not to abort their pregnancy).

Before entering Chicago, the price of gas was approximately $2.79 per gallon. Once I entered the very heart of Chicago, I saw a station selling it for $3.99. Was this magical gas? Would it give my car a turbo boost? A $0.99 bottle of water in the Indiana suburbs was $2.19 in Chicago.

The city may offer access to more pleasure and the ability to work in an air-conditioned office, but it's not for free. You must be bombarded with corporate propaganda, obsess about your appearance and the size of your muscles, and perhaps even take boner pills so that you can perform for a multitude of sex partners who won't love you. For your trouble, you get to spend two hours a day in transit to a job where you have to give fealty to the leftist cause of the month. Traffic in Chicago was so bad that I saw standstill traffic jams in *both* directions, a rare sight in Washington, DC. Why do so many people live in such a way? Why do they tolerate this degraded state of affairs? One of the main reasons is sex. Big cities offer the most opportunities to sleep around and get a "hot" sex partner. While many people profess a love of material riches or social status, those rewards are usually harnessed to achieve better sex. I wonder whether it is a stretch to say that most of urban capitalism is driven by the need for sex, a need that is nurtured and amplified within us by those who control the country culturally and politically.

My rash started to get intolerably itchy. I self-diagnosed myself as having scabies and went online to find a home remedy. Anonymous internet users claimed that tea tree oil is effective, so I went to a pharmacy, bought 100% tea tree oil, and applied it to my body, including my groin, which had several spots. I ignored the warning on the label that said not to apply directly to skin. Almost immediately, my genital member started to burn. I ignored that for a few minutes, but then it felt like it was on fire. I washed off the oil and noticed that my skin had turned bright red. In the past, I would have had a panic attack at my inability to fornicate. If I had a date planned later that night, I'd figure out the logistics of how to have sex despite such damage, perhaps by using two condoms simultaneously, but this time, I experienced no additional anxiety. It's not like I needed to use my reproductive system anytime soon.

The pattern of the rash, which now covered most of my body, began to remind me of the two times I had been bitten by bed bugs and experienced an allergic reaction. Even if I am bitten by only a few bed bugs, dozens of marks appear on my body. I rediagnosed myself as having bed bugs, which is a better affliction than scabies since it resolves on its own. I wasn't worried that the bed bugs had hitchhiked with me since I always closed my travel bag overnight when staying in hotels.

The Chicago dinner was attended by two men married to Ukrainian women, one man engaged to an American woman, and another who was single. Two were Orthodox and two were Catholic. I unwisely picked a steakhouse, so to maintain the fast I had to ask the waiter for "vegan" options, which was embarrassing. He recommended the veggie flatbread without cheese.

Before going to bed, I asked God to perform another miracle and completely relieve the itchiness so that I could give my talk the next day with ease. Unlike the request I had made in the car, this one was premeditated, done with a crafty heart. I could handle the rash on my own, but I wanted God to take away the discomfort. The next day, the rash was even worse. God had answered my prayer when I asked spontaneously, in the most humble way, but when I had my eye on the benefits He could give me, He said no.

Dr. Jones came to the event and sat in the front row. After my speech, he made impromptu remarks that showed his support for my new direction. He stated that a weight has been lifted from his shoulders because he didn't have to be the only one spreading a new consciousness based on the Gospel. I was flattered and hoped that I wouldn't disappoint him in the future.

An attractive woman attended the talk and sat in the third row. The first thing I noticed about her was her ample cleavage. A woman may be the nicest in the world, but if her sexuality is the most prominent feature being displayed, I have to assume that she was sent by Satan to tempt me. I avoided looking at her breasts during the speech, but during the Q&A session, when I was overly fatigued and itchy, I accidentally glanced at her breasts about half a dozen times. I don't think she noticed. She also behaved suspiciously, rapidly tapping on her phone as if taking copious notes. As long as the event wasn't sabotaged, I didn't care if she was a leftist spy.

After the event, I went alone to a famous pizza restaurant called Pequod's to get a deep-dish pie. The dough was twice as thick as a normal pizza, the cheese was heavy, and the sauce was overflowing to the point where it was all I could taste. I sent a picture of the pizza to my Southern Italian friend. He replied with disgust. In his mind, pizza should be airy and light, not a dense calorie bomb that gives you fatigue and heartburn. I agree that once you eat genuine Italian pizza, with its thin dough that practically melts in your mouth, American pizza is inferior.

For the happy hour the next day, I asked everyone to meet me at Buckingham Fountain, which was a poor choice since the fountain was so big that you couldn't recognize someone standing on the opposite side. Nonetheless, I gathered about 20 souls. They followed me to a nearby rooftop bar.

Once we settled in, a man in his mid-twenties challenged my Christian views. "How do you know God exists?" he asked.

"Because He revealed Himself to me."

"But you can't see Him."

"Do you believe in evolution as a mechanism of creating new species?" I asked.

"Yes."

"Well, have you seen evolution change species?"

"No, but we have the bones and the fossils..."

"...which are wrongly or maliciously interpreted by anthropologists. We both have faith in something we can't directly see, though I would argue that it takes more faith to believe that we spontaneously arose from a primordial soup than we were created by God."

He started raising his voice and shaking his head. He created straw-man arguments. He refused to agree on the dictionary definition of "atheist." He asked me how I could be "so sure" of my beliefs, or at least surer than someone who had figured it all out in his mid-twenties. His heart was hard, but I did want to hear his arguments for I knew I'd face them again. I responded to him as kindly as I could until politely bowing out of the discussion, stating that the opinions he held now would drastically change, sooner than he thought.

7

Lust

My next stop was Madison, Wisconsin. It was packed with homeless people, most of whom were young enough to work, with no obvious disabilities or mental disorders. From the look of their travel bags, they seemed to be on their way to be homeless somewhere else.

Madison was also full of attractive and naïve-looking young women thanks to the University of Wisconsin. My first experience with one was in a supermarket. I asked the female clerk for a bonus card to save a few cents on my shopping. She asked for my mailing address. When I made an offhand comment about being from "out of town," she interviewed me about where I was from and what I was doing in Wisconsin. Telling her that I was on a massive road trip was all that was needed for her eyes to open wide and give me a long stare. When a man receives such a look, intimacy is not far away. It would have been effortless at that point to get her number, but instead I got my bonus card and walked off.

Later while at a Starbucks, a series of young women who were alone sat next to me. Two were attractive enough, and starting a conversation with them as an out-of-towner would have been natural. There were more young women on the streets and many of them made eye contact. These women weren't the hottest I had seen, but they were cute and young. A six out of ten in Madison is an eight in many other parts of America, and based on the excessive public display of leftist catchphrases, I doubt they would have objected to casual sex. Maybe I received so much attention because the young men possessed an effeminate manner, making affirmative statements with the intonation of a question. The hours dragged on and the girls kept looking at me. They were dying to interact with a man! Why Madison has a flood of soy boys, whereas I hardly saw any in the cities of Ohio, Indiana, and Illinois, I do not know.

I knew that my lust could quickly be sated by the women of Madison, who were leftist enough to engage in premarital sex but not so leftist to be ugly. It reminded me of Poland, a country I had lived in for five years that had the exact same type of female. I could stay in Madison for one night and resist the temptation on willpower alone, but to live here would pose a great difficulty for me, because it was obvious that women would give me enough attention that I could unconsciously transmute into sex.

The women of Madison were so starved of masculinity that even a stony look could elicit their submission. In the afternoon I was on the street filming a homeless encampment for my travelogue. As I finished recording a clip, I heard the voice of a woman ten feet away saying, "Why is he doing that? He shouldn't do that." I put my phone away as she geared up to make another statement of complaint. Then I stood still and stared at her. Immediately, she looked away and stopped talking to her male friend, who didn't look at me either.

The temptation continued in La Crosse, Wisconsin, even though it had a fraction of the university students as Madison. In my brief walk through the center, a beautiful brunette locked eyes with me. I had the opportunity to approach her with a basic "Do you know where I can find…?" opener, but I let the opportunity pass.

I went to the fast-food restaurant Culver's for a meal. The young woman who served me was excessively friendly, as if she had targeted me specifically to release her affections. When I was leaving and walking out the door, she shouted after me to ask if I enjoyed the meal. She seemed eager to converse further.

At the cheap hotel where I stayed the night, the front desk was staffed by a woman with a thick Eastern European accent. Before I could ask her where she was from, she asked me. It turned out that she was from Iaşi, Romania, a city I happened to live in for three months, a fact that excited her. Arranging for some kind of date after her shift to "talk about life in Romania" would have been a foregone conclusion. I had been presented with a number of potential sexual opportunities for two straight days. In the past, I'd celebrate this fact and bless my luck, but now I cursed it and suspected some form of demonic attack.

If Satan wanted to get me, he could send an attractive girl to one of my events, and have her make it obvious that she wanted to engage in fornication immediately. It might seem that I was helping him by thinking this way but Satan already knew my weaknesses. He and his lieutenants had been examining me my whole life, and knew exactly how to trip me up. Without God's help, I had no chance, and would fail on the very first temptation, but with God's grace, I just might make it.

✝

The western border of Wisconsin is the Mississippi river. I decided to take the Great River Road up north to Minneapolis, Minnesota. I set my cruise control to 60 miles per hour, turned off my music, and silenced my phone's notifications to enjoy the ride, with sights of the Mississippi to my immediate left. Trees lined the back of the river behind train tracks that were still in use. This was what I imagined a road trip in America to be—a smooth ride with a nice view and the sounds of the wind and trains. Every half an hour, I'd slow down to roll through a little town, and then I'd accelerate again to cruising speed. I can complain about America all day, but there are not many countries that allow you to appreciate such beauty from the road. When I encounter the phrase "God bless America," it's for scenes like this, out on a country road while alone, away from the cities where beauty is choked by the weeds of modernity.

About two hours into my ride, I saw a sign that read "Scenic Overlook." I pulled over into a small parking lot and took a 20-minute nap. Then I got out of the car and walked to the edge of the fence to soak in the Mississippi River. I had learned about this river when I was young, reading about it in books like *Huckleberry Finn*, but nothing prepared me for its massive width. It looked more like a slow-moving lake, fully dominating and determining the landscape and the people who lived around it.

I sat down at a picnic table and noticed birds flying around the trees. I retrieved my binoculars and proceeded to identify six species—American robin, indigo bunting, Eastern bluebird, hairy woodpecker, Eastern phoebe, and bald eagle—all within an hour. This was my most profitable bird-watching session yet, and it was completely unexpected. My phone's navigation app hadn't brought me here like most of the other places I had seen. If I let the apps tell me where to go, I would end up where everyone else went, and then whine that the experience was "crowded" or "expensive." The only way I found this overlook was by following the road sign. What a risk I had taken to pull into it! It was like buying a product online without reading any reviews. Yet I knew that if there was no risk involved, it was likely I would be disappointed by another mediocre experience marred by the noise of the crowd.

It's safe to say that travel is dead, at least according to the classic definition that hints at an exploration of the unknown. Today it's just too easy. All risk is eliminated as you "explore" what amounts to a commodified, neatly-packaged experience that has already been devoured by the masses. Even worse is that travel has become more about collecting photos and videos, mostly of yourself in exotic places, than truly knowing the exotic.

With navigation, hotel, and travel apps, along with credit cards, it has become impossible to "fail" at travel. If anyone can do it, and no training or discernment is required to make it back home in one piece, it amounts to a prolonged consumer transaction.

I remember my first international trip in 2005 to Italy. I took traveler's checks, which I cashed in various Italian banks for local currency. That wasn't at all difficult, but it involved *some* planning and foresight. I remember having to ask around for train schedules and hotel recommendations. I went to train stations with all my bags not knowing whether or not I'd get a ticket. I walked into hotels and asked whether they had a vacancy, and if they didn't, I trekked to another one nearby. I had to hail taxis with my arm and pretend that I knew my way around so drivers wouldn't rip me off. I caught the tail-end of travel when reservations were not automatic and you were forced to interact with other human beings to gain information. Now anyone can be a "traveler" and have their status boosted on the internet. It has become an identity. The irony of my complaint is not lost on me, since I have profited from the traveler identity. Even now, I am putting out videos of my road trip and writing a book about it, so perhaps I am the problem, and my pride simply wants to look down on others who are less "authentic" than me where I get to define what is authentic.

I arrived in Red Wing, Minnesota, a city on the western bank of the Mississippi that borders Wisconsin. I stayed for only one night but I was impressed with the brick buildings in the old town. I considered walking through to film it, then climbing the bluff in the center that Tripadvisor declared the number-one thing to do in the city, but I resisted. I did not take video of the center or climb the bluff. Instead, I drove right out of town. As expected, feelings of regret followed. Had I really experienced the town if I didn't document it in some way? How could I say I had been there without having taken the 20-minute hike to the bluff? I wondered whether the way to break those feelings was to seek out travel only if it allowed me to strengthen my faith. If my spiritual relationship with God was not deepened through travel, it was entertainment, a way to pass the time. If I witnessed a beautiful sight and didn't immediately feel the compulsion to give glory to God, maybe I shouldn't have gone there.

†

The Mall of America opened when I was 13, advertised as the "biggest mall in America" with hundreds of stores. I was at that Generation X age when my friends and I hung out at the mall every week, so I often dreamed of going to this beautiful shopping center. Finally, at 40, my dream was granted. The mall was located in a suburb of Minneapolis, the city of my next speech.

I'm not sure what I was expecting when I entered, but it was a mall just like any other, with the same stores you could find on the East Coast. The only difference was the children's theme park in the center with carnival games and roller-coasters, without which I would guess the mall would be dying like most indoor malls in America.

If there is ever an act of terrorism in the state of Minnesota, I'm sure it will happen at the Mall of America. No other target will elicit as much public terror and fear, and just one month before my arrival, a migrant threw a young boy from its third-floor platform. The fact that the mall has a "no guns" policy makes it even more appealing to terrorists, who can start their reign of terror knowing that enforcement is at least several minutes away.

There was nothing to do in the mall except eat, buy clothing made in Bangladesh, and watch other people, many of whom were Somali women in full hijab gear. I bought three t-shirts, a straw hat, and two chocolate chip cookies. The mall got $50 out of me. Many people travel long distances to visit it, but now in the age of the internet you no longer need to go to the "biggest mall in America" to buy the junk you can buy just about anywhere else.

My Minneapolis event dinner took place downtown. A white man in his late twenties brought a small clipboard of questions for me, which greatly facilitated the evening's conversation. Whenever there was a silence, I would turn to him and say, "Another question!" Like many other men, he asked about finding a good girl for marriage.

"I date and am on all the apps," he said, "but the women have too many red flags. How can I find one that is worth marrying?"

"For a girl that is worth marrying, is she secular or religious?" I asked.

"Religious."

"Are religious girls on Tinder?"

"No."

"And where do religious girls go?"

"Church."

"There's your starting point. But the real issue is you have a spiritual problem masquerading as a material problem. I'm assuming you are not active in a church. You have little or no faith, and you're trying to bond with women who have little or no faith through secular apps that would repel any devout Christian. And from this process you hope that you will have an everlasting union full of love and happiness. Are you currently sexually active?"

"Yes, I sleep with women."

"And then when you sleep with these women, you enjoy the stupor that results, the sexual satiation. You become addicted to it. If I was getting serviced by a promiscuous girl who was a porn star in bed, the last thing that would enter my mind is finding a good girl. How could I, with the carnal sex act feeding my lusts and desires? So I just got hooked on the sex while fooling myself that I'm still on the lookout for a good girl, who, if she really was good, would run away from a man like me, and they did! Thoughts of the good girl rarely entered my mind, because look at the day, it's been a week since I got laid, and I'm getting hornier and hornier. I'm in a sexual emergency! I must hit the bars and achieve immediate orgasmic release! If you asked me to delay that pleasure for something greater, such as a family, I would tell you to stop trying to hurt my sex life. Stop being a prude. Ironically, being successful at scoring sex hurts you more than anything else when it comes to finding one girl. If you cut all that sex out, and masturbation as well, which is extremely difficult and can only be accomplished through God, your radar will suddenly change. You will notice good girls when they were invisible to you beforehand because you yourself are becoming good. At the end of the day, a man can only pursue sex or marriage, but not both."

"Or he ends up marrying the wrong girl," he added.

"Exactly. The solution is not how to find a girl, but how to strengthen your faith. Once you do that, you will encounter women with faith as well. Otherwise you'll end up like me, meeting all these girls and banging a lot of them while simultaneously whining about how hard it is to meet a good girl. I wasn't a good guy, so why would a good girl want to have anything to do with me? And the girls who I thought were good, who so happened to sleep with me within a couple of dates, were obviously not as good as I thought when I tried to pursue a relationship with them."

One of the guests was a Jewish man who had political clout in his city. Adam had scraggly long hair and an excited energy. He described how he helped elect the new mayor by connecting him with Jewish donors. He was well versed in the "conspiracy theories" of the day, so when the other guys ran out of questions for me, I started asking him a few.

"So Pizzagate, is that real?" I asked.

"Yes, and it's far worse than what you know. Have you heard

of adrenochrome? They put children in a state of fear so their bloodstream is flooded with adrenaline. And then they sacrifice the children and drink their blood."

"That really happens?" I had heard of the theory before but was skeptical.

"Yes, but the market for adrenochrome is drying up because of Trump. He has arrested thousands of pedophiles since getting elected. This is why certain celebrities like Celine Dion suddenly look gaunt, like concentration camp victims. They can no longer obtain adrenochrome and are experiencing withdrawal."

"So we're essentially ruled over by vampire pedophiles?"

"*Satanic* vampire pedophiles," he corrected. "The good news is that Trump is trying to dismantle this."

"Why doesn't he tell the public? He can make a speech and get the nation on board with him."

"Dwight Eisenhower tried to do that with his military-industrial complex speech. They labeled him a kook and nothing happened. Trump is acting as a folksy patriot. It's for show. Behind the scenes, he's fighting them. I expect things to unravel for the pedophiles next year."

"Do the pedos think they can get away with it?"

"The only way they can is if they start World War III. They believe that will cover it all up. If they don't start a war, they will be exposed, and it will be game over for them."

"And what is my role in this grand game?"

"To strengthen the family."

"But I don't even have a family."

"It doesn't matter. Remember when you were getting all that media coverage a few years back? They were actually promoting you. At a time you were still teaching promiscuity and casual sex, they wanted to send more men your way who didn't fit in with their feminist paradigm. A lot of men found you from those viral Return of Kings articles, didn't they?"

"They did. But wait, you're saying that their attacks against me, with those large mobs, were a way to corrupt men further by helping them engage in more casual sex?"

"Yes! You were a useful idiot without knowing it. You don't think they know that by attacking you, they promote you? They're not stupid. But have you noticed they don't attack you as much anymore? Why is that?"

"Because I stopped pushing sex?"

"Exactly. Now they're quiet, because by attacking you, people will encounter your Christian message, which they can't have. But when your message was free love, they promoted you under the guise of an attack. In essence, men who weren't corrupted through their direct liberal education and propaganda were corrupted by the liberated sex norms you promoted."

His theory was intriguing. When the media attacked me, only 1-2% of the mob would identify with my ideas and become followers. They would then go on to watch me teach a sexually liberal lifestyle which wasn't that different from the 98% or 99% of those who hated me, so I can agree that I was a dutiful soldier of the establishment by teaching men the same type of sexual norms that they taught women. If the media starts writing about you, whether positively or negatively, you're serving a purpose for them in some way. By attacking me, they energized their troops, advanced the main tenets of their agenda, and, if Adam was right, taught more men how to engage in seamless fornication.

After dinner, we went upstairs to the rooftop lounge. The pleasant view of Minneapolis was canceled out by loud hip hop music emanating from nearby bars and nightclubs, which attracted groups of women who wanted to drink and dance. My previous work encouraged men to go to venues like this. I taught them that they would feel strong and masculine by having one-night stands with women, whereas the type of pleasure-seeking I promoted was more in line with effeminacy and a lack of self-control.

✝

On the day of the talk, I arrived at the hotel where I had booked a conference room and immediately noticed that it was directly across the street from the largest gay disco in the city. I used it to get some cheap laughs during my talk to the 40 or so attendees.

While I didn't talk about God much during the main speech, most of my answers in the Q&A did revolve around Him. When someone asked me a question about achieving a materialistic goal, I was quick to highlight that it was a spiritual problem in disguise. Towards the end of the event, a man about 60 years old made loud sighs that were noticed by the crowd. He was handed the microphone and began complaining.

"I did not come here for all this God talk," he said. "I came here to hear about masculinity. Men are being attacked, and you're just going on and on about God nonsense. That's not what I paid for."

"I did advertise the talk would contain things I learned about life," I replied. "What specifically about masculinity did you want to know about?"

"I don't know. I just didn't come here for this. This was a waste for everyone here."

"Don't speak for me," a young man in the back said. "I came here for this."

The crowd started murmuring against the old man until he gave up the microphone and stewed in silence.

At past events, some men had left quietly during the Q&A, but it was impossible to know why. Maybe they felt the same as this man. In some way, I'm glad he had spoken up, because it showed everyone in the room how the same speech can be perceived differently. Afterwards, one man from the front row told me that he planned to attend church for the first time the very next day, and Adam asked me for advice on converting to Christianity. It's not up to me how people respond to my words.

It turned out that someone spoke to the disgruntled man during the intermission. He admitted that he was going to the Philippines to meet women. Because of his age, I doubt he was going to pick up girls, so I suspected that he paid for sex. If true, a man who was actively engaged in committing carnal sin was angry that my talk advised men to avoid sin. Of course he would be upset. This man wasn't going to turn to God anytime soon, but once he hit a dead end with meaningless sexual experiences, he might remember the speech he heard one summer day across from the biggest gay disco in Minneapolis.

After the event was over and I had said goodbye to everyone, I walked a few blocks to sit at a bar for a cheeseburger-and-fries dinner. Near me were an older white couple drinking beers. Behind them was a table of black men loudly gambling over dice. They had bills folded lengthwise and would toss them in the middle of the table before rolling. I looked at the faces of the old couple. They exhibited a grin of frustration, restraining themselves as best as they could while the black men didn't restrain themselves at all. The bar staff permitted their yelling and illegal gambling. I found this to be a fitting metaphor for what was happening in America. The way of life that the boomers coveted was disappearing, to be replaced by homosexuality, degeneracy, constant criminality, low-grade political violence, censorship, low-paying jobs, homelessness, profuse drug use, large-scale Third World immigration, and a host of other ills that had barely touched the boomer generation in their youth. They still had their wealth and their large houses in the suburbs, but once they died, what kind of America will remain?

†

There were two mass shootings over the course of 12 hours—one in El Paso, Texas that killed 20 people and another in Dayton, Ohio, a city I had recently driven through, that killed ten. The first shooter was purportedly a right-wing white male who hated Hispanics. The second shooting was by a purportedly left-wing male who wanted to kill "fascists," but who ended up killing people of various ethnic backgrounds inside a bar.

When reading history books about countries in decline, the narrative includes huge spans of time—"so and so country experienced great hardship during the years 1845 to 1857." Those 12 years may get a page of text, or only a paragraph, but that's over 4,000 days of violence, poverty, starvation, and suffering. America is in decline, and we have to go through daily degradations until it hits bottom, which could take decades. There will be mass shootings, political violence, outrageous corruption, and rounds of sinister social engineering. Things that were just an afterthought before, like going to the supermarket, will soon be a source of fear or concern. America is dying, and the only question is when the body will breathe its last breath. As the decay of the cities increases, it will begin to spread to the suburbs. As in the past, only those in the rural areas will be able to retain their way of life with the minimal amount of disruption, but what happens when rogue gangs start invading farmhouses for supplies? Or when SWAT teams with thermal imaging equipment effortlessly disarm the locals? It's tempting to prep for these times by building a bunker and stocking it with a million rounds of ammo and five years' supply of food, but that presupposes that God doesn't exist and you can save yourself through your own efforts. Without God, you will simply go mad in your bunker, cursing the world, surrounded by cans of tuna rapidly approaching their expiration date.

Should I be worried about my speaking events? If someone wanted to kill a group of God-fearing conservatives, my speech would be an ideal target. I had not received any threats, and for the seven events I had completed, the biggest mishap had been one man complaining that I didn't talk more about masculinity (i.e., fornication), but that didn't mean I was in the clear. Since I was in no way qualified to know the best course of action to take, I asked God. I prayed to Him to instruct me on how I should proceed and what exactly He wanted me to do.

The three options on the table were to cancel the events, hire security guards, or make no changes. I didn't have the right to cancel my events out of fear if God had willed those events for me, which I believed to be the case. Hiring a security guard was a sound option, but it would give the veneer of security as much as real security. The guard would be an obstacle for potential shooters, but with most of them using high-powered rifles, unless the guard had his weapon drawn the entire time, he would likely be caught by surprise and be the first person killed. Guards seemed more suited to deal with rowdy guests or those who tried to sneak in without paying. Last, I could simply continue, but wasn't that unnecessarily risky? Wouldn't a guard at least be of some help? While I didn't particularly want to die, I was more concerned about others dying under my watch. I would feel a heavy burden of guilt if they were killed before working out their salvation.

Sunday's happy hour would be the last one. Starting with Denver, I would tack a two-hour happy hour on to the end of the main event. I organized the happy hour at Powderhorn Lake on the southern side of Minneapolis near the Somali Museum. The online pictures of the lake seemed quaint enough, but when I arrived, I was greeted by a busy art festival. Dozens of artists manned booths to sell their work. On the northern tip of the lake, a DJ pumped out loud music beside a gigantic gay pride flag. Every party must now be a gay party. For the second day in a row, I had inadvertently picked a venue that featured homosexuality. Even if you're not gay or don't want to be gay, the gays will find you and shove their lifestyle down your throat.

After hanging out by the park and snacking on fried carnival food, we moved to a nearby craft brewery. We hung out and chatted by a wooden bar that was, as expected, decorated with gay pride stickers. Like with the previous happy hours, I entered dozens of mini-conversations. I remember one with a Lutheran. Early on in my Christian faith, which had been only a few months prior, I had a couple of heated discussions with non-Orthodox Christians concerning doctrine. I now saw that as pride. I decided that, in the future, I'd represent Orthodoxy as best I could, but I would not passionately debate or argue with fellow Christians. I maintained this rule with the Lutheran man, as different as our Churches were. He might not believe in everything I did, but that didn't allow me to not treat him as my neighbor.

8

Demons

There was a lot to explore in the state of Minnesota, but I had only five days until my next series of events in Denver. I drove right across it and into South Dakota, a state I had been to before. The small towns of South Dakota made me feel as if I were going back in time. You can find old motels that still have their "Free Television" signs ("Free WiFi" is perfunctorily added below). The bars are trailers that were plopped onto the dirt—only one per small town. Much of the road is gravel, and dust is constantly kicked up by pickup trucks. The cell-phone signal is weak and so is the internet. The best part is that there is no obvious degeneracy. No gay flags or even gays. If someone is gay in South Dakota, they have no choice but to go to Rapid City or Sioux Falls to practice their lifestyle, but those cities are so small that they will run out of partners within a few weeks (or days). They'll have to go further west to Seattle, Portland, or Los Angeles if they want to experience "love."

I've noticed that size is a function of degeneracy. The more populated an area, the more synergy it facilitates among degenerates, and they start to attract other degenerates from smaller towns. Like a series of creeks or mountain streams feeding a large river, the degeneracy becomes a rapid. South Dakota, because of its small size, can serve only as a small stream to other areas.

Unfortunately, feminism took hold in South Dakota a long time ago. The men may act like men, but the women also act like men. The latter are large or tattooed, usually both, and there is no sign of Christianity in the form of modest dress. If an area is saved from one form of degeneracy, it's invariably affected by another, and the many men who spend the bulk of their adult lives trying to find an uncorrupted land will search in vain. I see all my travels of over a decade as just one big temptation that took me away from leading a Christian life close to my parents in Washington, DC. I rebelled by traveling around the world and all that accomplished was throwing over a decade down the drain. Even if I went on to find the perfect town with good living and Christian women, I could enjoy it for only a day or two before leaving, because home is where my family is. They are the only roots I have left, and if I needed to move, I would have to take them with me.

South Dakota is a flat state, full of prairie land that is suitable for cattle ranching. Driving west on I-90, a dead-straight road with a pleasing speed limit of 80 miles per hour, I called my friend Jeremiah, an army vet who was ten years younger than me. He was injured in combat while serving in Afghanistan and received a pension that, for a long time, funded a lifestyle of travel and fornication, but he turned to God shortly after me and was now someone I could talk to about the faith.

"I told my pastor about you," he started. "He said, 'Oh, your friend could be in trouble.'"

"Why's that?"

"Since your faith is so new, you could backslide into your old habits."

"Everyone says that," I replied. "I agree that this trip could end in disaster. There are a lot of potential traps."

"They told me the story of Bob Dylan. He experienced something similar to you, but then his friends sucked him back into the world."

"I'm careful," I said confidently. "I maintain my daily prayers and abstain from alcohol, which usually gets me into trouble, though I am having trouble maintaining custody of my eyes. I still look at women to get pleasure from their beauty."

I wouldn't recommend someone new in the faith to undertake the kind of road trip I was doing. If I had to do it all over again, I'd probably wait a year before attempting it, but it was too late now.

I visited the Badlands National Park on the western side of the state. The park is composed of rock formations that the French explorers who first found it thought were so useless that they called it "bad lands." Scenic overlooks throughout the park offered endless views of reddish-brown rock mounds with horizontal stripes, sometimes broken up by green prairie. The rocks were uneven and raggedy, almost lunar in appearance. In their own way, the rocks were beautiful, perhaps one of the most beautiful sights I had ever seen. Only God can make rocks beautiful.

The National Park Service did everything they could to re-move God's glory through their informational placards. They stated the age of the park as if it were a fact, not a theory, and explained with precision how the rocks developed through various geological processes. One placard claimed that the Badlands was 500 million years old. They lied to us about the war Jeremiah fought in, and now they were going to tell me the story of what happened half-a-billion years ago?

Millions of children who visit the national parks receive a dose of propaganda through these secular lessons. It normalizes a narrative that the earth is so old that evolution from molecular soup to human consciousness is the only story of humanity. It could very well be the case that geologists have tapped into God's method for creating the Badlands, but it is only a method of which He is governor. Beauty is not a spontaneous or random natural process, but an event guided by the hand of God.

However old the Badlands is, God created this. It's His, and so all glory for it must be given to Him.

I undertook two small hikes that afforded me time alone with the rocks. I was even able to find a shady nook where I could sit and stare at them for some time to appreciate their splendor without the taint of lust or passion like when appreciating a woman's appearance. The latter begets the desire to take her body while in a state of mindless passion, to have her as my own. I get excited by a woman's beauty, am pleased by it, and imagine the acts of fornication that I will do to her, and if that desire is not satisfied, I can simply masturbate to the virtual women on my computer screen who look like her. The cities are so void of natural beauty that men become enthralled by the artificial beauty presented through makeup, fake nails, and skin-tight yoga pants. Such beauty is not meant to glorify beauty itself, or even God, but to be used as bait for a process of extracting sexual pleasure, excitement, or wealth. Women clearly advertise their intent to extract, but men still become addicted to their false beauty, because they are hoping to extract themselves. I used to see women in the city as the ultimate reason for my existence, but all of them failed to satisfy. I was dying of thirst and then dove into the ocean to drink saltwater, only to wonder why my thirst remained. Unless you acknowledge the deficit in your soul, and turn away from mere simulacrums that defy God and towards the clear springs of life, you will always remain thirsty because all material rewards are saltwater.

Admiring the rocks could not damage my soul. I could not keep the rocks for myself. Satan could not be glorified through them. Unless I learn to recognize a woman's true beauty—the internal beauty that stems from her faith—temptation will never escape me. I will always be a slave to the pleasure I get from my eyes.

†

I traveled to Rapid City, South Dakota. It was nice enough, but its old-time feel clashed with the tattooed "artists" and assorted liberals who were in the process of taking over the city center. I can't believe there are so many of them and that they're all over the country. About a year before, I fantasied about moving to Rapid City, a place I had never been to before, based on scant information I read about online, but that was just another temptation. When I'm going through a difficult period in life or not experiencing pleasure, I fantasize about something that I believe will give me pleasure. The cabin in the woods was another temptation in response to the initial difficulty of doing the tour. I was obsessed with it for several days until Dr. Jones remarked that my plan sounded like a nightmare.

I noticed a large presence of Harley Davidson motorcycles. I was told that the Sturgis Motorcycle Rally was in progress, which explained why motel prices were three times above what I expected. The city of Sturgis was only an hour from Rapid City, and when I got closer to it upon traveling to the town of Deadwood, there were more motorcycles on the road than cars.

In my mid-twenties, I owned a Kawasaki Ninja 500 sportbike. With an engine size of 500cc, it was considered a beginner bike, but it was plenty fast. For two years, I rode beyond my skill level and had several close calls on the road that could have ended gruesomely. I got the hint and sold the bike. Now that I was seeing motorcycles everywhere, I became captivated. I wanted a naked street bike, one that looked cool. I researched the bikes online and imagined riding one. I would have to retake a motorcycle safety course and buy new gear and... another temptation! I knew what my mind was up to, but it was hard to resist. The road was tough, especially without the usual pleasures I had depended on in the past, such as women, caffeine, alcohol, and Twitter trolling, and now I had nothing that could release dopamine. My eyes were uncontrollable, starved for pleasure. I couldn't stop checking out the figures of women in my vicinity, even the gray-haired librarian who worked at the Deadwood library. She was at least ten years older than me.

I walked on Deadwood's Main Street. The city was illegally settled in the late 1800s as a result of a gold rush. Men went into town to buy supplies and partake in drinking, gambling, and sex with prostitutes. It was the sort of lawless place that inspired many Western movies. Instead of men flocking to mine gold, there were hundreds of men on their motorcycles flocking to have fun and share in their mutual "biker" identity. The only price of admission was a Harley Davidson bike, leather gear, a couple of faded tattoos, and a penchant for drinking. These men didn't have a tribe of their own, one based on blood and faith, and so they allowed the Harley Davidson Corporation to create one for them. They looked at each other not as fellow consumers but fellow tribesmen.

For a long time, my identities had been traveler, player, and writer. To be a traveler, I had to leave my home and spend tens of thousands of dollars in foreign countries. To be a player, I had to be a consumer of bars, cafés, restaurants, and clubs while seeking transient, sterile relationships with women. To be a writer meant feeding my pride and puffing up my experiences and abilities to receive compliments, status, money, and fame. All were material, all damaged my soul. If just one sentence of this book brings you closer to God, it is more valuable than all my previous writing put together.

I drove through the Black Hills of South Dakota, which offered forest as far as I could see. It also contained Mount Rushmore, one of the most popular tourist attractions in America. I had little interest in going, since I had already been burned by the famous pizzas of New Haven and Chicago, but since I was so close to it, I coughed up the $10 parking fee and went. When I squinted at the tiny faces of the four presidents from what seemed like a dozen miles away, I immediately regretted my decision. I stayed for two minutes then left.

I drove through the Black Hills and then the grasslands of South Dakota. The number of cars on the road steadily decreased as I entered Wyoming, where it seemed that all of civilization had ended. As far as I could see, I was the only person on the road, and only infrequently did I encounter other cars and trucks. My cell phone lost all reception. For the first time in my eight-week trip, I was alone. A tinge of fear entered my mind. What would happen if my car broke down or if I had a medical emergency? I'd be in real trouble. And that's how I knew that Wyoming was a great place. No one to bother you, no policemen with their speed traps, no billboards advertising boner pills. Just you, the road, and the grazing cattle. I honked at them many times to get their reaction, but they never looked at me. I felt blessed with total peace, away from man.

The driving got tough at night. With no road lamps, and countless signs denoting deer crossings, it took all of my mental energy to concentrate on the road. If a deer did appear while I was driving at high speed, I would have no time to stop, and trying to would probably be even more dangerous, since it would lower the front end of my car enough for the deer to fly through the windshield.

Still far from Cheyenne, I saw a lone red light in the distance. It was too small to be a car. Was it at the top of a tower? I couldn't make out how far off it was, but it was definitely getting closer. It could have been a drone or a slow-moving aircraft, maybe even a government experiment. I started getting concerned that it would appear right in front of me, so I slowed down. It went farther away from me and then it got closer again. This went on for at least 20 miles, until I finally got close enough to the light. It was a motorcycle. In the pitch darkness, with no one else around, a common thing had taken on an ominous appearance. Immediately, I knew that it would take a certain kind of character to live in Wyoming. With so few people around, you'd never be sure if you were safe and on the well-worn path.

Cheyenne itself was similar to the small cities in South Dakota but with much less degeneracy. People weren't unnecessarily loud and drawing attention to themselves. The men were masculine. They looked like they knew how to jump-start a car without first double-checking on YouTube where the connectors went. I did see a GOP campaign office that had pro-Trump signs out front. In liberal cities, they would have to remove Trump from the window unless they wanted to be firebombed.

It took only one night in Cheyenne to confirm that Wyoming is the best place I've been to in the United States, for the simple reason that it allows a man to be a man without living like a rat. As long as you don't have the desire to fornicate with other rats, be entertained by other rats, or be close enough to them to contract various diseases of the body and soul, Wyoming will allow you to spread your wings and soar like a phoenix over the most beautiful land in the country, and with only 600,000 people in the entire state, you can be as alone as you desire. You can live in a small city like Cheyenne or buy land and pretend to be a rancher. Or become a park ranger. Or work in the energy sector. There are unlimited opportunities for a man who doesn't want to sit in front of a computer all day. Best of all, the prices are affordable, from food and gas to real estate. If my family was willing, I would relocate all of them on a nice 50-acre plot of land, but they are set in their ways, so somewhere close to them in Appalachia on the Blue Ridge Mountains, which is sort of a mini-Wyoming, may be the answer for me.

The only problem with Wyoming, and this could be a deal-breaker for most men, is that there aren't many women. If you go alone, there is a high chance you will stay alone. If you've dedicated yourself to the spiritual life, and remain in the company of Christ, that may not be a problem, but then again, I wonder whether your chances of meeting a good woman in Wyoming are worse than in New York City. The latter has millions of women, but they exist in a deeply fallen state. They are there because they don't want to take on the traditional role of a God-fearing housewife. They don't want to have a big family. It's a deception to think a larger number of women—especially good-looking women—means it will be easier for you to find a wife. It could be just the opposite, because what leads to a successful union is not the quantity of available women but their faith in God. The big cities tend to attract women with no faith, who move from the little towns of South Dakota and Wyoming to worship at the altar of Satan, whether they realize it or not.

†

I wanted to go to Yellowstone National Park. Since it was peak season, indoor lodging was over $250 a night. I came up with the idea to camp instead. I could surely buy a tent and sleeping bag for under $250, which meant that camping for just one night would pay for itself. I began researching how to camp. I made a list of all the supplies I would need. Unlike buying a motorcycle, this would be a totally practical decision since I was saving money and putting myself closer to nature, but just to be sure, I asked God whether it was okay for me to start camping. I didn't see any reason why He would say no.

A few hours later, I went on to YouTube to watch camping videos. I was recommended one by a man who had hiked the entire length of the Appalachian Trail, which typically takes five or six months. He went on about how he was always searching for new hikes and adventures. He hated to stay still and always had to be on the move. He even criticized people who desired to work a stable job. Here was a man who, instead of getting closer to nature out of necessity or to build a relationship with God, was doing so out of novelty and pride, to have a lifestyle that keeps him occupied while being able to judge others. I watched more videos by people who made such a false idol out of nature that they developed a lifestyle around it, in a similar way I had done with sex. So even nature can allow the sin of pride to enter a person's life? But isn't nature just a gift from God? Yes, and sex is also a gift from God, but I experienced firsthand how it could be used in a way that opposed God. Any inherently good act can be perverted into evil when separated from God's intended purpose.

With this insight in mind, I accepted that my urge to camp was yet another temptation. I was already on a mission and now I wanted to take on a new mission. My desire to learn how to camp would divert a large amount of energy away from my speaking tour. The camping temptation was more dangerous than the cabin or motorcycle temptation, which was future-oriented, because a small mishap while camping could jeopardize my entire trip. Permission to camp denied. I decided that any idea or thought which led me away from my spiritual mission was in all likelihood a temptation.

✝

Driving into Denver, I saw signs for Aurora and Littleton, two places I remembered were in the news for mass shootings. In America, you are just as likely to know a city for its massacres as for its beautiful landmarks.

The Denver dinner was attended by one lapsed Catholic, one Protestant who was considering whether or not to convert to Orthodoxy, and two men in the Orthodox Church in America (OCA), an independent church that was spun off from the Russian Orthodox Church. One was serving active military duty in what I surmised involved high-security clearance. I'd met many men like him before, and since they couldn't divulge specific information, I had to read between the lines. Throughout the night, Chris repeatedly stated that he was relaying his "personal opinion" as a citizen, but of course I knew that his "personal opinion" was influenced by what he saw at work. I asked him questions to elicit opinions that could serve as a soft confirmation or denial of a particular theory I had.

"Last week, I talked to an insider," I started, "and I asked him if Pizzagate was real. He replied that it's worse than what is known. Would you say that his response is accurate?"

"In my personal opinion, that is accurate," Chris replied.

"Would you also say it's accurate that we are essentially ruled by satanic pedophiles?"

He paused for a few seconds. "I would say that's accurate. I can say that many high-level commanders have committed... suicide... based on information they received that the public does not know. The scale of human trafficking in the United States is immense."

"Is it likely that Federal agents are attending my tour, to see what I'm speaking about and to discern the vibe of my audience?"

"I would imagine there has been at least one Federal agent on your tour, probably more."

The Catholic of the group, who was the youngest, expressed surprise at the revelations, but I was just getting started.

I said, "I believe that the CIA and possibly the DEA are arming and training Mexican drug cartels to destabilize Mexico to encourage hordes of people to come into the United States in a way that serves the immigration agenda. Would you say that is accurate?"

"In my personal opinion, that is accurate. Every agency has a black ops budget that is funded through illegal activity. For example, there are soldiers in Afghanistan who wonder why they are commanded to protect poppy fields."

"The CIA is not known as the Cocaine Importing Agency for nothing. And what's with all the rash of UFO media reports that have been surfacing? Navy pilots have been granted permission by the Federal government to share sighting stories, which tells me that the government itself is behind the UFOs in some way. Is it safe to say that the military has advanced technology that we don't know about?"

"I can only state that there is technology in existence that is way more advanced than what is known, by a very large degree."

"Why don't they reveal it?" I asked.

"Because they don't want the enemy to develop countermeasures. They will only use it if they have to."

"This ties into Operation Blue Beam."

"What's that?" the Catholic asked.

"It's a scheme to simulate a supposed alien invasion," I replied. "In order to defeat the interstellar 'aliens,' the government will say that we need to unite with the world. We will then be ruled by one government and one diluted religion. There's also the operation to simulate the rapture, a doctrine many Protestants believe. Through advanced technology, people will be lifted off the ground and a Jesus-like figure will be anointed as God to bring the whole world together in one government, but he would actually be the Antichrist." I turned to Chris. "Are these operations real?"

"I cannot confirm or deny their existence, but I can say that a lot of the truth is already out there, perhaps 85% of it. Only problem is there is no context to connect those truths, so when you hear of a theory in isolation, it's not easy to understand how that fits together with what they want to accomplish."

"And what do they want?" the Catholic asked.

"Complete control," I said. "They want you to be a slave. They want to direct your behavior, actions, and even thoughts. Everything you do must be controlled by them."

"Correct," Chris said. "And they are doing it through the smartphone. There is technology in the phone, which you can see in public patents, that can emit certain wavelengths."

"For mind control?" I interrupted. "I had heard of technology that could control your thoughts."

"Yes. It is my personal opinion that they can put thoughts into your mind. There is a reason that new phones have batteries that can't be removed."

"Interesting you say that. I turn off my phone at a certain battery level, and then when I turn it back on, the level sometimes drops by 3% or more. My previous smartphones didn't do that. I would have to watch a video for at least 20 minutes to drop the battery by that amount."

"Even if your phone is off, it could still be in operation."

"So they control you indirectly through marketing and algorithms into consuming certain products and internet content, and now you're confirming—through your personal opinion—that they can also put direct thoughts into my brain that seem as if they're coming from my voice. This is the same power that demons have. I have also heard that the government has done extensive experiments with psychedelics to receive technology from the demons. The demons share things with humans who have evil intent, the humans apply it, and, sure enough, it works."

"It is known that Hillary Clinton had séances," Chris said.

I mostly watched YouTube videos about Orthodoxy, so why was the top recommendation for me the other day an atheist video titled "Walking away from faith"? Google was recommending videos to disrupt a faith that they knew was growing based on my watch history.

There is a finite number of demons but a growing world population. To scale up their evil, maybe the demons have given some of their abilities to humans they control in order to maintain a satanic world system that appears to be dragging people into hell.

"How about Edward Snowden?" I asked. "How is it possible that a media organization like The Intercept, owned by a connected oligarch, Pierre Omidyar, can publish NSA secrets without getting shut down? Is Snowden a CIA spy? Is The Intercept some kind of front?"

"Snowden did have links to the CIA," Chris replied. "If there is information out there that the government doesn't want out there, it would be removed. Otherwise, it serves a purpose for them and allows people to be led in the way they want. That purpose may not be immediately obvious."

"So basically all the information that is presented to us, especially in the news, is information that will not harm the government?"

"I would say that's accurate."

"I have a friend who is connected to the very upper tiers of power. He once took a photo on his phone that he shouldn't have. It involved a powerful government politician. He told me that within a day that photo was wiped from his phone. Is there technology which allows that?"

"In my personal opinion, that is possible."

I was a bit demoralized that Chris confirmed many of my theories. That doesn't mean they're necessarily true, but I believe they are. It would have been nice if he had told me that I was wrong and the world wasn't as evil as I believed it to be, but those denials didn't come. Satan rules this world, and there is a long line of human beings who want to work with him to receive rewards in this life, and I'm sure it has always been this way, only on a smaller scale and without the aid of technology that allows new evil ideas to spread around the globe in a matter of days.

"Are there any good guys in the government?" I asked.

"There are a lot of them," Chris replied.

"So why don't they do anything?"

"Well, you see what happens to whistleblowers. They are defamed and sometimes killed. Or they commit an impossible suicide. It's not easy to fix a corrupt system. Also, if a white hat wants to do the right thing, he has only one bullet in his gun. It is my personal opinion that white hats want to wait for the crucial moment so that their efforts won't be done in vain. Anyone who has information that genuinely threatens those in power, white hat or not, will be killed."

The very next day, the top news story in the country was that Jeffrey Epstein had committed suicide in his jail cell.

†

The itchy rash I thought was a reaction to bed bugs had become worse. I'd wake up in the middle of the night to scratch my body so vigorously that I was creating bloody sores. I didn't remember that from my bed bug experiences. I decided to go to an urgent care center a few hours before my Denver talk.

The doctor took my history and examined the rash on my body. "And you've had this rash for how long?"

"About 16 days."

"It could be scabies. Let me prescribe you a cream for that. You only need to put it on twice."

Scabies is a mite that burrows under your skin with the intention of squatting there indefinitely. The itchiness is a result of your body's reaction to its feces. So I had completed two lectures while possibly infected with scabies and was on my way to do a third. I could add that to the list of my life's accomplishments. It would take a lot more than heart palpitations or scabies to stop me, Satan! Men around the country expect a talk from me, and that's what they will get.

The city of Denver was far more liberal than I had imagined. It had numerous homeless people and drifters occupying all parts of the city, and many of them seemed of working age like in Madison, Wisconsin. The normal population showed off tattoos and other degenerate styles, such as excessive piercings and colored hair. When it comes to an American big city, there is little variation from one to the next, and the only real identifying trait of Denver was a clothing style that said, "I'm about to go for a short hike." But the strongest memory of my stay was getting served a cup of tea at Starbucks by a man with the voice of a little girl while his coworker right behind him was a gigantic man, at least 6'4", wearing poorly applied makeup.

About 25 people showed up at the lecture, including three women who came with their significant others. After the speech, a man who arrived late came up to me and asked whether I had seen the protesters outside.

"What protesters?" I replied.

"There were five protesters, four women and one man, if you want to call him that. They held signs that you are a rapist and were yelling against sexism."

Giddy with excitement, I exited the room and rushed towards the front of the hotel. I looked outside but they were gone.

"Were they unattractive?" I asked.

"Yes, they were large."

If there were protesters in Denver, I expected worse in Seattle, Portland, San Francisco, and Los Angeles. The prospect of bigger protests got me thinking whether I should start concealing venue details from ticket holders and walk them to the hotel from a neutral meeting point. I had done this in 2015 when I had trouble in Canada, and while this counter-terrorist maneuver had allowed the events to proceed, it fostered a high degree of tension. Now that women were coming to my events, I couldn't see this as a reasonable option. I would take basic precautions, such as revealing the venue only the day before to ticket holders, and hire security if necessary, but I wouldn't try to guarantee an outcome. Besides, if protesters shut down an event, it would garner more attention for my tour's other stops, so let the Lord's will be done, whatever it was.

The next day, I was invited to attend the Liturgy at St. Herman's Orthodox Church in Denver, an OCA church. For the first time, I heard the Liturgy in English. You'd think it would have greatly enhanced the holiness of my experience, but it felt just about the same as if I had heard it in Classic Armenian or Old Slavonic.

After the Liturgy, I stayed for coffee hour and was introduced to many parishioners. The priest of the church, Father John, approached me and I gave him a five-minute rundown of my life story. He approved of my current path and I received his blessing. Now that I didn't have to do a separate happy hour on Sundays, I could become more like a pilgrim.

9

Mountains

I'd heard of the name "Rocky Mountains" but never knew where it was or what it contained (besides rocky mountains). It is right on the northwest doorstep of Denver. I decided to visit while using the resort town of Estes Park as a home base.

On the first day, I visited Bear Lake. I knew it would be crowded when I saw an electronic road sign saying that the Bear Lake parking lot was full. I went anyway and was greeted by a large swarm of people trying to enjoy the lake in their own way, such as by playing pop music through a Bluetooth speaker or yelling across the lake to hear their echo. There were also many families with loud young children. I don't have children, but if I do, I will instruct them to use their "quiet voice" while in a park so that the lonely bearded men can lose themselves in nature, something I could not do at that lake.

I got on a trail to Alberta Falls. On the way, side trails allowed me to be alone. I took one to a small rapid and sat on a rock facing the water. I relaxed for 20 minutes until a family came by to take pictures of themselves.

When I made it to Alberta Falls, I climbed the rocks to get a better view. I was hit by the distinct smell of marijuana. I suppose the falls were not relaxing enough for that person, and he needed a chemical to add to his mountain experience.

The next morning I woke up in my cabin room. I looked out the window to enjoy the mountain view. I wouldn't have minded staying for at least a week, just reading and relaxing, but I couldn't linger. I was on a strict schedule. The trip was like experiencing an appetizer sampler where I could have a bite here or there but no more. How else can you do a USA road trip? If I wanted to meander, I'd have to block out two years because of how massive the country is. The best you can do is get a taste of the country and then use that to plan future trips that focus on just one area, but chances are you'll get so full from the appetizer that you won't have any room for the entrée.

I've learned that when you're in a national park and see a bunch of cars stopped by the side of the road, there is a large animal nearby, usually a moose. Often it's just one animal, but early on day two of exploring the Rocky Mountains, it was a huge herd of elk grazing on a meadow. They were rather close to the road, not afraid of the human presence. At least a fifth of the herd was baby elk, and they looked cuddly enough that you could walk up and pet them. It was difficult to soak in the majesty of the elk with everyone around me taking pictures, but I did feel blessed that I was able to see God's creations in such a way.

It was hard to tell while driving, but I was steadily climbing to the highest point in the park. My ears popped every time I swallowed. I parked the car near a trailhead to experience my first alpine tundra hike. I made sure to walk in slow motion so as not to tax my body. I didn't mind that little children were passing me by. The first hike was easy enough, but the second one involved a steep flight of stairs. I carried on like an old man. This strategy paid off because I made it to the scenic view without any breathing problems, unlike many others. My goal is never to break a sweat or get "exercise," and I seem to be a natural at that. A sign posted at the peak signified that I was at an elevation of 12,000 feet.

The mountains were so beautiful, yielding such intense pleasure, that initially I had to limit how long I would look at them. When you're used to city life, as I am, and you don't normally see natural beauty, you have to brace yourself when it comes. The phrase "glory to God" automatically came to my lips as I meekly turned my head from one captivating view to the next. I had ignored all the informational placards around the park that offered theories on how these mountains and valleys had been made. The glory goes solely to God, not to "natural forces," which are merely means to God's ends. I didn't want to hear how old the mountains were, or what purported glacier was here eons ago. God created this beauty, and He created it for us, and on this day He allowed me to witness it for a brief moment of human time. What more could be added? I couldn't carry the mountains home with me, no matter how many pictures I took. I could sleep on the mountains and prolong the appreciation of its beauty, but even if I moved on top of them, I would eventually adapt to them. The once-hidden mountain would then become as forsaken as the air I breathe.

I moved to Rio de Janeiro ten years ago because I loved the beach. I imagined going to the beach every day, but after just one month I became tired of the beach, immune to its sounds and heat. This is why God hides from us, and reveals His presence only sparingly when we're in need of Him. If God were everywhere, we'd turn Him into an idol, an ornament that we'd occasionally glance at, a golden calf we'd dance around. We would take him for granted like we do with the creations of this world, even our own parents. His divinity would be lost through constant accessibility. We'd start looking beyond Him for answers that allow us to experience more pleasure or meaning. Unless we take a road trip up the mountains, we cannot understand their majesty, and unless we take a spiritual trip to God's mountain, we cannot fully accept Him into our lives. It is in His infinite wisdom that He hides from us, and only at the end of our spiritual journey, when we cry out to God that we choose Him over the world, will we be able to experience Him in complete fullness.

✝

I drove to Glenwood Springs, Colorado, another resort town that serves as a jump-off point for a variety of nature activities. I decided to visit Hanging Lake, a small body of water fed by a waterfall located 1.5 miles up on the edge of a mountain. I turned the hike into a walk, going so slowly that I'm sure many people thought I was physically disabled. I was even lapped by people who arrived 45 minutes later on the next tour bus. I stopped often to soak in the views, aware that the lake itself might not be worth such a hike.

I arrived at the lake feeling rather refreshed, and although it was pretty, it did not hold the other tourists for long. They took their selfies, sat for three minutes, and then headed back down. I wondered whether they were disappointed that yet another goal they had achieved could not add to their lives, let alone sate them for ten minutes. I identified a bird in the trees and then took a long nap on a bench to the sounds of the waterfall.

The drive to Moab, Utah would take four hours. My plan there was to visit Arches, a national park that features huge stone arches. I had never before spent such long periods alone, and on most days of the trip I talked only when recording my video travelogue. I was getting quite used to the isolation, and enjoyed not being disturbed by people. I remember when I broke up with my girlfriend in 2017 and how upset I was at not having a companion to speak with daily. If I find a woman today, I will initially be chafed that my alone time is gone, but soon get used to her presence and begin to crave it.

Arches National Park was similar to Badlands—it contained a lot of big rocks in a small area. While Badlands featured a uniformity of rocks, Arches featured a uniqueness of them. Every section of the park had a distinct rock structure to look at, often in the form of narrow columns that seemed ready to topple over or big rocks resting precariously on smaller rocks. The highlight was the arches. Somehow, the middle bit of a rock formation was missing, leaving only an arch. To explain how an arch had been formed, the National Park Service's brochure threw everything at it: earthquakes, glaciers, ice freezing and melting, heat, erosion, and wind. Their theory, which they presented as fact, was that earthquakes sectioned the rocks, ice cracked them in certain places, and then the wind, over the course of hundreds of gazillions of years, eroded the rock that was once underneath. It's very possible that it could have happened in this manner, but what bothered me was their arrogance that it had to be this way and no other. God wasn't mentioned at all. It's as if He didn't even exist.

Just like in Badlands, the park was set up to be explored by car. You drive to one scenic point, take your pictures, and then drive to another. There were also trailheads to view some of the arches by foot, but there wasn't much motivation to hit those trails when the temperature was 100° Fahrenheit. I walked two short trails and that was enough, especially since they were extremely crowded with chattering tourists. While facing one of the arches, trying to understand the graciousness of God creating such a marvel for me to enjoy, the last thing in the world I needed was human speech, yet one man was talking loudly about which biotech firm he worked at. Another old couple was discussing the location of the parking lot they had to get back to. Spanish and French tourists were going on about this matter or that in an elevated volume. If I was in charge of the Park Service, I would have a "No talking" rule enforced by Cossacks armed with whips. If you talk, you get a lashing. On the bright side, no one brought a portable speaker, so it could have been worse.

I took a short hike to "The Windows" arches. The name made me remember the Lil Jon rap song "Aww skeet skeet," which advises men to dance around a room, from the window to the wall, until women allow them "skeet," a slang word for ejaculation. The song became popular right after I graduated from university in 2001. I heard it dozens of times in clubs and parties and because I consented to being exposed to the song, it was burned into my brain, surfacing while I tried to admire God's work. While a song like this might not affect my behavior directly, for I didn't experience a sudden urge to dance in a dank room seeking pleasure from women, I felt tainted. It's too risky to watch a Hollywood movie or listen to pop songs. Immoral ideas or catchy lyrics will enter my mind and refuse to leave, no matter how many decades have passed.

I sat in a shady nook near a large arch. Not long after, a woman with red hair came into view. Her left arm was completely covered in tattoos and her right calf had a six-pointed red star. Her body was thin enough, so in my old days, with sufficient alcohol, I would have attempted to fornicate with her. She milled around the arch longer than the other tourists. Based on the experience of my past life, I got a suspicion that she was horny and presenting herself to me in a way that would encourage me to initiate contact. She climbed a rock and got even closer. After a few minutes, she got down from the rock and started to walk away, but when she was directly opposite me, only 20 feet away, she looked at me and said, "It's quiet." Well, not anymore! I gave her a nod but did not open my mouth. Discouraged, she left.

My imagination whirled to action. In the past, I would have started a banal conversation while trying to identify something about her that could sexually please me—maybe her mouth, her breasts, or her butt. Then I would scheme for a way to get her into a private room for a fast score, to receive orgasmic pleasure and also a story that I could tell my friends or to the world online. I could brag about sleeping with a girl and—*enough!* Those days are over.

I found a picnic table and prepared a spinach salad and bagel sandwich. A bluebird flew close to me and I identified it with the aid of a pocket bird guide. After lunch, I had a three-hour drive to Salt Lake City. I was feeling tense and knew why: I was traveling too fast and seeing too many sights. Just two days ago, I had been in the Rocky Mountains, but it might as well have been two weeks ago. Nature is beautiful, but I was seeing new sights before processing the previous ones. Was I just collecting sights to say I had seen them? Was I going to parks just to gather video for my travelogue, to write about them for this book? At the same time, I was missing so much. For every park I visited, I had to pass on at least five worthy contenders. West of the Mississippi River is stacked with so much beauty that the fear of missing out was strong, but at the same time, if you are tense and fatigued, you can't possibly enjoy what you end up seeing. Yes, I could say that I had been to Arches National Park, but I had been staring at the clock the entire time, concerned about a long drive that I didn't want to make. I knew the answer was to slow down, but how could I when Grand Teton and Yellowstone had yet to be explored? I would visit them just to visit them, to get the pictures, and then I could slow down.

†

I arrived at Salt Lake City, which is surrounded by mountains and spectacular views. And that's the best I can say about it. I went for a walk in the downtown area and was greeted by a homeless woman splayed on the sidewalk. Large groups of homeless with camping chairs and baggage had set up primitive camps on the grass, their eyes glazed over. Denver seemed to have homeless drifters, people who wanted to hang out and smoke weed instead of work, but the homeless in Salt Lake City appeared more… authentic. They coincided with numerous billboards offering help for addiction to opioids and other drugs. Restaurants and important buildings were protected by security guards who quickly rushed over to confront anyone in rags who crossed an invisible boundary into the "good" area. I made the mistake of believing that Salt Lake City's nearly 50% Mormon population would make the city something of a Christian oasis, just like I thought the Amish would impart their faith onto the city of Lancaster, Pennsylvania. Salt Lake City was plagued with the same problems as anywhere else, and judging by the drug and homeless problem, it was one of the worst cities I had seen.

After the event dinner with three men, one of whom was Mormon, we strolled through the garden of the Mormon Temple alongside friendly couples and respectable adults. It was hard to imagine that only three blocks away the homeless were finding a way to inject their drugs, and one block away were bars filled with hordes of tattooed men and women with ear gauges and other trappings of rebellion. Holiness doesn't magically rub off onto the non-holy. If someone makes the free-will choice to transgress God's law, it matters little if his neighbors are devout Christians. Those neighbors can serve as a positive example, but faithfulness or morality must be taught, accepted, and acted upon to result in salvation. Otherwise, you'll have nothing but condemned souls right outside the Christian's door.

Fifteen people came to the lecture including several Mormons, both former and active members. During the Q&A, one told us the trouble they were in.

"Right now the church authorities are mainlining the culture. This will cause a lot of damage in the future when it filters down to the faithful. Families are getting much smaller. Five or six children used to be common but now it's two or three. Women are adopting the ways of secular women. They're getting more sexually curious, and it's not uncommon to hear of girls who cheat on their boyfriends when they're abroad for their two-year mission. The boyfriends come back and marry their girlfriends without any idea what they've done in their absence."

"This sounds like Army wives who cheat on their husbands fighting abroad," I added.

"Yes, it's no different. And race is playing a factor, too. Newly converted Mormons are Hispanic and African, and they're turning out to be more conservative than the whites."

"Do you think the Mormon Church has what it takes to resist the culture?"

He paused for few seconds. "No, I don't. I'd give them 20 years."

Another Mormon I met agreed with his sentiments, saying that many men were leaving the church because there was so little "meat" to the faith. He said, "Mormonism comes down to following a lot of rules that are disconnected from the faith. So you do all these things and you're a 'Mormon,' but then people start looking for loopholes to the rules, or they start breaking them because doing so is supported by the culture, and then you have no faith left."

After the event, I sought out my post-event reward of a cheeseburger with fries. I picked a burger bar named Lucky 13, and was immediately shocked at the level of degeneracy on display. A requirement of the waitresses seemed to be that they possess several tattoos. One was covered from head to toe, in addition to over a dozen randomly placed piercings on her body. She looked so unhuman that I had to turn my head away in revulsion. A customer had a tattoo that covered his bald head and came down his sideburns and chin to form an ink beard. The Mormon faith surely hadn't rubbed off on them.

I started to wonder whether Satan sent the most degenerate people he could find in the United States to Salt Lake City to counteract the faith of the Mormons. If that was his plan, it was working, because, unlike the Amish, who were still putting up a good fight against the modern world, Mormons were starting to blend in with the culture as a whole, and the odds that someone who had grown up in the Church would later become gay or a leftist with a face tattoo might be just the same as for the rest of the population. Otherwise, how could I make sense of the fact that Salt Lake City has a gay pride parade that is in the top ten based on size in America when the population of its metropolitan area ranks in the fifties?

It became clear to me that the Mormon Church is more of a social bubble than a faith. It is highly involved in people's lives and provides a means to shield them from the world. As long as Mormons stay within the bounds of their institution, they will hardly be tempted by the turpitude around them, but that bubble is under attack by aggressive secular trends, internet pornography, and swarms of Californians moving into Utah to promote the same liberal policies that caused them to flee their state in the first place. The bubble is becoming more like a sieve.

A bubble is necessary to resist the evils in the world, but one that exists in the heart instead of the physical world. Christians must learn the hard way how to resist Satan's temptations, and that will surely include a degree of falling, or, in my case, an extensive degree of falling. The Mormons are so sheltered that temptation can almost be eliminated, which means that men can grow up to believe in a blue pill Disney fantasy yet still create big, healthy families, but I'm not optimistic that they will be able to continue in this fashion for much longer.

†

On Sunday, I picked a Greek Orthodox Church to attend, but the day before I received an email from a reader inviting me to Saints Peter and Paul Antiochian Orthodox Church in downtown Salt Lake City, led by Father Justin, an American convert to the church. I accepted his invitation and went to the Liturgy at 10am. I was immediately struck by how many children there were—they made up at least one-third of the laity. They made so much noise I had to strain to pay attention to the priest, a good problem for a parish to have. The noise of the children, however, encouraged the adults to chat among themselves, and the priest admonished them three times to quiet down. It would have been easier for him just to carry on, to get things over with, but I could tell he wanted to complete the Liturgy in a way that was most respectful to God.

In his sermon, Father Justin warned his congregation against giving their children a tablet or smartphone to consume mainstream entertainment. It would only distance the little ones from God. He also spoke against the excuse of "not having time" for prayer and attending both Vespers and the Liturgy. He said, "If you attend the Liturgy every Sunday, and Vespers on Saturday night, and also participate in the feasts, that only comprises 2% of your life. That should be the most minimal commitment you make in serving the Lord." I did the calculation for myself and included my daily prayers. It came to 3.3%. I would imagine that many monks exceed more than 30%. Of course the number itself is not the goal, but it is a sign of how seriously you are taking your spiritual life. If the number is much below 2%, you run the risk of forgetting about God in your daily life. The pleasures of the world will start to take you. If you only attend a two-hour church service on Sunday without any prayer, if you're only "a Christian within the four walls of the church," as Father Justin put it, you're dedicating 1.2% of your life to God. That's simply not enough, as indicated by the many people who attend church regularly but live wholly secular lives.

I was starting to understand how hard it must be to serve as a parish priest. The salvation of dozens of people was in Father Justin's hands, and he couldn't be with them while they were tempted every day of their lives. Most Orthodox saints seem to be monks, but the priests are the unsung heroes of the spiritual world. They are the front-line defense against Satan, while the monks are the Special Forces that can direct concentrated fire on evil in the form of ceaseless prayer.

I stayed for the coffee hour and talked with a few men who knew of my work. I was starting to get recognized more inside

Orthodox churches than anywhere else. I waited patiently for the crowd to die down so that I could talk to Father Justin.

After most of the people had left, Father Justin approached me, still in his black vestments. I introduced myself and told him my story, including how I went to Holy Cross Monastery in Wayne, West Virginia and received guidance.

"Did you talk to Father David?" he asked.

My eyes popped out of my head. "Yes, why, that's the monk I talked to."

"He's my friend from college!"

West Virginia and Utah were on opposite sides of the country, and I hadn't even planned to be in Father Justin's church until the night before, but such was God's joyful providence. I exchanged contact information with him and received his blessing. I left the church and got in my car, grinning from ear to ear at the little "coincidence." Every day, I used to seek out pleasure in the world, but all I have to do is wait for God to give it to me in innocent forms.

After the Liturgy, I went to The Original Pancake House. I thought the church was crowded but the restaurant even more so, mostly with young adults. I couldn't help but notice a heavy concentration of obese individuals. Near me a couple ordered four meals to eat between themselves. Food is an addiction for many people, and on that day they depended on pancakes, omelets, and bacon to feel good in the moment, but they will gradually have to eat richer foods in larger portions, with the resultant diabetes, heart disease, and other ailments. Sex is no different. The hangover from sex is guilt and anger, and to relieve those effects, you numb yourself with more sex, or more extreme forms of pornography, often in conjunction with alcohol, and the cycle repeats until you run out of ways to feel good.

Orthodoxy was giving me the tools to resist pleasures of this world. After a weeklong fast, where I did not receive enjoyment from food, I could enjoy a stack of pancakes and hash browns without hurting myself, instead of it being just another shot of a drug to keep me going for another day, or just another hour. If I was faced with temptations to experience pleasure, I could pray the Jesus Prayer, but without Christian tools, how would I make it? My day would consist of chasing one high after another.

When I lived in Poland, I would start the day with a big dose of pleasure—coffee and a chocolate croissant. I would then work in a public café where I could gawk at beautiful girls. Then I would go home and make a rich lunch of ham, cheese, and eggs. I would put on popular music to lift my mood. Then I would go back outside to another café to complete my work while staring at more girls. Dinner would be another rich meal containing meat, topped with a cookie or piece of cake. I'd shower and then head out for a night on the town to meet women while drinking alcohol. If I was horny and did not succeed in picking up a girl, I would masturbate. To do just two or three hours of work, I had to envelop my day in almost nonstop pleasures. Ironically, it was at that time, when I was most addicted to pleasure, that I believed I possessed a high level of willpower, whereas I was nothing more than a dumb animal.

10

Photographs

I left Salt Lake City and drove five hours to Jackson, Wyoming, right on the doorstep of Grand Teton and Yellowstone national parks. The main attraction of this area was Yellowstone, but I first wanted to get a little taste of Grand Teton. I drove into it and parked near Phelps Lake. It was past 7 p.m. when I arrived, so I hiked fast to beat the night. My heart rate elevated substantially. Other hikers were going in the opposite direction, including one man who was carrying a canister of bear spray on his belt. Mine was in my bag, but if I was suddenly attacked by a bear, I probably wouldn't have time to retrieve it, remove the safety clip, and spray the furry creature. I took out my canister, armed it, and put it into my back jean pocket.

I was nervous. Multiple signs advised me to "fight back" if a bear attacked. Fight back against a bear? I used to feel totally at home in a nightclub, Satan's number-one venue for tempting souls at night, yet here I was in nature, as close to God's creation as you can get, and I was fearful. A bear could maul my body but not my soul, at least, unlike what happened in the years I experienced comfort and carnal satisfaction in places of the night.

Right before I reached the lake, where I sat alone for a short while, a couple passed me. The woman, in her early twenties, wore a white hair bonnet and loose-fitting blue dress that went down to her ankles. The man behind her, perhaps a year or two older, wore a flannel plaid shirt. Since his beard wasn't shaved at the mustache, and there was no horse and buggy parked in the trailhead lot, I assumed they were Mennonites and not Amish. They both gave me a slight smile and I returned the favor. No words were exchanged, but through their modesty and meekness, I could feel their faith, and from that faith alone they possessed a genuine beauty that would have gone completely unnoticed by me only two years before.

I used to think beauty came from careful manipulation and sculpting. A woman was beautiful if she put on makeup and a sexy dress on a thin body, and a man was beautiful if he got a cool haircut and worked out in the gym to make his chest and biceps bulge. But through their efforts, which were guided by the trend-makers of the day, they were distorting their bodies to appear pleasing to people of the world. The faithless seek to please the faithless. There is no humility in their pursuit, no trust that their natural appearance is what God intended. They send you a flash of their manipulated beauty to elicit an instant "Ooh," a rapid feeling of desire, but what is behind it? I can place a sugar cube on your tongue, and you will receive immediate satisfaction from its sweetness, but it will last only for a moment.

The Mennonite couple structured their entire life to serve God, and it came across plainly to a man who was attempting to do the same. The monks were beautiful, not because their beards were scraggly and long, but because God was flowing through them, and as a result, I felt a spiritual delight when in their presence instead of a visual pleasure that is simply a neurochemical high. If a person prays daily and avoids sin, if they put God first, as Christ has commanded us to do, how can they not be beautiful, regardless of what's on the outside? You can have the deformities of a crab, but if you possess pure faith, I will see your claws as a gift from God.

I used to sculpt my beard carefully and trim my body hair because I knew that worldly women liked a man who had cosmopolitan bodily habits. Putting on a mask of false beauty allowed me to attract women who also had false beauty. I always met my perfect match. Now the hairs on my body were getting so long that they curled, covering my back, stomach, and shoulders. My beard line was creeping up so high on my face that it was approaching my eyeballs. In each travel video I uploaded, at least a dozen people commented how unattractive I looked. I had to trim my beard to look "good," they said, and based on that, I knew they spent hours every week fussing with their beards and faces and bodies. Worldly people are trying to appeal to other worldly people to play the casino game of dating and shallow compliments. *If I manipulate my appearance in a way that I think others will like, maybe someone will love me.* This will fail; only the most transient of relationships will result. She got bored of your muscles. He got bored of your body. She found a man who will stimulate her for a month longer than you did. Time to work on your appearance some more, time to improve your confidence and spin the roulette wheel once again, but the house always wins. Satan has perfected all the games in the casino and will make sure you don't walk away a winner. The only way to win is not to play his games at all.

†

I had to drive through Grand Teton to reach Yellowstone. I made only one stop, at a Catholic chapel that resembled a wood cabin. Inside, a lone stained glass window illuminated the nave and statues of Jesus and Mary. I figured this chapel would be safe to pray in unlike the Freemason-inspired church in Valley Forge, and did so for a short while until I noticed pieces of paper on the pews. I picked up one and read it. It was a request from Pope Francis to pray for "immigrants and refugees." How modern of the Pope to have the same cause as CNN and the New York Times. Would it be okay for him if I prayed for my fellow Americans who were destitute and homeless? How about those who were dying every day from opioid addiction? It seemed to me that Pope Francis's request was based more on global politics than the needs of my neighbor. Irritated, I ended my prayer and left the chapel.

I had come to this part of the country for Yellowstone so I hurried through Grand Teton, a decision I would later regret as I was greeted with innumerable tourists in the former, mainly from China, making it feel more like an adult amusement park than a nature park. In Yellowstone, I had so little time and so many potential landmarks to visit that I was paralyzed by what to do. I visited Lewis Falls first, a pleasant waterfall near the south entrance of the park. I went to West Thumb Basin to view its colorful hot springs then to the Grand Prismatic Spring to view hot steam rising from turquoise waters. They were perfectly made for photographs, and I, along with the hundreds of other tourists, took many, but that's all I walked away with. Since seeing them had not involved a hike or a climb, they didn't feel earned. When beauty is roadside, you will attract only the most basic, camera-toting tourists.

I knew I couldn't have all that nature to myself (though I did have Phelps Lake to myself in Grand Teton), but there has to be an unspoken agreement that you don't disturb the experience of others. That's hard to do when you have little children, but when adults are speaking loudly, like the Chinese tourists were, your attention turns to them instead of nature. Prayer does not come to my lips when it feels as if other people are speaking directly into my ear—as when an American girl who was angry with her boyfriend abused him with a profane tirade. I knew that I needed to park my car, get a backpack, and start walking away from everyone else into the backcountry, but I didn't have the time. Maybe I shouldn't have gone at all. Visiting a botanical garden with a gray catbird resting beside me had given me more enjoyment than touring the mighty Yellowstone.

I went inside a gift shop and bought a stuffed elk that I named

Burt. While driving through Yellowstone, I positioned him in my car so that he would have a view. I said a few words to him before I caught myself and stopped. I talk a big game about liking my solitary time, but there are occasional bursts where I just want to talk, and if there is no one to talk to, a stuffed animal will do.

For my second day in Yellowstone, I forced myself to see a thermal formation with a steam vent, then the canyons, and then a close-up view of another waterfall. I did these things not because I needed to see them—I much more needed to sit on a sofa and catch up on my reading—but because I would've felt guilty otherwise. I knew that attempting to avoid a negative, such as guilt, would not lead to anything positive, but the thought that I might never enter Yellowstone again wouldn't leave my mind.

I still hadn't seen a large mammal when I pulled into a picnic area to have my lunch. Before exiting the car, I glanced through the rearview mirror and saw a huge bison only 15 feet behind me across the road. I got out of my car, admired his shaggy head, and started taking pictures with my phone. As I did so, a group of picnickers saw the bison and came closer. Then drivers passing by, seeing that a bearded man was filming something on the side of the road, slowed down to do the same. Within only three minutes, there was a traffic jam and multiple people hanging out of their cars trying to get photos and video of the land beast, which didn't seem to mind the attention. He'd sometimes shake his head, and at one point he scratched himself against the bark of a small tree.

Even though the park warned visitors not to get within 25 feet of a bison (and 100 feet of a bear), many people ignored the warning, getting as close as ten feet to take a picture of them-selves with the bison in the background. It wasn't just young people doing it but boomers as well. I was witnessing—and taking part in—a compulsion to capture something novel or interesting on camera to show it to other people in order to receive attention, praise, or compliments. Going to a park and "experiencing" nature has become so twisted through technology that it is now a means to receive status. People who are attractive enough don't need to use nature in this way, and can just take pictures of themselves in their cluttered bathrooms and receive plenty of "likes" from online admirers, but a person like myself has to capture the video and add insightful commentary to get the attention flow going. In some ways, I was worse than the selfie army, because I would share a video of the bison and include links to my tour web page. I monetized the bison! And he wouldn't even get a cut of my ticket sales.

I felt a vague sense of self-disgust. Of course I was annoyed with all the picture takers—they reminded me of myself! But I needed to do this, I reasoned, to help sell tickets to fund my expensive trip, but if the only way I could experience the country was by exploiting the bison, was it worth doing? If I couldn't document my trip through writing or video and I couldn't tell anyone about it, would I still have done it? How would my life be if I couldn't take any pictures of anything, or write about anything? How would the lives of others be if they were never allowed to take selfies? How much does all this incessant documentation feed our pride? *I'm cool or special because I have pretty eyes and I saw this and did that.* Was this entire trip just a vain deception to keep my pride elevated, to be the focus of attention?

The words of Father David came to mind. He had said I was in danger as a new Christian. I was a spiritual baby undertaking a journey full of traps and temptations. I could see myself becoming paralyzed by the thought of whether what I was doing was right or wrong, healthy or damaging. The best I could say was that I was more faithful to God in word, deed, and thought today than I had been yesterday, and might even be helping others revive their faith. I shouldn't be so hard on myself. God has given me gifts, and I was finally using them for good.

✝

I headed to Missoula, Montana. The countryside of Montana looked quite similar to Wyoming, as they both have roughly the same population density of six people per square mile. They have cities where you can be with other people, but also stretches of land where you don't see anyone for miles. Compare that to my home state, Maryland, which has a population density of over 600. The city I grew up in, Silver Spring, Maryland, has a population density of 9,900. I grew up in an environment made for rats. I was conditioned to have people surround me at all times. Their noise became something like a security blanket—I needed the music, cars, and people around me to feel normal, and only when I started to hit my late thirties did I begin to shake that security blanket and crave the quiet life.

I didn't have time to walk through Missoula since I had to be in Seattle for my next event. To split the 475-mile drive, I stopped in Spokane, Washington, a metropolitan area in the east of the state with roughly half-a-million people. Superficially, based on all the new buildings and construction, the city appeared relatively wealthy and successful, but quickly I noticed the homeless problem. The parks were being used by vagrants who slept openly on the grass with their bags, and the downtown public library was essentially a homeless shelter. A quarter of the library patrons either looked slightly homeless or were definitely homeless. Many were there with foam pads, sleeping bags, blankets, and even tattered luggage. At least two of them had a loud, productive cough. I found an isolated area to complete my day's work and perceived a subtle odor of urine. While working, I periodically stared at the face of the librarian sitting at the information booth. She was in her fifties, with short white hair and glasses. Her face was one of concern, bordering on sadness. She had picked this job because she loved books and wanted to help others read, and instead she was more of a social worker, monitoring the homeless and enduring the stench.

I took a break and walked to the restroom. The sign on the door forbade me from using drugs. I imagined that if I intended to break the law, a sign would not stop me. Inside, the lights were a dim blue to make it difficult to identify a vein to inject drugs. A pair of dirty jeans were by the sink. Long hair shavings were sprinkled everywhere. Additional signs warned against the penalties for drug use.

The romanticized notion of homelessness is that someone is down on their luck and needs a bit of help to get back on their feet, but the reality is that people are choosing a life of addiction, disease, and squalor. On one hand, I have sympathy for this level of suffering, but on the other, I'm sufficiently realistic to know that this problem can't be solved simply by throwing money and social programs at it. The problem of the homeless is spiritual. The homeless are living in sin, in intoxication, gluttony, and sloth, with no desire to stop or choose the mainstream alternative of being a good capitalist citizen and participating in a different set of more socially acceptable sins (greed, pride, and lust). More homeless shelters, needle-sharing programs, food programs, and sympathy won't change that these people have, for the most part, chosen to live this way, and only want enough help to maintain their lifestyle. Local governments will continue to write checks for new homeless shelters or put up signs in the library while we walk over them on our way to eat or work. Maybe we can even pretend that there is no problem, and our society is just fine the way it is, until it finally blows up.

In Europe, I had gotten used to working in cafés or libraries, and had come to expect a certain level of quiet and comfort in those venues, but in America, public spaces that were originally intended for the community are becoming homeless shelter annexes. Normal people flock to their manufactured suburban town squares with security guards or just stay home. I can't help but think of my time in Brazil over a decade ago. During the day, the downtown of Rio de Janeiro was a chaotic jungle of businessmen, beggars, and thieves. At night, the homeless would set up their temporary shelters on the sidewalks, only to remove them the next morning to repeat the process. It appears that America will take this route, and you will only venture into a city if you absolutely have to, with headphones on, ignoring the human misery and decline that surrounds you.

†

The first thing I noticed about Seattle was all the Teslas and Subarus. Luxury German automobiles were also common. In the Midwest, such as Wyoming and Montana, there was more status in having an ancient pickup truck than something new and shiny.

I explored downtown Seattle and the area around the University of Washington. More women had short, blue-colored hair than anywhere else I had been. There were more tattoos, more piercings, more granola stylings where it was hard to tell the difference between a homeless person and someone who wasn't, more soy physiognomy among the men, including one man at a restaurant who talked to me in a sing-song female voice. Had he been born like that or did he take hormones? It was hard to say.

Liberals in Seattle seemed to take their ideas all the way. As liberal as people on the East Coast had become, they still possessed a degree of vanity that prevented them from going over the edge, albeit by a very small degree, and I guessed that Washington, DC would have degraded noticeably by the time I made it back in the winter.

I stayed in the Kirkland suburb across Lake Washington. To drive into Seattle, I crossed a toll bridge that cost over $6. The price changed depending on the traffic, for it was only $3 to return later that night. That's the utopia that big cities offer—an expensive toll on a short bridge to avoid longer bridges that are stacked with traffic all day long. Even if I was successful and worked for Microsoft or Amazon, with a $200,000 yearly salary that included stock options, once I adapted to my Tesla and luxury home that was 90 minutes away from the office, what would be the real benefit? How could this material excess compensate for living in Babylon where the closest sanctuary to your home was a shopping mall with chain restaurants?

I held the Seattle dinner downtown. Three men attended, including a practicing Christian. He was in his mid-twenties and ready to receive benefits from the world, which meant going to Ukraine to find a wife.

"I've been studying Russian for many hours a week," he said. "I hope it will help me to communicate with the women when I get there."

"That's a good effort," I replied, "but did you ask God if He wants you to go to Ukraine to find a wife?"

He stared in the distance for a moment. "No, I didn't."

"So how do you know that you should go there? Where did you get the idea for that?"

"Well, I figure my odds are highest if I go there, since the women here are not very traditional."

"I agree with you. Your odds will be higher there, but if you solve the problem of gaining a foreign wife, from that new problems will be created. Where will you live? How will your children fare without one-half of their grandparents around? What happens if you bring her back to the United States and she changes for the worse because of the culture? What happens if you decide to live in her country and your parents get sick and need long-term care? You're looking at the most immediate problem, finding a wife, without considering what happens after. Only God knows what happens after. I would pray to Him, or at least seek spiritual guidance, before attempting the difficult task of going abroad for marriage."

Americans are not used to asking for guidance before undertaking a major task. The ego has a will of its own and can rationalize anything as prudent when it's really a temptation. God did give us intellect and free will, so we don't have to ask Him for everything, but for the things that could potentially lead to sin or involve major life changes, I don't see why we shouldn't.

The next day, I sat in the hotel lobby to read a book (it was more comfortable than my cramped room). A porcelain young woman with dark hair milled around nearby. I was taken aback by her beauty and looked at her repeatedly. Lust surged into my body. I could no longer focus on the book. Perturbed, I got up and moved my seat so that she was out of my field of vision. This was the first day of a new attack of sexual dreams, including one where I suckled on the large breast of a nurse who was treating me for some sort of malady.

In attendance at my Seattle talk was a man more famous than me—Owen Benjamin, a stand-up comedian who had been blacklisted by the entertainment industry for not kowtowing to the transgender agenda. He moved away from Los Angeles to Washington state where he set up a homestead with his wife and kids. Although our lives were completely different, we had come to similar conclusions about the establishment's agenda. After the talk was over, I had a short conversation with him as others looked on. He left early but not before inviting me to come to his homestead for goat's milk.

I conducted the Q&A and then made the rounds to talk to as many guests as I could. One was a humble woman a few years younger than me who was turning more deeply to Christianity. She handed me small gifts that I could use on the road. She was single and asked for advice on finding a man who wouldn't fake interest in a relationship only to bow out shortly after sex. I reminded her that dating doesn't work and is never suitable for finding a spouse unless you can endure dozens or hundreds of failures that destroy your ability to connect with one person. I advised her not to date at all, and that if a man was willing to commit to her for life, he could surely wait until marriage to have sex with her. If I ever get into a situation where I meet an ideal girl who insists we "fool around" just a bit before marriage to see whether we're "sexually compatible," I would have to reject her, and if she gets upset, that must be a sign she's unsuitable, because a woman who has identified a man she can spend the rest of her life with can surely go a year or so without any sexual activity.

I can't say for sure that there was strong sexual chemistry between me and the woman, but there was enough that the old me would have insisted we continue the conversation in a bar. On some days, I can resist the greatest of temptations, which gives me the confidence that I've permanently overcome all my passions, and then on other days, I can't even glance at a woman without flashes of sex entering my mind. Because I retain the memories of my past sexual experiences and the pleasures they gave me, I know that I can never become complacent.

I developed a fast rapport with another guest. Sean and I were about the same age and we both came from a broken home (his parents split up when he was two and mine when I was nine). We both pursued women excessively, including foreign women from Ukraine. After the event was over, I offered to give him a ride home. We stopped by a restaurant for a late dinner, where he told me the story that put him on the path to God.

"I was on vacation in Thailand when I met a beautiful Ukrainian girl in a nightclub. We exchanged numbers and I slept with her a few days after that. I didn't use a condom and she got pregnant. She decided to keep it, and now I have a daughter."

"It's a man's nightmare to impregnate a girl from something like a one-night stand," I added unhelpfully.

"But I wanted to make it work. I didn't want to repeat the same mistakes of my parents, and she was very beautiful. So I found a job in a country near Ukraine and we moved there and started raising our daughter. There were many red flags. She wanted a nanny and a maid, she had many slutty friends, and on and on, but I didn't want to give up. Then one day we were walking on a seaside promenade as a family and she was giving me attitude for no reason. She insisted on interrupting the walk to sit down and craft a long text message to someone. I asked her what she was doing and she said, 'I have to wish my friend Happy Muhammad Prophet Day.'"

"Uh-oh."

"I didn't remember her having any Muslim friends. She was on her phone for a long time until I got fed up and took it from her. I started going through the messages. Turns out she was texting a guy who worked at the mall. Their messages were explicit, about the things they wanted to do with each other, and if she wasn't already sleeping with him, she soon would."

"Ouch."

"The marriage was over. I failed to overcome my past. My attempt at a family ended just about in the same way as my parents. Now I see my daughter twice a year."

The most amount of pain I have seen in men is divorce when children are involved. It rivals, if not surpasses, the death of a parent. "All you can do is pray for your daughter," I said.

"I do, every day."

Our food came, served by a male waiter who wore makeup and acted more feminine than most women in the restaurant.

I traded war stories with Sean, including the exceedingly foul women I had slept with. Even though I was recounting the stories from a position of regret instead of glory, reliving my sex memories was creating the same physiological response as watching pornography. I was inadvertently fueling the tempta-tion, which meant several more nights of sexual dreams and difficulty in maintaining custody of my eyes when attractive women crossed my path. It took my conversation with Sean to understand that I must permanently turn away from sin, including memories of things that had happened a long time ago, no matter how much I might regret them.

11

Homestead

I drove to Owen Benjamin's homestead, still in Washington state. I'd seen glimpses of it through his live streams and imagined it to be a huge farm, but it was reasonably modest at about five acres. He had a large garden and all sorts of animals, including chickens, goats, alpacas, geese, bunnies, and Silkies, which are extra feathery chickens from China. I imagined he required a small army of workers to maintain the operation and asked whether he hired anyone to help, but just he and his wife worked on the homestead while raising two young boys.

If the family is the best unit of organization for raising humans then a homestead is likely the best space for that organization. It keeps the family busy and entertained, promotes teamwork that strengthens family bonds, blocks out pernicious urban influences, and keeps the family close to nature while lowering their financial burdens. Without a family, however, growing so much food would be excessive, so for my potential homestead, I imagined having a few chickens and maybe a little garden for my use. I would add numerous bird feeders, a birdbath fountain, and comfortable seating to watch the birds.

Owen showed me how he milked goats. First, he opened the main gate of the goat pen and selected which goat was to be milked. The goat already knew what to do—it ran to the milking area, which had a container of food. As the goat started eating the food, Owen locked her head in place with a metal bar to ensure she couldn't escape. While she ate, and derived pleasure from the food, which I assumed was tastier than her normal feed, Owen squeezed her udders to extract milk. The goat didn't seem to mind at all, and when there was no more milk in her body, Owen unlocked the goat and drove her back into the pen. I wondered if what I had just witnessed was a metaphor for how humans are controlled.

We are given access to a pleasure, whether food, sex, money, or fame, and then we gorge ourselves on this pleasure while our life essence is drained from us by unseen evil. After we get our fill, we have less will and strength to live righteously or serve our family and community, because all we can think about is feeding again. Does the goat know she's being milked? She must, since she can surely feel a man's hands on her body, but if the pleasure from the feed is strong enough, it doesn't even begin to bother her. For a long time, I had been obsessed with pleasing myself, never noticing that my head was locked into place by a metal bar. All the while, Satan had been taking away bits of my soul for his use, garnering far more from the exchange than I had.

Owen's wife prepared a dinner of asparagus, baked salmon, and salad. I dined with them and their two sons. Owen was an intense man. I could tell that his mind moved quickly, providing him with various thoughts and jokes in rapid succession. I had the idea that stand-up comics merely crafted jokes, and when not doing so they were just like normal people, but Owen created jokes spontaneously one after the other. He created one joke about Osho, the famous Indian guru whom I had considered a mentor for some time.

"I was into Osho because he taught how to reduce the effects of your ego," I said, "but while he was doing that, he was feeding his own ego by building a dedicated following, sleeping with his female admirers, and accumulating expensive watches and cars. His teachings always had a loophole to allow you to do whatever you wanted, that maintaining any will to resisting sexual urges was needless, but because he spoke so slowly, it seemed like there was real wisdom there."

Owen replied, "So if you just put his speech to 2x speed, he sounds like a pervert who's trying to get laid like anyone else?"

"Yes! He grooms his female audience to just 'let go,' which means to sleep with him."

"He's like a Sheryl Crow song." He then recited the lyrics in Osho's glacial cadence: "If it makes you happy... it can't be that bad." He refined the joke further for his live stream the next day. His fans then remixed it by morphing Owen into a floating swami beside trippy visuals. I was satisfied to serve as the inspiration for a comedian's joke.

Owen had been connected to Hollywood for some time, even dating actress Christina Ricci of *The Addams Family* fame.

"Is everyone in the industry controlled?" I asked.

"Definitely, especially the higher up you go. And they do it in a subtle way when you start auditioning for roles. They treat you like dirt. You may not even be finished reading a script and they yell, 'Next!' You want the prize of the role so bad, and you become more determined to get it. You decide to do whatever it takes, to accept the abuse, and soon you just hope for them to compliment you. You start to crave their attention and validation, so before you even get hired for a role, they already have you."

I imagine that when auditioning actors are asked to perform a sexual act for a role, or to come by the producer's house at night for a "reading," they are more than eager to comply.

"Most of the male actors in Hollywood are gay," Owen went on. "The ones that appear most masculine are compensating. So many famous actors were abused badly when they were children. Their mothers didn't care, and whored them out for the money."

"This is why it's so hard for me to watch a Hollywood film. I know that the actors and actresses were sexually humiliated, and the child actors were abused. I can no longer suspend disbelief that I'm watching a fictional movie, and instead think of the casting couch. I remember when Leonardo DiCaprio finally won an Oscar and at the same time was shilling for global warming even though he flies around in private jets. I knew that they had him and were essentially directing him like a puppet."

"Even I had a handler. My manager was my handler. All managers are handlers."

"How does that work?" I asked.

"Every comic gets a development deal with a studio that usually goes nowhere, but they hang it over your head. I had a development deal with Disney and made a joke about Mickey Mouse. My manager called me and very politely told me that sharing the joke was a bad idea. So I couldn't speak badly about Disney. The higher up you are, the more limited your speech. The whole operation is a grooming program. They groom you for your own humiliation, to control everything you do in public, all because you desperately want their money and fame."

"Is there anyone else in the public sphere you like?"

"Not really," he replied. "There's you, Vox Day, and E Michael Jones. Most everyone else is lying or controlled in some way."

Owen's wife took care of child-raising and household duties. Not once in Owen's presence did she whine or try to put him down in a subtle way, like so many American wives do. In exchange, he brought home the bacon. I saw their union as something that could serve as a template for myself, at least in a way that my divorced parents could not. It makes the most sense for a man to nurture his masculinity and for a woman to nurture her femininity while raising children in a Christian home away from the city.

I spent the night at Owen's house. The next day, his neighbor came by with his son on an ATV. They were about to slaughter a pig.

"You know how to kill a pig?" I asked jealously.

"I've been doing it since I was a kid."

"I've never killed my food before."

"Well, when you buy it in the store, someone else is killing it for you. Look at Owen's chickens." He pointed to the chicken coop. "On a commercial farm, they don't have that much space. They're stuck in a little box. So you treat the animal right, feed it right, and you kill it right."

I imagine that if I killed my own animals, I would eat less meat and not waste any parts. I would save the chicken bones and use them to make a broth or soup. When you don't see what the animal had to go through to provide you with food, it's easier to take it for granted.

I peppered Owen and his neighbor with questions about building a homestead and how self-sufficient I could be in times of crisis.

"You want to have enough food to last a month and a half," his neighbor said. "Because when disaster happens, everyone is going to hit the highway and get stuck. They will be easy pickings. My wife and Owen's wife know how to can and garden. We have animals that will give us food for many months."

I thought of my mother, who lived in an apartment building not far from a major highway, and my father, who lived in a townhouse a few miles away. They did not have more than two weeks of food stored and hardly knew their neighbors, let alone possess a plan to endure conflict. They would have to be the ones hitting the highway, but where would they go? They didn't have a mountain hideaway or safe house. If a major conflict broke out in the United States within ten years, and my parents remain unprepared, the responsibility would fall on my shoulders to keep them safe.

Before leaving, Owen gave me a few shirts from his merchandise store, and I gave him a prayer booklet. I prayed that he and his family could endure the trials to come, and made my way south.

✝

I had to stop by Mount Rainier, the thirtieth tallest mountain in North America. I drove through Mount Rainier National Park, found a scenic viewing area, and milled around for half an hour to take the obligatory pictures. There were lakes and little mountains nearby that could be appreciated with a hike, but I was too tired and short on time. I noticed that I felt relaxed if I drove through a park, even if I didn't spend any time walking or hiking. When there aren't a lot of cars on the road and the scenery is beautiful, you can't help but feel serenity, but when you're in the middle of urban traffic, it's torture.

I stayed overnight in Packwood, Washington, on the south end of Mount Rainier, a somewhat touristy town that serves as a jump-off point for people wanting to experience the big mountain. Despite the excessive leftism of Seattle, Packwood was ultra-conservative. There were men in dirt-covered jeans getting into and out of pickup trucks devoid of secular bumper stickers. A flea market tent in the middle of town flew multiple Donald Trump flags. I walked up to the tent and saw "Make America Great Again" hats on sale. They seemed to be knockoffs, but I bought one for $15 anyway. For a social experiment, I may have to wear it in the middle of a liberal city, though saying "liberal city" is a bit redundant.

As in Pennsylvania and Ohio, just because the major cities of a state are liberal enough to turn the state blue during elections (by voting for the Democratic Party), that doesn't mean there aren't conservatives in other parts of the state. The rats are huddled tightly in major metropolitan areas, keeping each other warm, united in their hatred for tradition and heterosexuality, while the conservatives control over 80% of the country by landmass, with the knowledge of how to live and operate on that landmass. Even if the United States tips over into being a majority blue country, that doesn't mean the war for the soul of the country will be over. In fact, that may very well mark the beginning.

Soon after meeting Owen Benjamin, I received an invitation from Cody, a YouTuber in Oregon with a popular homesteading channel named Wranglestar. When I put his address in my navigation app, I was presented with three potential routes. The fastest went straight through Gifford Pinchot National Forest, so naturally I picked that.

Driving into the forest, I hardly noticed any cars. Why wasn't this two-lane road used as a major north-south artery from Washington to Oregon when it was in great condition? Soon it turned into a one-lane road, but still perfectly drivable for my sports car. Then 15 miles further in, the road turned to gravel. No big deal, I thought, because I had to go only 15 more miles until making a right turn onto what I suspected would be a major road. I didn't much care for the gravel dinging the underside of my car, but it wouldn't last for much longer.

The gravel road had some huge potholes and bumps that I was careful to avoid. Eventually, I made it to Council Lake. I parked my car beside a handful of four-wheel-drive vehicles and went for a walk. So the way to get away from the crowd was to drive down a long gravel road… good to know. I got back in my car, which was coated with dust, and continued on the road. Very quickly, I encountered huge craters that I had to inch over slowly, and then the road split as if ruptured by an earthquake. Missing road was replaced by a collection of large rocks. Could my car, which had a clearance of six inches, make it across? I looked at the navigation app, which said I needed to go only two more miles until making the right turn. There was also the option of turning back, but that would take too much time. I decided to go for it.

I crossed the broken road at an angle. *Cruuuunch*. Was that the oil pan? I might have to get that checked out. The road only got rougher after that, but I was so close to the turn. Finally, the sound of the soothing female voice of the navigation app filled my car: "Turn right." But when I looked right, I didn't see a road. Instead I saw a sign that said "Trail" beside an exceedingly narrow rock path. This was the "road" that the app wanted me to take? I knew I could not pass and yelled out a string of obscenities to the trees.

I sat in the car, debating what to do. There were other roads to take but I didn't have any mobile signal to pull up driving directions or even a map. I looked at the time—nearly two hours had passed since I left Packwood. I was supposed to meet Cody in 90 minutes, but that was not going to happen. I had no choice but to make a U-turn and go back the way I had come, first over the blown-out dirt path and then the rock crossings. When I passed Council Lake, I looked up and saw a huge mountain—Mount Adams. Its entire peak was covered in snow. Normally, I would have recorded it with my phone, or at least stop the car to admire its beauty, but I was too tense. I appreciated it from the corner of my eye and continued back on the long gravel road until it became paved again. Once I got a signal on my phone, I called Cody to update him on the fact that I would be a day late. I had wasted three hours because I listened to the app. If I had paid closer attention, I would have noticed that the two-and-a-half-hour route I had chosen covered only 60 miles, yielding an average speed of 24 miles per hour. A rear-wheel-drive sports car was ill-equipped to handle the terrain, to say the least, and I can only imagine the "dumb city slicker" judgments from those in pickup trucks and SUVs who witnessed my folly. Yes, I was a dumb city slicker, but I was learning, and one day I won't be so dumb.

The next day, Cody picked me up from a strip mall in Hood River, a scenic town that had a disproportionate number of gay flags. The trust fund kids were coming, Cody remarked, trying to change the town so that it suited their lifestyle requirements.

Cody told me his story. He had lived in Portland and had pursued women and money until he inevitably hit a wall. Having been raised in a devout Christian household, he went back to his faith, which eventually led to marriage. He and his wife wanted to raise children in a good environment, so they left Portland, first to a suburb, and then to a plot of land on the side of a mountain. Things had gone wrong while trying to build a home. He had to sell the land, nearly extinguishing his life savings in the process. He had been in dire straits when his son was born; not much money was coming in and he had no stable home for his family. Then one day he had come across a house that was not for sale, and through a series of providential steps, he had been able to obtain the house and the surrounding land for a good price. He has worked on that property for many years, documenting the improvements on YouTube. His channel took off, providing his family with a steady income, and now he has one of the most popular homesteading channels on the internet, aided by his smooth narrator intonation and natural story-telling ability. A daughter was later welcomed into the family, and from the outside-in, he was living the dream on a productive piece of land.

After lunch in the downtown area of Hood River, he drove me to his 60-acre property that has a view of Mount Adams, the same mountain I had driven by the day before.

"The economy of this area is built on forestry," he said. "These Douglas firs are the best timber you can find, and Oregon is full of them, but the business has slowed down, mostly because of environmentalism. What the environmentalists used to do was drill a hole in the best trees to insert a tube of ceramic. Then they'd cover up the hole. When a logger would try to cut that tree, the ceramic would break his chain saw. If he cut down the tree without hitting the ceramic, it would make it to the sawmill, and that causes the saw there to explode. Many men have been killed because of it."

It was hard to believe that some people put trees above the lives of other human beings.

"Now they log mostly smaller trees that don't garner much protest. The best trees get shipped off to China, since they pay a premium price, and the rest is for the US market."

"If I buy a big piece of land with a lot of trees and want to sell them, how much could I get?" I asked.

"I'm sure you've seen those logging trucks. A truck full of trees, depending on the quality of the wood, can get you around $9,000."

We walked through a particularly dense part of his forest. "During the winter, we ski through the trail we're walking on. The little dog of ours you saw is small enough to walk inside one of the ski tracks. It's a nice activity to do with the family."

We rounded back up near the house where he showed me a barn full of equipment, tools, and various projects in progress. He also showed me a woodworking shop with even more tools. From watching videos on Cody's channel, it's clear he has a mechanical inclination. He enjoys the automation that equipment brings, along with fixing that equipment and completing mechanical projects.

Just like with Owen's land, there was no shortage of things to do. When you're an urban dweller, you don't think of what your apartment or house can provide. It's a shelter and a place of mild comfort that must be compensated every day or two by the excitement of city activities that usually involve alcohol. You pay for rent, you eat food prepared by others, you watch entertainment made by people in Los Angeles and New York City, and you live life as a consumer. A piece of land is different—it gives as much as you put into it. From its dirt comes food, either in the form of vegetables or grass for animals, and the waste from the animals goes back into the soil to keep providing you with food. The landscape affords you with views and relaxation, a sort of natural meditation. You can ski on the land, shoot on it, ride vehicles on it. You can erect a big pool or place a few bird feeders to watch nature. The limit to what you can do is limited only by your creativity and local zoning ordinances.

I was fascinated by how different personalities interface with land. My friend in Kentucky, who has a full-time job, uses his piece of land as a respite from the world, tinkering around here or there with his orchard and greenhouse. Owen uses his land to provide a big portion of the family's food needs. Cody, with his engineering mind, uses his for work and leisure, mastering tools and machinery to allow him and his son to steward so many acres.

I fantasized about what I would do with a plot of land. I was too far behind the curve to duplicate what Cody had achieved, and I didn't have a family to help me take care of the animals Owen had. I'd probably be more like my friend in Kentucky. My writing keeps me busy, so I'd stick to the basics—a few apple trees, a modest garden, three egg-laying chickens, an outdoor dog, and perhaps a path through the wooded area with strategically placed bird feeders, along with comfortable garden chairs strewn throughout the property. Every day I could putter around the land for an hour or two and then find a chair to read a book before going back indoors to write. The foundation of my life has already been set—I was given a gift of writing, and would continue to do that, but instead of going to bars or cafés to be around strangers as a way to decompress, I would sit near my garden and watch the birdies.

I asked Cody whether I should buy land that already had a house or buy an empty piece of land and build on it.

"A few years ago, I would have told you to buy an empty piece of land, since it would be cheaper to build than buying an existing home, but things have changed. Regulations and building costs have gone up to the point where it's now cheaper to buy land that already has a home. You want someone else to do all the hard work of serving it with water and electricity, and even if the home is not exactly what you want, you can improve on it. We gutted our home and remodeled it. You can always make changes."

"I plan to first rent a home in the general area I want to buy land in," I replied. "I want to get a feel for living away from the city before buying something. It's possible I may find out that a half-acre plot is all I need instead of the five or ten acres I'm dreaming of."

"That's exactly what you should do. When you rent, make sure to start talking to people. Go to local events. Ask them about land that's for sale and if they would consider selling it. Some people don't list their land with realtors because they don't want someone to change it. If they get to know you and trust you, they may sell to you at a cheap price, because you will take care of what they've loved for so long."

"My first step is to buy a four-wheel-drive vehicle," I said. We were sitting in his living room and I glanced at the tops of my socks. They were covered in nettles and other debris from our walk. "Actually, the first step is to buy a pair of boots."

"There will be no end to it. Wait until you get the land—there will be a million projects that you can think of. It's very easy to make an idol out of a homestead, so be careful. Right now I'm overwhelmed with stuff. I have so many things, yet I crave simplification."

"So through your land, what's the end goal?"

He looked up and spread his arms. "To be ready when Jesus returns."

I smiled at his answer. He might get distracted with this project or that, but his heart was fully turned to God, and so I was sure he could overcome any material obstacle that came his way.

Even with writing, the problem of never-ending projects is present. While I'm writing one book, ideas for several more books come into my mind, along with ideas for articles, live streams, and new websites. I could easily spend a lifetime being distracted by these projects, especially if they were secular in nature, and place greater distance between me and God as a result. If I ever got a piece of land, I would have to be extremely choosy about which projects to embark on.

Cody's 14-year-old son walked into the room. Cody already spoke glowingly about him and the abilities he had learned on the homestead. I wondered whether I should be embarrassed that in a crisis I would be dependent on a teenage boy for survival because of my lack of skills. I find solace in the fact that I'm not the only hipster doofus out there, but it will still be humbling when I ask rural folk dumb questions and they look at me wondering how I even managed to survive this far.

Cody had told me that his son had an urge to move to the city when he got older, not necessarily to get away from the country but to try a different experience. I felt it was my responsibility to give him a warning.

"I spent just about all of my life in the cities," I began. "I attempted to extract all the pleasures and enjoyments from them, but now that I'm 40 years old, I can't stand them. I can't wait to escape from them for good and move to a homestead similar to what you have, to experience the peace and quiet away from all the weirdos, crime, and temptations that allow me to harm myself. Even worse is that the city gives you no real skills. I'm an expert at using a computer to make money from the internet, but that's about it. I would need to hire you to teach me how to live out here."

"I don't know about that," he replied sheepishly.

"I don't even know how to use an ax. That's the level I'm on."

"Okay, maybe I do know more," he grinned.

If he lives in a city at some point in his life, at least he'll have warnings from his dad and his dad's friend in mind. When I was his age, I didn't even know there was an option not to live in the cities. I spent most of my life moving from one to another, extracting pleasure and novelty from a place before packing my bags and looking for fresh blood to suck. I had thought that was the point of life.

Cody brought out a rifle and shotgun and asked whether I wanted to shoot. I chose the shotgun. We went to his backyard while I pretended to spot "zombies from Portland." I neutralized them all with superb accuracy. I'm not much of a gun guy, and I don't see myself killing another person, but I'm told it's a necessity on a homestead. Aggressive animal pests may need to be dispatched and there is often no police force that is on duty 24 hours a day.

"In addition to guns, you'll also need a dog," Cody said. "Dogs are like security systems. They can sense other animals or people nearby before you can. It's especially important if you have children." I already planned on getting a guard pug so that wouldn't be a problem.

Before leaving, Cody said he wanted to give me a gift. He took me to his woodshop and handed me a massive ax. Sensing my ignorance, he said, "Be careful, it's extremely sharp." I thanked him for his gift and hoped that one day I would learn how to use it.

As soon as I had finished with the degenerate stage of my life, God was sending me family men to get me ready for the next stage. *Here's how to have a family. Here are the skills and knowledge you need to know. Here's the template I want you to follow.* When I had been busy in the cities, I never received an invitation from a family man to visit his homestead. Even if I had, how could I have accepted when I needed to spend my free time prowling the bars for new sexual prospects? Besides, what would I have done in the country? Walk around on the grass? Was there even fast internet?

†

I drove into downtown Portland for the Friday dinner. I had some extra time to kill so I went for a walk after parking my car. In previous cities, it had taken time for me to notice the somewhat concealed homeless problem, but in Portland it was revealed immediately. I saw homeless people loitering on sidewalks, their belongings stored in nearby shopping carts. For the first time, I even encountered homeless tents set up right on the sidewalk. I witnessed a police officer on a bicycle roll by a tent without saying anything. Wasn't it illegal to set up shelter anywhere?

For over a dozen blocks, I saw more homeless people than non-homeless, and a lot of them were women. Many were covered in brownish-black grime. Their faces were vacant. Debris and soiled foam mattresses were strewn throughout the streets. The scale of human misery was hard to take in, but it seemed that the non-homeless weren't bothered by it. The homeless hangout spots were not far away from happening cafés and restaurants, many of which displayed the gay pride flag. Just half-a-block down from a homeless shelter, one café displayed a sign stating "Trans rights are human rights" and "White supremacy has no place here." From what I witnessed, the last problem that Portland had was white supremacy.

Liberals can't solve the problems they create, so instead they focus on imagined problems that will provide an unlimited supply of activism and opportunities to spite God. Declaring war on white supremacy is the same as declaring war on jealousy—it's a war that can be waged forever. As long as you can find a white person doing well in life through their own labor, you can argue that white supremacy exists and feel justified to engage in mass censorship while giving power to politicians who make the problem even worse.

I met up with four men in a restaurant that served standard pub fare. One made fun of me for being hairy and the other trolled me with silly questions. Normally, I don't take kindly to such behavior, but I controlled my pride, since they had paid me $250 each. For that amount, you can mildly insult me once. I had noticed that when first meeting me, some men insisted on asserting a subtle form of dominance, either through an excessively strong handshake or making a mild joke at my expense, but after a couple of hours, their "alpha male" tone subsided. Maybe they wanted to make a strong first impression.

Towards the end of the dinner, I noticed that multiple transsexuals were walking by our table on the way to the bar. I asked the waiter whether there was a "special event," and he eagerly stated that every Friday was drag queen night and we should join. What used to be found only at the circus was now eagerly promoted at the local restaurant.

My curiosity got the best of me, so after the dinner I went to the drag queen party. On the stage, a man dressed up as a woman danced in twerks and jerks. Several more trannies wearing wigs, layers of brightly colored makeup, and high heels rooted him on, waiting their turn, proud of looking like grotesque monsters. The crowd cheered louder than the display of talent on the stage warranted, as if they were supporting a school play performed by mentally handicapped children. I want to say it was repulsive, but it was more in the realm of the absurd. It made no sense why men were pretending to be women, no sense at all. I could stomach it for only one minute before leaving.

I began the walk to my car. The number of homeless outside seemed to have tripled in only a few hours. It was like one giant sleepover. They were lying side by side with their sleeping bags and blankets, leaving little space for pedestrians. The smell of urine was overwhelming. All of this was right next to the restaurants and bars with crowded outdoor patios. And what were the tattooed leftists doing there, within sight of the encampments?

Partying! They were celebrating! Celebrating what, I do not know. The drug abuse? The misery? The mental illness? Those in the bars were using drugs too, so why would they judge the homeless for doing the same? And were they not also miserable, needing to participate in the outrage of the day against racism or what have you to get a pathetic dopamine kick? As for the mental illness, I'll leave that for you to judge. They don't mind the homeless because the homeless are like themselves. They may be able to party next to the stench of urine, but for me it was too much suffering and nihilism. The city of Portland was too much.

If I had worn my new MAGA hat, I have no doubt they would have given me dirty looks or worse. I was the offender, interfering with their epidemic of urban rot. Their ideas, activism, policies, and votes had helped to create this. Their weaponized use of political correctness, equality, and atheism destroyed anyone who tried to fix it. Just a week previously, while in Seattle, I had read a news article about a sidewalk in front of the city courthouse that was soiled with urine and feces. The council members argued about how to clean it, and when someone suggested power-washing it with a hose, a councilman disagreed, saying that hoses were used against black people during the Civil Rights era, implying that it would be racist. Attempting to solve the problems that leftists create is "racist," "sexist," or some other nonsense. Soon it will be impossible to fix any problem.

Once Satan gets a firm foothold in a city, which he accomplishes through servants who choose a life against God, it's over. If you're in a small town and gay flags are popping up in storefronts, the satanic infection has arrived. Either treat the infection or flee to safety because it surely won't cure on its own. Americans are too spiritually weak to put up a fight. Maybe a few pockets of the country will stand up, but based on what I was seeing with my own eyes, it is too late. We'll get to watch the slow, painful decline. Mass shootings here and there, more drug use and homelessness, more public displays of sodomy and other degeneracy, more political violence, and an inexorable decrease in the standard of living. Satan won't stop until every space on earth is turned into a living hell, and even if you run for the hills, which I plan on doing, he'll find a way to molest you there. Changing locations is not enough to protect yourself, as I learned during my years in Eastern Europe where everything American simply followed me like a shadow. A man of the purest faith can make it anywhere, city or countryside, but I still have a long way to go before I can say that is true of myself, so the countryside it is, where at least Satan won't tempt me daily with vices that I'm still trying to overcome, or so I think.

†

The Portland talk was attended by approximately 30 people. There were three women, including one who, while friendly, was dressed provocatively. Would God send me a woman whose appearance made me think of her sexual attributes before her faith? I remembered back in Indiana when I asked my young date not to wear anything sexy. For future dates, maybe I should not tell a woman what to wear, just to see what her instinct is. If she wears something revealing, I can take out my prayer book and begin preaching the Gospel to her, but by revealing this in print, aren't I allowing women in the future to trick me by dressing modestly on our first meeting? If a woman likes you, and knows what you like in a woman, you may be as good as finished! Men simply were not designed to decode the numerous manipulations that women throw at them.

Sean drove from Seattle to attend the talk in Portland. The next day, he and two other men from the event joined me for Divine Liturgy at St. George Antiochian Orthodox Church. All three were not baptized as Orthodox but were considering it. Afterwards, we joined the other parishioners for coffee-hour fellowship. The priest came up to our table and I briefly told him my story. He looked at me with a blank face. It turned out that his English was limited since he had only recently come over from Syria as a Christian refugee. He sat with us and talked through a translator. While he was a sincere and faithful priest, how could I communicate with him if I needed spiritual guidance? I told the other guys that they should try a couple of other Orthodox churches before making a final decision.

Later, Sean and I went to the Grotto, a Catholic shrine visited by the faithful from around the world. A part of a hillside was carved out and filled with a replica of the Pietà. During the summer, Mass is said in front of it. There was also a garden above the hill that we walked through, with various carvings and statues placed throughout. Most praised Mary. She is most deserving of praise, and I'm not one to take away the blessings meant for her, but it did seem more voluminous than what is done in the Orthodox Church. (I could only imagine what a Protestant would think.)

I sat down with Sean on a garden bench in front of a walking maze that was etched into the concrete. We watched a man follow his woman through the maze and then go for a kiss at the end. She hesitated. Sean and I exchanged a knowing glance.

He took out his phone and showed me a picture of his daughter. "Look how my ex-wife dresses her." His daughter had on a skirt that was a bit too short, enough to be concerned, but not enough to hop on a nonstop flight to kidnap her to safety.

"How old is she?"

"Six years old."

I looked off into the distance. "Your ex-wife is going to teach your daughter everything she has learned—how to act seductive, trick men, manipulate them, gain favors from them. The next decade or two will be a lot of pain for you. The best you can hope for is that your daughter moves in with you while still a teenager."

"I go see her in a few months. Even when I'm there, the ex-wife tries to sabotage our time together. I love my daughter so much, but this is hard."

"And when you hooked up with her mom, you probably thought you were on top of the world due to how beautiful she is."

"I thought I was the king. I showed my friends photos of her and they replied that I'm 'winning' in life."

"In Psalm 51 we admit that we were conceived in sin. My parents had me out of intense passion, which I inherited. It remained with me for a long time until God gave me the strength to fight it. I hope your daughter can realize the same, though you may have to watch her fall for a long time."

Both Sean and I possessed a double dose of lust, eagerly traveling around the world to sleep with women. God had given him a daughter, whose love had enhanced his life in a way that I only slightly comprehended, but with a bad woman. How does God decide which trial is more fitting for one man compared to the next? The seeming randomness of life can be hard to understand until you believe that everything that happens to you is for your own spiritual benefit.

After the Grotto, Sean wanted to show me the hipster part of Portland so that I could shoot some video clips of gay pride flags, but I was too tired and had to bid him farewell. I went back to my hotel room and intended to nap for 20 minutes but ended up sleeping for hours. My body was hitting a limit. I was running out of gas and barely halfway done with the trip. I asked God to give me endurance for the remainder of the tour, but it would be unreasonable to expect Him to turn me into Superman. Something would have to give.

12

Temptation

I stopped by Crater Lake National Park in the south of Oregon. The lake itself was the product of a massive volcanic explosion. A vestige of the volcano remained in the middle of the lake, its crater filled with peacock blue water. The National Park Service provided a newspaper that explained how the lake had been formed, but I made sure not to read it. I didn't want my mind to be polluted by the theories of man.

The lake possessed immense beauty, but the color of the water and the rocky shoreline reminded me of bits and pieces of other parks. It was novel but not truly so. I had no connection to it, no immediate spiritual feeling. It was just another place to record with my camera. Woe to those who have idolized novelty! If I was dependent on achieving novelty through nature, I would be bored only two and a half months into my road trip. There is only so much variety in the world, and if you require variety to experience pleasure, you will exhaust yourself in no time.

I stayed in Crater Lake for only two hours and then continued my journey south. I made it to Red Bluff, California, a dusty town I used as a launchpad to St. Herman of Alaska Monastery, founded by Father Seraphim Rose (born Eugene Rose) and a friend of his. Father Rose was an American who converted to Orthodoxy from Protestantism after experimenting with Eastern philosophy. Once he accepted Orthodoxy, he turned away from a wicked relationship. At the time, around the late 1960s, there were very few Orthodox books written in English. He began the process of translating and printing them on a manual press, and would go on to author several important books that added to the Orthodox intellectual canon, particularly for believers in America. He is widely venerated and seen as a candidate for sainthood.

I arrived at the monastery and strolled through the grounds for a few minutes until I was approached by Brother Alexei, a Russian novice (someone who is in the process of becoming a monk). We sat down in the garden. He was hesitant to give me guidance. "Most of my knowledge is theoretical," he said. Three Russians traveling from Arizona joined us. One was a monk and another a priest. Brother Alexei gave us a tour of the grounds that included structures Father Rose built. His wooden cabin was even smaller than Henry David Thoreau's on Walden Pond. I sat on Father Rose's bed, which was more like a bench, and at his desk. The icons on the wall had not changed from the time he was alive. When I researched buying land with a house, I envisioned a two- or three-bedroom dwelling, but did I really need that much space? Father Rose's cell, along with the cells of the current monks, couldn't have been more than 150 square feet. Their dwellings were so small and austere that I imagined I could construct them myself despite not having any building experience. All their structures were off-grid, relying on solar power, and the collection of Toyota Land Cruisers the monks used to get around the mountain were ancient. I peeked at the odometer of one and saw that it had 288,000 miles.

Going to a monastery challenges the notion that you need a certain level of material comfort to worship God. In fact, money is the obstacle, and the disparity between what you need and what you want can be quite large. As a single man, I thought I needed a half-acre plot of land with a few trees and a wooden shack to live in, but even that might be too much. Everything else that could be added, such as electricity and internet, were wants, and were likely to be a hindrance to my spiritual development.

We visited Father Rose's tomb. Brother Alexei retrieved incense and a censor. The visiting Russian priest led a prayer for the reposed. I had to look towards the others to know when to cross myself during the prayer. Then we went to the main church to conclude the tour.

Later, I went to the bookshop. The first thing I grabbed was the *Orthodox Study Bible*. I had a copy of the *MacArthur Study Bible*, the gold standard of study Bibles for Protestants, but I am not Protestant. There were many more books to choose from, but I remembered how many dozens of unread books I had waiting for me at my mother's house. I looked at the collection of icons and bought two, one of Father Rose and one of St. Herman of Alaska, the missionary who brought Orthodoxy to America in the late eighteenth century. I wanted to fill my future home with icons, so I had to start somewhere.

The monk who manned the bookstore gave me a tip: "If you have time, walk two minutes up the hill. Behind the cross on the left are the mountains." I took his advice and climbed the hill, passing by a workshop and a monk's cabin. The shrubs on my left cleared to reveal a 10-foot tall cross and a striking view.

I didn't want to return to the hotel, so I stayed at the monastery for Vespers (a small evening prayer) and then dinner. I joined five other pilgrims and 12 monastics to eat a kind of vegetable puree with salad and bread. It was Wednesday, a fast day, though I doubt the monks ate meat on non-fast days. During the dinner, the life of a saint was read by two monks in succession. When it appeared that everyone had finished eating, Father Damascene, the abbot of the monastery, rang a bell, gave an update on church happenings, and assigned the monks their duties for the next day. When everyone began to get up, Brother Alexei interceded on my behalf and asked Father Damascene whether he could talk to me. He had a group of visiting parishioners who were a priority, but he reluctantly agreed to sit with me in the dining hall. He seemed irritated, so I gave him the short version of my already short life story and then fell silent.

"I have two questions," Father Damascene began. "First, do you masturbate or use porn?"

"No, nothing," I replied.

"Good. And secondly, do you intend to convert to the Eastern Orthodox Church from the Armenian Church?"

No one else had asked me that question before. "I haven't given much thought to it," I let out. "Most of the religious materials I study are Eastern Orthodox, since there isn't much in English from the Armenian Orthodox Church."

"But you're not receiving communion from the true church. I don't know your family situation, but it would be a no-brainer for you to convert."

He then went into a prolonged theological discussion of the Christological issue that caused the Armenian Church to schism in the sixth century. It came down to the nature of Christ and how his divine and human natures were mixed (or not mixed). I didn't understand most of it. Father Damascene was passionate about the issue, stating how the Oriental Orthodox Churches, of which the Armenians are part, are flat-out wrong. I didn't know how to respond. I knew that I was receiving God's grace even though I was in a "schismatic" church, so was it really necessary for me to change churches? How about my mother, with whom I want to attend church in the future? I knew Jesus Christ calls us to place Him above everyone, even our family, but was it God's will for me to change churches? Maybe God was speaking through Father Damascene, so I would have to wait and see whether I received further guidance on this particular issue. I was comfortable during an Armenian Liturgy, but also comfortable during Eastern Orthodox Liturgies. If my Armenian ethnicity had been stronger, such as being able to speak the language, I might have taken offense at Father Damascene's advice, but I was open to serving God's will in a way He saw fit.

A monk poked his head into the dining hall and informed Father Damascene that he was needed for the Compline service. He excused himself. I followed him into the church, now lighted only by candles. After the service, Father Damascene sought me out and said he wanted to recommend a book for me. We went to the bookshop and he grabbed *On the Providence of God* by St. John Chrysostom. We sat in the bookstore and I gave him an update of the trends I had noticed in the secular world. As we talked, many monastics came up to Father Damascene to receive his blessing to go to bed.

"I feel a pull to monasticism," I said. "How would I know that it's the right choice?"

"If you're coming to monasteries, that is usually a sign that it could be suited for you. I look at you and would say you have a 50% chance of becoming a monk... maybe even greater than that. God will let you know in time. Things in the world won't work out, no matter what you do, or you will find it hard to live among secular people."

"I figure I'll go back to the world for a couple of years and see if I meet a woman to marry."

"You could also try to be a monk in the world, because here it can be very hard. I mean, you have no will. Most people cannot handle it. You can stay in a monastery for a few months to see if you like it. It's not a sudden decision."

I had spent my entire life fortifying my will, making decisions for myself, and only recently had I relaxed that will to submit to God's will as it has become known to me. I could see how submitting to the will of an abbot would be even more difficult. To get permission to go to sleep, for example, would require an incredible level of humility that I don't have. I also suspected that I would be chafed by the social nature of the monastery. I'd have to work with other monks and be part of a community. Maybe being a monk in the world would make more sense. I could use the money I'd saved up to isolate myself from others in a log cabin not too far from my parents and work on my salvation. Whatever the case, God will eventually let me know.

Father Damascene gave me his blessing and I drove back to my hotel in Red Bluff. Precisely when I had been pessimistic about finishing the tour, God graced me with a holy mountain that encouraged me to endure.

†

On the way to San Francisco, I stopped at the public library in Orland, California. I had learned to read the reviews of libraries online to ensure I picked one without a homeless problem, and with a rating of 4.8 out of 5, the one in Orland passed the test.

It was a small library with only two work tables. I sat down at one and began working. About half an hour in, a young woman entered. She wore a modest skirt and white blouse. Her hair was long and her body thin. From what I could see of her face from a distance, she was rather attractive. I suspected that she was Slavic. As she lingered by the front desk, my desire for her increased. I stopped working. She walked to the opposite end of the library, disappeared for ten minutes, and then walked out. The temptation was gone, or so I thought, because only a few minutes later, she came back into the library, walked in my direction, and sat in a chair right next to me. She took out her smartphone. I had written books on how to approach women in this very scenario. The urge to talk to her was becoming impossible to control, and although sex wasn't on my mind (yet), I craved an interaction with her—with any beautiful woman.

"Maybe you are bored and would like a book to read," I said. She looked in my direction and smiled. I pulled out *On the Providence of God* from my bag. "I got this from the monastery not far from here." When she reached out to grab the book, I noticed a large tattoo on her arm. I examined her face more closely. It was weathered and full of dark shadows. Was she a drug user? She took the book and then complimented my t-shirt that depicted an intelligent grizzly bear smoking a pipe. The game was on, as they say, but I didn't want to play it. I wanted my book back. When I had seen her walking around the library, I created a fantasy of her as an attractive, meek woman, but the reality was much different. In the past, I could suspend reality and treat her as an idol until we entered a bedroom, thanks to the aid of alcohol, dark lighting, and insatiable lust, but those things had gone.

She got a call on her phone. "My social worker is here," she said. She handed my book back and said goodbye.

For many years, I had walked up to random girls and figured out a way to talk some of them into my bed, but now I could see how insane that behavior was. How could any woman consider a random man for sex? Surely, she had grown up around countless men. She had met many men through her family and friends. Why couldn't any of those men pass muster? So she had thrown all of those men away, but would allow one who appeared out of nowhere, on a street or in a bar or on a dating app, to fornicate with her? The men who were connected to her in some way through her social circles didn't meet her standards, but this random man whose last name she would likely never know potentially could? Any woman who is even considering a random man must be in a state of rebellion. She is trying to punch above her weight, just like the man who thinks that, with a little bit of time in the gym, a good haircut, and some useful pickup lines, he can pluck a beautiful girl from thin air to be his. It's a delusion, and I bought into it for a long time.

How about the woman who is eager to date a foreign traveler? I spent five years in Poland where I searched for "the one" while fornicating on the side until she would arrive. There were tens of millions of Polish men who shared the same language, religion, and traditions of any girl. Innumerable Polish men were orbiting each one, even the ones who were not that pretty. And yet she said "no" to all those men to sleep with me, a man who couldn't even give her a direct answer to why he was in her country. Why would she do so unless she was ready to throw away her traditions and ancestry? In fact, she was the perfect match for a man who was doing exactly the same thing.

†

I met with four men for my event dinner in the Cow Hollow neighborhood of San Francisco. After all the news articles I had read about San Francisco being the outdoor feces capital of the world, the neighborhood was surprisingly clean and tidy. I saw not a single homeless person. That could be due to the fact that rents for studio apartments started at $3,000 a month. Many properties were priced at over $10 million.

One man who came to the dinner had just got out of college. He told me that he was ready to leave the United States and travel the world like I had done, eventually settling down in a foreign country with beautiful women.

"Don't do it, it's a trap," I said. "I wasted a decade abroad, and now I wish that I had stayed in the States all along. You can create a million reasons to go, thinking you're making the right choice, but it's a deception."

"So what should I do instead?"

"Live near your parents, within a day's drive of them. They are healthy right now, I'm guessing, but when they get older, they will need you, and you will not be able to help them if you're in a foreign country. Do you have siblings?"

"Yes, two younger siblings."

"You also will be able to serve as a role model for them. The world is changing so fast that your parents don't understand what is going on in today's culture, but you have this understanding. You can help steer your siblings away from danger, but while abroad, you won't be able to do this as much."

"But it's very expensive here. It's cheaper to live abroad."

"You can find a rural area to establish a homestead for cheaper than living in a foreign city. You don't need to live the big city life. It's still possible to live economically in the United States, but you will not be close to the action. Now even if you follow this advice I'm giving you, you'll hit many roadblocks. You can't find a woman. You're bored. Your parents are overbearing. Things can happen that make it hard to sustain what I'm telling you, and that's because I'm giving you advice based on the world of the material, since you are not yet a man of the faith. I suppose I'm doing you a disservice, because following a plan without God will fail in the end. The real answer is for you to first seek God. Once you turn to him, you will see that being close to your family is the obvious choice, and He will help you overcome any difficulty that is thrown at you, but without God, you will want to seek pleasure and novelty as soon as the going gets tough, and you will ultimately regret your decision to stay here. With God, you can bear the right choice, no matter how hard it is. So really, you need to ask me how to get close to God, not where to live. God will tell you specifically where to live."

Around that time, another guest had to make a phone call. His parents lived on the East Coast and had health problems that needed constant monitoring. He had hired a nurse to take care of them. That might reduce the problem of them getting the health care they needed, but it wouldn't do much to reduce the emotional burden and pain of having ailing parents living in a far-away location.

"I'm sure you were thinking of finding a beautiful girl abroad to marry," I said to the young man. "But why would a good girl marry a man who left his family because things were a little tough at home? Isn't that a red flag for her? If you can't stay with your family, whom you're related to by blood, wouldn't it be easier to leave any random girl you meet in another country? The truth is that a good girl wouldn't marry such a man. She would run away from him, and the only reason she would consider him is that she's running away from something herself. She's his mirror reflection. You do not want to meet a girl who picks you while you're living life in the wrong way."

"But how about if I stay here and don't find a girl?" he asked.

"Don't worry about it! Have faith in God and He will give you what you need. You don't know what you need. You think you know, but you don't know. Everything I thought I needed took me away from God and put me on the path to ruin. You're a fool, just like I am, and without a spiritual foundation to guide you, you will flounder from one bad decision to the next. If it's God's will for you to be married, you will be married. It's as simple as that, and it's not dependent on your effort, on talking to one thousand girls around the world to find one you are deceived into thinking is good. It's about serving Him as faithfully as you can. He will send you a woman when you're ready if He believes a wife is important for your salvation. And all you have to do at that point is to be a man and ask her out to begin a courtship."

"How do I turn to God?"

"Tomorrow during my talk I will detail how it happened to me. It's different for every person, and I don't want to share a method, since a method does not exist, but the most basic step is showing faith and humility to God and talking to Him through prayer. Faith will be based on prayer, going to church, and reading the Bible or other spiritual texts. A priest could better guide you when you're ready."

As the dinner wound down, the restaurant transformed into a loud bar. We went for a walk outside, and I noticed huge groups of attractive young women everywhere. How was this possible? I had thought San Francisco was full of blue-haired freaks. One pretty woman even came up to our group and asked me for a high-five. "I can't," I replied, "you may have germs." She frowned and walked off.

A group of four girls walked by, followed by a group of five, another group of four, and then a group of six. "Is this some kind of joke?" I asked the guys. "There are good-looking women everywhere. Did one of you pay these women so that I could later say San Francisco was great?" All wore the same uniform of tight pants and minuscule top that revealed just about everything. Their hair was straightened and their faces were coated with makeup.

We stood beside the entrance of a popular lounge. For every guy waiting in line, there were three girls. It seemed like the sort of "paradise" I had sought in the past, but I only had to remind myself of the day before in the library to know that this was an illusion created by Satan. The women had spent many hours to look good on the outside to serve not God but their desire for fornication and pride, seamlessly enabled by alcohol.

When a woman is immediately pleasing on the eye, I must assume there is nothing beyond that. If a girl is faithful to God, why would she put on a uniform that allows men to imagine fornicating with her? No, she would dress modestly, and conceal her sexual beauty for her husband. The women out in the streets can show me their butts and boobs all they want, and there is a good chance I'll glance or even stare because I'm weak, but I will do all that I can to starve the passion.

†

On the day of the San Francisco talk, my scabies rash came back. Some of the red spots, including a big one in my groin, re-activated and started itching again. It appeared that the rash had never fully healed, causing me to doubt that it was actually scabies, but the talk had to go on.

I drove downtown near the Tenderloin area. It was as bad as Portland. Mentally ill and drug-addicted homeless were loitering, talking to themselves. I saw two men whose pants were hanging off their legs, revealing their butt cheeks. The familiar mephitis of urine hit me as I walked past alleys. This must be the new normal for large parts of the city, tolerated by those who live in it as long as they are still able to fulfill their material desires.

Approximately 65 people showed up for my talk. There were seven women, the first time their presence tipped over 10%. One wore an exceedingly erotic outfit with high heels, revealing the complete shape of her body. I tried my best not to look. During the Q&A portion of the event, she publicly asked the following question: "Is it important to give your boyfriend deep-throat blowjobs?" The audience laughed and murmured. One man shouted, "She's trolling!" Predictably, a sexual image entered my mind.

After the Q&A, I had the opportunity to talk with most of the guests privately. When only ten people remained, the sexy woman approached me. We sat close to each other and she asked me for advice on her relationship problems. She felt that she was running out of time to find a husband and needed to employ a special tactic to hook a man. I replied with my stock answer that her problem was not in dating or sexual technique, but her faith. She was depending on her beauty or knowledge of men to get a husband instead of depending on God and… I was overcome by her sweet-smelling perfume and glanced at the top of her exposed pinkish-white chest. What was I saying again? I closed my eyes for two seconds and when I opened them, I noticed that I had developed an erection.

She said, "I'm going to a bar down the street to hang out with my friends. I hope you can join." She then handed me a slip of paper with her phone number. I put it in my pocket. Immediately, I thought of the itchy red spot on my genitals, thinking that sleeping with her would be difficult because of that reason. Maybe she had good intentions, and would absolutely refuse my sexual advances upon meeting her at the bar. I gave her a hug goodbye. I enjoyed feeling her body against mine. I played out the scenario of joining her at the bar and then taking her to a room. I fantasized about the bodily ecstasy—as fleeting as it would be—that would follow. As she left the room, I stared at her legs. The passion burned. I wanted to fornicate with her.

For another half-hour, I talked with several other men, but I had trouble concentrating. Her number was in my back pocket. I said goodbye to the remaining men and carted my event gear back to my car. I went to a nearby diner. She was all that was on my mind. Finally, it struck me that I should pray. I recited the Jesus Prayer until returning to my hotel room. I reached into my back pocket and felt the piece of paper. I took it out, and without looking at it, in case my subconscious would memorize her number, I tore it into a hundred little pieces.

I woke up many times throughout the night in a state of arousal, desperate to masturbate, but each time I would recite the Jesus Prayer and wait until I fell back asleep. In the morning, I felt like I hadn't slept at all.

†

St. John's Armenian Church was located on the hills of San Francisco away from the grime and filth below. The Liturgy was conducted by a priest who was a few years younger than me. At the end of the service, I venerated the Gospel while the priest held it, and then he turned to me and said, "I was told you would come." An Armenian man who knew of my arrival in San Francisco had told the priest to look out for me.

When the service was over, I approached him and relayed an abbreviated version of my life story. He gave me his blessing to stay on the right path. I was asking him some questions about church practices when a woman interrupted our conversation.

"Did I forget to bless the table again?" the priest asked, exasperated.

"Yes. They're waiting."

In many Orthodox churches, a requiem is done 40 days after

someone dies, involving a special prayer at the end of the Liturgy followed by a fellowship meal. I got in line for food in the banquet hall and a little old lady said hello to me. I told her that I was half-Armenian and visiting from Washington, DC. She got excited and immediately introduced me to a young woman who was half-Armenian as well. I piled my plate with Armenian food and sat at their table.

The young woman was cheerful and kind. I guessed she was in her late twenties. She had a professional job and lived alone, paying $2,000 a month to rent a studio apartment.

"Do you know how to cook Armenian food?" I asked.

"Not really." She mentioned the names of two dishes that I didn't recognize. "I'm a vegetarian now because of ethical reasons. I don't like how animals are treated in industrial farms."

"I just visited a couple of homesteads. When you raise animals, you can treat them properly and make sure there is no undue suffering when they die."

"It's also not good for the environment to eat too much meat."

"What do you mean?" I asked.

"It uses more resources and puts a strain on the earth."

"The earth is just a rock," I said, matter-of-factly. "When Jesus returns, the earth will go with it, so I'm not sure if the earth needs our protection."

She broke eye contact with me, a hint for me to stop, but I continued. "Our environment was given to us by God. We can appreciate nature to get close to Him, but I'd be careful about making a god out of nature." I couldn't help but think of the Portland tree-hugger types I had come across and their deification of Mother Nature. I assumed she would understand my point, but she ignored me and started talking to other people at the table.

The night before, the temptress at my event had claimed she was a Christian, and this Armenian woman was obviously a Christian, but it seemed they had allowed the secular world to adulterate their faith.

Just because a woman attends church or declares herself a Christian, it doesn't mean she has strong faith, or at least the same intensity of faith as I do. All I can assume is that she has at least an intellectual belief in God and a desire for a more spiritual life, but when it comes to her lifestyle, all bets are off.

I wondered how strong a woman's faith had to be for me to proceed with courtship. If she believed in God and went to church but was a liberal when it came to everything else, was she a worthy candidate? I didn't yet have the ability to discern whether or not a woman's faith was genuine. I imagined that if I did meet a worthy candidate, I would have to ask God what to do.

As the fellowship ended, Father Ash came by and sat next to me. I felt comfortable with him since it was likely that he had gone through the same sort of Generation X upbringing as I had. One of the first questions I asked him was if there were any Armenian monasteries in the United States.

"No, because after the genocide and communism, the church was badly hurt. We went from 10,000 priests worldwide to a low of around 1,000. Today we only have 2,000. The monasteries still remain as holy sites, but monks cannot receive pilgrims. In this restructuring phase, the monasteries are a luxury. Parish churches are given more priority."

Maybe I could start an Armenian monastery in America, I thought, but I didn't dare suggest it out loud.

"Do you feel that things are getting worse?" I asked. "It seems like evil is spreading, such as with the transsexual agenda that is affecting children. Are we approaching the end times?"

"The world is always doing evil. We have to put things in context and look at early Christian history where it was a death sentence if you declared yourself a Christian. There were many waves of persecution by dictators and governments, and in more recent times there have been Armenian martyrs. Today, you can openly worship Christ and not be persecuted like in the past, so I don't know if I can say that things are worse."

We moved to the outside of the church. Father Ash's large pectoral cross shimmered in the sun.

"Be careful," he added, "about becoming despondent at what you're seeing. Despondency is a tool of the devil. He wants you to believe that nothing can be done and evil will only get worse. Anything that causes you to lose faith, or see yourself or the world as irredeemable, must be corrected. That's the wrong path."

I looked on the bright side. I could openly declare myself a Christian, practice my faith, and visit churches and monasteries all over the country. I could speak about Christ to people in hotel conference rooms and write about Him in books. I am negatively affected by people who choose evil, but that has always been the case. I could always decide to turn away from evil-doers and towards Christ.

I started to wonder whether I was serving up a plate of despondency to my followers. By telling them that the cities were failing, and that future conflicts were inevitable, was I helping them spiritually or was I merely fear-mongering? If you keep God close, does it even matter what the world does? Persecution and martyrdom can be seen as a way to serve God instead of something to be feared. What is there really to fear, anyway? If the world is going good, you can worship God publicly and privately. If the world is going bad, you can worship Him privately, and any trial can be welcomed as a way to please Him. Why was I so concerned about the future?

After church, I drove to The Mission neighborhood to get footage for my travelogue. It wouldn't be a stretch to describe it as an outdoor shrine to diversity and sodomy. Anything homosexual or non-European was displayed as desirable. Cool young people with a multitude of micro-identities strolled by trendy restaurants and cafés while ignoring the presence of the homeless. Nose rings were especially common among the women.

I decided to be hip for a moment by walking into a crowded café named Ritual Coffee Roasters. When I see the word "ritual" in a neighborhood full of gay pride flags, I think of satanic rituals, but no way could it be that. I looked at the menu and noticed their logo—an arc and a star against a red background. I immediately thought of the Soviet Union's hammer and sickle insignia. I tried to ignore this association and proceeded to wait in line. I looked around and saw a mostly homosexual clientele using Apple devices. I began to feel like I was in a doctor's waiting room of people awaiting the results of an HIV test. I left without placing an order. I would later find out that the owners did indeed receive inspiration for their logo from the sickle and hammer on the flag of the Soviet Union. Real edgy to use a political system that killed over 20 million people as inspiration for your hipster coffee shop in a capitalistic country. Did they serve organic fair-trade coffee in the gulags? Maybe they should research that.

I found another café that had no homosexual or satanic identifiers. I tried reading a book but couldn't help overhearing other people's conversations. One couple in their forties was on an internet first date. They had moved far away from home and reviewed all the countries they had lived in before deliberating where they should move to next. I was highly pessimistic that they would develop a meaningful relationship. Then I overheard two black women talking. One said, "Doctors don't prescribe painkillers to people of color because of discrimination, but that's really a good thing because then they don't get addicted to the drugs." Two other women near me were discussing their recent dates while exchanging pet memes on their phones. One had plastic wrap over a fresh tattoo on her neck.

I tried my best not to judge these people, but it was clear to me that The Mission was a place to worship the world and all its pleasures, delights, and false gods, if not the devil outright. All major cities have such a neighborhood because Satan has a template for how he wants to corrupt the cities. Being gay on the West Coast, it turns out, is not that different from being gay on the East Coast. Being a female in rebellion on one coast appears the same as being in rebellion on the other (minus the nose ring). It's almost as if the American city is devolving to the point where its entire purpose is to spite God.

13

Decline

I made a stop in Monterey, California, the site of Cannery Row, made famous by American writer John Steinbeck. During World War II, demand for canned sardines skyrocketed and many businessmen set up shop in Monterey. Business thrived, bringing many jobs to fishermen and packers, but demand eventually dried up and the last cannery closed in the early 1970s. Like most things of prior acclaim, it is now a destination for tourists to view historical buildings before purchasing souvenirs, overpriced clothing, and Mexican tacos.

I walked to the shoreline and identified a bird as a western gull. Oh yeah, I had forgotten that I was a bird watcher. To watch birds, you have to sit still for some time, but after crossing the Mississippi, I'd had to cover a huge amount of ground in a short time. The ego of my past, which had planned the trip, wanted to see the entire country just to say that I'd done it, while the soul of my present would rather sit and watch the birds in peace.

I left Monterey after only one night and drove through Big Sur, a group of parks on California's coast. There were endless miles of natural coastline shaped by rocks, cliffs, and small hills. Multiple vista points allowed me to soak in the beauty, which initially was overwhelming just like in the Rocky Mountains. I had to pace myself when viewing how the endless ocean runs to the shore and crashes against mammoth rocks that rise hundreds of feet from the earth. If there is objective beauty, which I believe

I found in Big Sur, there must also be objective love and truth, and to believe that all that came about by accident would take a level of faith surpassing that of even the Apostles.

In the middle of Big Sur, I visited Pfeiffer Beach, a beach with purple sand hidden behind hills and forest. I walked to the left edge of the beach and climbed the boulders, settling right beyond the reach of the splashing waves. I sat for an hour, cheering them on as they collided with the rocks, giving glory to God for such magnificence.

On the night journey to my hotel in San Simeon, a beach village south of the park, I drove like an idiot. I took a turn too fast, almost veering off the road, and I overtook five cars at once on a two-lane mountain highway because I was too impatient to pass them one at a time. God might be blessing my trip, but it would all be over if I attempted to push beyond my strength and abilities.

†

During the day in San Simeon, I walked to the beach. I saw only four people, including a man with a golden retriever that kept running up to me to say hello. The beach was too wet for sitting so I took a stroll over the rocks and found a small patch of hard grass. Using my day bag as a pillow, I lay down and listened to the waves for some time, drifting in and out of sleep.

Later in the day, my head felt heavy like it was under pressure. I was nauseous and had trouble standing. I had been on the road for nearly three months and had not taken a day off. Even on this day of beach relaxation, I still had three hours of computer work to complete. I decided to lighten my travel itinerary. I would stick to the California coast and skip the Joshua Tree National Forest and the San Bernardino National Forest. It would be okay if my travel videos were less interesting.

I hit the road for Los Angeles as early as I could. At only

2pm, I started encountering heavy sections of traffic when I was 60 miles outside the city. By 3pm, it was full-blown rush hour.

The hotel I booked in the Bell neighborhood of Los Angeles was suspiciously cheap. I found out why when I arrived: it was located in Mexico. I was the whitest person in the area. People stared at me as if wondering, "Is this gringo lost?" I had lived in South America for a year-and-a-half, so I have no problem living around Hispanics, but what struck me about the ones in Bell was that they were rapidly adopting the style and slang of the American host culture. Most had tattoos and, from my eaves-dropping in a Starbucks, talked just like the characters in mainstream television shows and movies, albeit with a slight accent. They wore yoga pants and ate just like an American would.

I hear a lot about how Hispanic immigrants are more con-servative and God-fearing, but what about their children? And their children's children? The rulers of this country know that any conservatism of Third World immigrants will be neutralized within a generation thanks to a pervasive and all-encompassing system of social engineering. You can import the most conserva-tive people in the world, even members of ISIS, but their children will get addicted to porn and then leave comments on the Instagrams of attractive women imploring them to show more boob. The oligarchs don't care how incompatible Third World immigrants are, because they know that the generation or two after them will be fully on board with their agenda.

I drove through Skid Row, a section of the downtown area where the homeless had created a parallel society consisting of hundreds of tents plopped down on the sidewalks, with various smaller tents tacked on to make additional living space. Portable speakers played mostly 1980s rap, signifying when the inhabit-ants came of age. The odor was violent—much of the area smelled like an open sewer. Driving through a massive cow farm is less offensive. There were several people in wheelchairs, rolling on the road, dangerously close to traffic, and numerous others staggered around having conversations with themselves. A part of me felt guilty for filming the scenes of degradation for my travelogue, but at the same time I wanted to present an accurate reality for people who live far from Skid Row, that this was what would happen to their city if it went the wrong way. One should not take clean streets and healthy people for granted—it's only a result of good, which disappears when faith goes by the wayside.

I thought that the tent cities would abate once I left Skid Row, but they persisted in the downtown area, even directly opposite the headquarters of the Los Angeles Police Department. Most of the homeless preferred setting up their tents near the on- and off-ramps to major highways. Even in Hollywood, a mythical place where stars are "born," there were furled tents on many side-walks, along with numerous homeless who would camp there after sunset.

Hollywood was a great disappointment. There was no gran-deur to it, no beautiful actors or actresses. It was simply a tourist trap with numerous souvenir and costume shops that catered to the same sort of person who thought the Las Vegas strip was exciting. I could imagine the young people who left their homes to "make it" in Hollywood, only to discover that it was almost certainly a bigger dump than the place they'd run away from. That should've been a clue that trying to improve your life by running away from home was an illusion, but like me, they would have to waste many years before coming to this realization.

I passed by a few movie studios. Are they where aspiring actors and actresses were sodomized for a chance at fame? I saw a few young women dressed in a sexy manner—were they on their way to an audition where Mr. Goldman would promise them a role if they fornicated with him?

Hollywood is where broken people go to trade their souls for a heightened material existence. They degrade and foul them-selves under the influence of lust, power, and greed before a select group of gatekeepers who control the best roles and parts to produce sordid content that modifies the beliefs and behavior of those who watch it. At some point on the street, I glanced up and saw a billboard for a new show called *Evil*. Based on a true story.

The only highlight of my entire Hollywood experience was seeing Donald Trump's star on the Walk of Fame. I thought it would be mobbed by protesters, but I was the only one who noticed it in a dense crowd of tourists.

The Friday night dinner took place in West Hollywood, an exceedingly homosexual area, an observation that was becoming tautological. My guests were all secular, so I didn't steer conversations to God as much as at prior dinners. They wanted advice on how to "succeed" in the material world.

I got into an argument with the youngest guest, who had not been out of college for long. Like other men of his age, he needled me a bit, first giving unsolicited advice about which deodorant I should use and then saying he believed I had "mommy issues" based on his reading of my book *Lady*.

"And why do I have mommy issues?" I replied.

"Because your advice was over the top."

"Which advice?"

He demurred. "I can't remember."

"I can take a criticism, but if you can't explain it, then it's just an insult."

"I didn't take notes on it, so I don't remember."

I let it slide, but he insulted me again later. I told him that he had a problem with authority and needed to have more respect for his elders. It devolved into a back-and-forth debate that was unbecoming of my attempt to be more humble. After a few minutes, we resolved the issue and apologized for our behavior. This skirmish was edifying because it signaled to me that I still had a lot of pride to work through. A kid insulted me—so what? I could humbly ignore it and then, if necessary, withdraw from the conversation, but the problem with these dinners was that, since the guests had paid me a sizeable fee, I had to provide the advertised product (a three-hour meal) even if I felt the urge to run away from them.

The dinner ended and we all took a walk through West Hollywood. There was a handful of posh bars where the city's beautiful people congregated, and I admit that the women on display were attractive. If I lived in the city and was younger, I would go to one of these bars and work mightily to sleep with such a girl. Then on Monday or Tuesday, she would go to an audition and immediately sleep with a casting director or a Mr. Weinstein. A lot of the men who use Tinder or go to bars try to perfect their look and muscles to sleep with these women, but the gatekeepers don't need to play that game. They have what fallen women truly want. You, on the other hand, only have what they want for a night or two.

†

I booked the LA event at the Los Angeles Athletic Club, a fancy gym in the downtown area that doubles as a hotel. When I booked venues, I usually went with the cheapest option that was centrally located, because my guests needed only so much luxury while sitting on a chair and listening to me talk. Even with that strategy, once I added drinks, snacks, state taxes, local taxes, hotel taxes, and automatic gratuity, the average cost of a conference room rental was usually over $1,000.

In attendance were many Proud Boys, a men's club started by *Vice* founder and entertainer Gavin McInnes. His club was initially formed as a joke but began to grow in influence as they pushed back against Antifa violence and Silicon Valley censorship, even to the point where they began to provide security at conservative events. The media took notice and, of course, painted them as a violent right-wing extremist gang, which had been enough to put them on the radar of the Feds. Leftists are allowed to be politically violent, but those on the right are blocked from even existing.

The speech and Q&A went off without any mishap. Most of the audience seemed receptive to my spiritual message, a surprise since they were living in the epicenter of hell. Before we moved rooms for the meet-and-greet, I packed up my equipment. Then a staff member came into the room and briefly filmed me with her phone without saying anything. I found that behavior odd, but couldn't figure out why she had done it.

I had booked the venue until 10pm. There were still over a dozen guests remaining as the time approached. Then a few minutes before 10pm struck, the banquet manager aggressively demanded that my guests gather their things and leave. I approached him and said, "According to my clock, it's not yet 10pm, but you are asking people to leave. Is there a reason you are doing that?"

"Event is finished, it's time to go," he replied, not making eye contact.

"But it's not 10pm."

"Party's over. You have to leave."

One of the Proud Boys overheard the exchange and said to the employee, "Are you autistic?" They began arguing, but the worker remained firm. It didn't make sense to me at the time, but later I remembered the other worker who had filmed me.

In my event kit, I had a printout of Clown Pepe, a green frog with a rainbow hairstyle that represented the "clown world" meme. If I was in a jovial mood before an event, I'd tape the meme somewhere in the conference room. The worker hadn't filmed me but the Clown Pepe meme. I believe that it had triggered her, making her think that we were neo-Nazis. She had told the other staff members that racists had booked the room, hence the rude conduct at the end. After getting kicked out, many of us went to a restaurant down the street and enjoyed another hour of conversation. Thirteen events in, if this was the worst treatment I would have to face, I couldn't complain.

The next day I went to St. Leon's Armenian Cathedral in Burbank. The cathedral represented the Western Diocese of the Armenian Church (the Eastern Diocese cathedral was in New York City). Around 400 people were there to experience the Liturgy. Up to that point, I had never seen so many Armenian people under one roof. Many men vaguely looked like me. Unlike in my little Washington, DC church, there were dozens of good-looking young women, many of whom dressed slightly inappropriately. It's not uncommon for Armenian women to cover their heads with a scarf in the name of modesty during the Liturgy, but if below the scarf I could see a snug dress, tight jeans, or a cut-off shirt, it defeats the purpose. If there was an attractive girl in my field of vision with an accentuated rear-end, I had no choice but to re-position myself so that another person would block her from my view.

Through my mom, I had been in contact with Marta, the widow of my late uncle. She found me in the cathedral when it was time to receive communion, which took about 30 minutes because of the sheer number of people. Not only is there traffic on the LA roads, but also in the communion line, and that traffic spilled over into the parking lot, which seemed like a Mercedes-Benz dealership. Every other car was a luxury automobile. I couldn't expect a parish church to be as ascetic as a monastery, but it was clear that the LA lifestyle had rubbed off on the Armenian population living there.

I went with Marta to meet with her two sons, my cousins, and we went to an Armenian restaurant in Glendale, a city with a large Armenian population. According to my cousins, most of the patrons in the restaurant were new arrivals from Armenia. Their culture seemed similar to Ukrainians or Russians, with the macho man appearance of the men, who were often balding and overweight, toting a man purse of some sort, alongside the hyperfeminine appearance and princess behavior of the women. They were not "cool" like whitewashed Armenians who have mostly thrown away their culture and adopted the attitudes and behaviors of the West. While the assimilated Armenians look down on the "FOBs" (fresh off the boat), the lives of the latter seem more in line with masculine-feminine polarity than the androgynous behavior of Americans.

My older cousin, Vartan, was 38 years old, and the other, Hagop, was 34. If I shaved, I would look just like the younger one—we both have the same facial shape and skin tone. I look at pictures of my Iranian father's family and don't look like them at all, suggesting that I received most of my physiognomy from my Armenian side. Vartan and Hagop's father had died a decade ago, so they knew what I was going through with my sister's death. I don't find it particularly difficult to talk about my sister's death to strangers, but if the person I'm talking to had known her personally, the emotions come out in a flood. I said only a few words about it.

It turned out that my cousins knew practically nothing about the past 20 years of my life. When I gave them an update of my worldly travels, philandering, and authorship of numerous sex guides, they were shocked. "I thought you wrote books on computer programming!" Vartan said. They did a Google search for me on their phones and couldn't believe what they saw. Vartan gravitated towards my Wikipedia entry and Hagop my YouTube channel. I'm not proud of what I've done, but at least with family I didn't have to worry about being harshly judged. I imagine I could commit a heinous anti-Semitic crime and still be accepted by them.

The three of us had zero children, a typical outcome for first-generation Americans. Our parents did not understand that the new country they moved to for opportunity and comfort would render us sterile. We had to learn how to live in the new world, but all we really learned was how to remain in a state of suspended adolescence, chasing daily pleasures while postponing commitment and obligation, and I had pursued those pleasures more excessively than them. Our parents came here, had us, and that was that, an Armenian lineage terminated. The only purpose of it all was to have a higher standard of living, but the cost was death of the family name. While I'm not going to use the preservation of my line as a motivation to rush into a marriage, it's hard not to lament that evil is winning. Our ancestors overcame numerous tragedies in the past to maintain their families, most recently the Armenian genocide, but we couldn't overcome pornography and casual sex.

After eating lunch, we returned to Marta's home. At some point, Vartan asked his mother for water. She groaned a bit and then I said, "If you get the water for him, it…"

"…tastes better!" Vartan knew exactly how I would finish the sentence.

"Wow, it's almost like we're related." We both laughed while his mother got the water.

Even if I didn't have an immediate rapport with my cousins, we were bonded by blood. The roots of our lives were connected. So many trivial disputes and dramas that would come about with random friends met through a shared hobby just wouldn't happen with cousins, even if we lived completely separate lives. It's too bad we were on opposite coasts. After my parents repose, I will have very few relatives left in America, and will need them in my life so that I don't lose touch with who I am.

†

I had been in contact with a female follower who wanted to meet me. I had no idea what Layla looked like or how old she was, but I agreed to meet her since she was a devout Catholic. After spending time with my cousins, I drove to a Korean tea shop in San Gabriel.

She arrived shortly after me. She was pretty. Her facial structure appeared vaguely Slavic. She wore jeans, a black turtleneck, and a thick pectoral cross. If she were a man, people might confuse her with a priest and ask for a blessing.

Even if we were about to hit it off completely, the date would not end in intimacy. I wouldn't even call it a date but a marriage interview. If our values were compatible, and we didn't find each other's demeanor or appearance disagreeable, we could continue. Compare this to dating, where everything can be disagreeable, but as long as the alcohol is flowing and we are both in a state of lust, sex can proceed.

As we got to know each other, I couldn't identify anything that would prevent her from becoming my wife. Her age was acceptable (mid-twenties), and she had turned away from the world in the same way as I had. She had made mistakes, but nothing that prayer and faith couldn't help resolve. Her demeanor was submissive, and there was no other objection I could think of. Most positively, she wasn't bothered by my past, and based on the way she looked at me, I suspected she was attracted to me. Best of all, her parents lived only a few hours away from mine. We would have no problem raising children to be relatively close to all their grandparents. I was very pleased that I had gone out to meet her. Then I asked her a question.

"Do you have a tattoo?" I stirred my tea, waiting for the "No" so I could develop the exciting fantasy of her becoming my wife.

"Yes," she replied. "It's on my chest." She then lowered her turtleneck and revealed a large tattoo that started at the bottom of her neck and proceeded down to her breastbone. I don't want to describe what the tattoo was at the risk of removing her anonymity, but it was a tattoo that most men wouldn't want to see when having intimate relations with their wife.

My heart dropped. Internally, I went into a state of shock. I couldn't believe that this woman, who checked off nearly all the preliminary boxes, had a tattoo. It wasn't her fault that I absolutely hate tattoos on women. They disgust me, because so many of my shameful sexual experiences had been with women who had them. Even a tiny tattoo on a girl's ankle, one that was barely visible, would give me pause, but I would see this one every day. Unless Layla had a closet full of turtlenecks, and planned to suffer the heat of every summer, and even shower in a turtleneck, this tattoo would always be visible, so just like that, I could no longer consider her a prospect.

I wondered whether she could tell that my disposition had changed. I tried to pretend that everything was fine, but I could hardly look her in the eye. Instead, I stared intensely at my tea as if I were expecting a frog to jump out of the cup. I didn't want to get close to a woman if there was no prospect of a future together.

I started to drop hints that I had a lot of work to do, and not long afterwards I gave her a ride home. Because we were naturally compatible, we talked in my car for another half-hour while the engine ran. We agreed on so many things, and I did not doubt that if we did get married, she would follow my lead within our "little church." In the name of honesty, I told her that her tattoo was an issue for me because I hated them, and left it at that. She graciously accepted the critique. I gave her some of the sweets I had bought at an Armenian bakery earlier in the day and said goodbye.

It was hard to sleep that night. Could I throw away a potential wife just because of a tattoo? Even if she may have been sent by God and was ideal in just about every other way? Yes, I could! I really hate tattoos! Was it possible that I subconsciously found her unsuitable and had picked on the tattoo as the most proximate cause? That was a possibility, but I had felt a stab in my heart only when I laid eyes on her bare chest. She had other flaws that might scare off men, but they weren't permanent as was that ink drawing. Layla even had practically no sexual experience, but I would rather accept her having ten sexual partners, or maybe more! Her tattoo was an absolute deal breaker. I couldn't overcome it. It will take a miracle for me to ever get married.

14

Immigrants

One hour south of Los Angeles was Laguna Beach, a resort city made famous by reality television. The beach itself was pleasant and clean, but with much work to do, I didn't have time to enjoy it. Instead, I took pictures and watched the shorebirds for a while before heading to a Starbucks with my laptop.

The template Americans use for how social interactions should proceed is television and movies. They copy what the actors are doing on screen, mimic behavior seen on the red carpet, and use that as a model for interacting with others. This is most apparent in the reality television stars, who are trying to be like the big stars in Hollywood, but because they are not real actors, they come across as phony. Now, so many people are trying to copy the reality TV stars, to become a copy of a copy, that the consumers at the bottom of the social hierarchy are totally confused about how to behave. I noticed this most strongly in Laguna Beach, where an over-manicured population behaved with their friends and family as if they were being watched by a television audience. Their expressions were overly exaggerated and they laughed one second too long for things that were hardly amusing. Unsure of what they were saying, or even who they were, they used an uptalk cadence that made it difficult to discern whether they were making a statement or asking a question. And they all did it. I had seen this sort of behavior among some of the millennials on the West Coast, but in Laguna Beach it was the default personality.

This fakery is necessary to fit in. Others must believe that you are cool, wealthy, and popular, and since both sexes have the same social goals, wholly disconnected from faith or the creation of families, both sexes act the same. Besides clothing and hair length, there was no other pronounced delineation. The citizens of Laguna Beach were converging into one gender, totally confused about their biological identity and the purpose they had to serve as mature adults, but as long as they were accepted into an artificial tribe modeled on television, as long as someone laughed at their joke or listened to their dramatic story involving Taylor and Riley, both of whom could be male or female, enough dopamine would be released to soothe their malaise for the moment. Even the streets were fake—grass medians on roadways were watered throughout the night. Flora that was not native to the area or conducive to the environment had been brought in and propped up with effort when the natural beauty would have sufficed.

More pronounced were the conspicuous displays of wealth. Many homes were valued at well over $10 million. Supercars were common. While walking by a beachfront area near a private resort, I saw a sign on a picnic table that read, "Reserved for my beautiful bride!" The table would have provided a fabulous view of the upcoming sunset. I looked online for how much it would cost to lodge his bride: rooms started at $1,000 a night and went all the way up to $2,500, but none of that included dining at the exquisite in-house restaurant with its Michelin-rated chef or partaking of the spa amenities that were meant to force skin cells to release "anti-aging" molecules.

I guessed that the couple was there for a weekend, and since his bride must feel content that she had made the right choice in a husband, he wouldn't dare put her in the lowest-priced room and betray a potential peasant background. For a three-night stay, including food, excursions, and dermatology therapy at the spa, I estimated that he had spent at least $7,500, and I could only guess how much more he had spent on the wedding. The wife, no doubt beautiful, must have been certainly pleased to be treated like a princess, and the story and pictures of her wedding weekend— including the view of the sunset from the picnic table—were sure to inspire the appropriate level of jealousy in all of her friends.

I couldn't help but think of how I would spend my honeymoon. My wife and I would drive to the nearest cabin in the mountains, pay $200 a night for the mountain view, and make peanut butter and jelly sandwiches. I would dedicate myself to her, protect and provide for her and the family, and attempt to deepen our faith in God to ensure our salvation, all in a meager home that prevented worldly temptations from entering. Do I have any takers? Far fewer, I imagine, than the man who had taken his bride to Laguna Beach.

Many men worry about getting married because they're scared of losing all their money, but I have to ask, why do you have so much money? Did you accumulate it by serving God or mammon? A lot of married men delay having children because they want to be "financially secure," thinking it will make family life safer and more comfortable, but security can never be guaranteed, and I argue that it's mainly through material difficulty that a family bonds. It's through the hard times that they count on each other instead of depending on daily leisure activities, expensive psychologists, gigantic homes, and digital entertainment beamed onto iPhones or cinema-quality television sets. If Laguna Beach is an indication of how the children of rich parents turn out, confused even about how to talk to other people, puffed up with pride because they occasionally get invited to the right party, then living in worldly poverty, dedicated to God, may be the cure.

✝

I drove inland to a San Diego suburb named Escondido. If you give your city a name that can only be pronounced properly by Hispanics, you've sealed its fate. More than half of the population was Hispanic, and with that came the Mexican restaurants and shops. Many parts of suburban Washington, DC also have a large Hispanic population, so I felt almost at home.

If you use the faulty language of the left-right dichotomy, I am a "conservative." I'm supposed to dislike the huge influx of Hispanics coming into the country since I didn't vote to live in Mexico, but it's hard to hate them. I've never been bothered by a Hispanic; they usually keep to themselves. First-generation immigrants are blue-collar workers, similar to my parents, and family-oriented. Some even possess a strong Catholic faith. Unlike the people in Laguna Beach, they don't ache for fame and status. I know that wayward Hispanics are capable of gang activity and excessive drinking, but those problems have impacted me far less than the thuggery of African-American youths, the demented wrath of white female feminists, or the political censorship of Jewish liberals. If I were to construct an enemies list, Hispanics would not be on it, but as a man who is frustrated at the direction America is going, who else can I direct my anger but those who are most visible? The elites at the top are untouchable. I can't see them or shout at them. The Federal offices and synagogues bringing in all the immigrants are out of my reach. I have complained about the Jews online, but they got me banned from multiple platforms. So I'm left attacking gays, Black Lives Matter zealots, and feminist women who preach for abortion on demand. For good measure, I'll make mean comments about Africans stewing goat heads all day or Mexicans living 20 to a house. The problems in America are so deep and intractable that any target I attack won't touch the root cause: the few men at the very top. Besides, can I even blame the Third

World people who are coming to America? Their countries are being ravaged—or have been ravaged—by American foreign policy, and the border gates are left wide open with the carrot of amnesty hanging right above their heads. Why wouldn't they pursue their self-interest? If I'm mad at their presence, it would be better to channel my anger at the enablers of immigration instead of those desperate hordes at the bottom who truly believe they are seeking a better life. But those enablers are above the law. If I get within a hair of hurting them, they will destroy me.

Downtown San Diego wasn't half bad. The streets were tidy enough and the homelessness was a fraction of what I had seen up north. I never picked up on a fecal scent. The people were just as tattooed, if not more so, but they were relaxed. The entire city was tolerable, even livable. Whatever stereotype I had of California was most represented by San Diego than anywhere else in the state. As a bonus, I never entered a state of disgust or sadness that necessitated prayer. I imagine it will take about three more years until that is achieved, when the demoralization sets in and people lose the will and ability to solve the problems that are rapidly approaching.

The nights were getting cooler so I bought a black plaid jacket. It made me look like a Hispanic. I imagined wearing the jacket to my sister's house and greeting her with "What's up, cholo!" (Cholo is a slang term for an uneducated urban Latino.) She would laugh and say how ridiculous I looked in the jacket. But she was no longer here for me to make that joke. After my nightly prayers, I crawled into bed and thought of her. The pain of her death was still strong, and the passage of time was doing little to take it away, and I didn't know whether I wanted it to be taken away.

✝

I had to drag myself to the San Diego speech. I was lying on my comfortable hotel room bed watching YouTube videos with no desire to leave. For the first few events, I couldn't wait to arrive at the venue, and my energy was so high that I had to take measures to calm myself down, but now I had to gather the strength merely to get dressed. Thankfully, when I started to speak in front of an audience, the fatigue subsided and I was able to give a speech that in some ways was better than the preceding ones, but as soon as it was over, all I wanted to do was lie down. Hopefully, it wouldn't happen that on the day of a speech I came down with some kind of psychosomatic attack that prevented me from speaking at all.

Forty people came to the San Diego speech. The wonders of modern media and the internet make it easier than ever to spread your message around the world, but it's face-to-face where you have the strongest impact. People feel your energy, convictions, and faith in a way they simply don't through a video, podcast, or book. Those other formats are better than nothing, but when you want to convey something of the utmost importance, doing so in the flesh is the best option.

Two Navy men came. I asked for an update on how their branch of the military was doing.

"Not so great," one said. "Once they allowed women to serve, the men have become distracted with trying to get laid. If you put a girl who is a five out of ten on a ship, she is treated like a model. Tons of men chase after her. It reduces unit cohesion because now the men fight with each other for the woman."

"If we get into a war with Russia or China, would we win?" I asked.

There was a long pause. "I don't see how we could, because things are getting worse. Our combat readiness is too low."

"The problem for you two is that at some point you will be asked to commit evil in the name of serving your country. I talk to other men in the military and it seems that that time is coming, and you'll have to make a decision between your beliefs and your duty. Have you put thought into that?"

"We're getting out. We have just a little more time to serve, so hopefully we won't have to make that sort of decision."

If good men like these were racing for the exits, I wondered what that said about the future strength of the American military, let alone the country.

On Sunday, I was invited by a follower named Michael to attend his Orthodox Church, but I decided instead to attend the Armenian Church in San Diego so I could at least partake in communion. The church was visually pleasing from the outside, and I encountered nothing abnormal upon walking in, but when I entered the narrow nave and found my seat, I noticed two huge LCD screens flanking the Holy Altar. They displayed the words of the Liturgy in both Armenian and English so that we didn't have to use the service books that were available in the pews. What was this… a karaoke bar? The only thing missing was the animated marker that danced from word to word as the priest and deacons chanted them.

I tried my best to avoid the screens but they completely dominated my field of vision. I used the service book instead to follow along with the Liturgy. Five minutes went by but I simply couldn't lose myself in the worship. I looked at the other parishioners. Were they bothered by the televisions? How long had they been in place? Had the diocese granted the parish priest permission to install these monstrosities, or had the priest done so on his own authority? I looked at the priest. He was older, maybe in his early sixties. Boomers! I glanced at the exit. I was ready to leave, but it was time for the Kiss of Peace, where a holy kiss sent from the altar, between the two televisions, starts a chain that proceeds to all the other parishioners. After it was over, I headed for the exit. I couldn't worship in a church that reminded me of a pub. I had previously thought that I would leave the Armenian Church if they did something as drastic as allowing women to serve as deacons or priests, but it was clear that my bar for disdain was much lower than that. I could tolerate an organ and a PA speaker system, but not televisions.

I walked outside the church and stood for a minute, thinking about what I should do. I could give up and go sightseeing, but I really wanted to attend the Liturgy. I decided to try St. Anthony's Antiochian Orthodox Church, the one I had been invited to by Michael. By the time I got there, communion had taken place and the service was nearly over. Michael found me quickly. I lit a few candles, venerated an icon, and kissed the cross while Father John held it.

During the fellowship, I sat with Michael and his friends. They shared their conversion stories. I told them about my experiences in other Orthodox churches and monasteries. Then Father John came to our group. I told him my life story and he gave me his blessing.

As the fellowship died down, one of the guys went to his car and returned to give me a large bag of oranges. I'm not a fan of citrus fruits, but I graciously accepted. When a man of God gives you a gift, it's best to accept, since he's effectively a messenger of God. I might have been short of vitamin C due to my travel diet, and God was advising me to eat more citrus.

After church, I dragged myself to La Jolla, a popular beach to the north of San Diego. It had ten times as many tourists as Laguna Beach. The sea lions who came to the shore to rest were inundated with women posing with them. The photos were usually taken by boyfriends or husbands. I had once been that guy, taking a photo of my beautiful Polish girlfriend on the shores of Croatia, and then we had broken up. She had uploaded those photos to various social networking platforms to show off her beauty to other men. I wondered whether a woman needs to have her photo taken to please the man she loves or to please other men who are waiting in line.

To get away from the weekend crowd, I went to a café and

ordered a rooibos tea, my favorite non-caffeinated beverage. I sat down on the patio near three women.

"Our home is so small," one of them said.

"Mine too!" another added. "We only have three bedrooms and I have two kids. Did you know that Theresa has two kids and lives in an apartment? I don't know how she does it, but I need at least four bedrooms. We're saving up now for a down payment, because I need a bigger house!"

I got up. I can't read or focus when the worldly concerns of others are blasted into my ear canals. I found a table inside, near two women working quietly on their laptops. I began reading my book, and then a few minutes later a young woman and an Indian man sat at the table next to mine. They began talking about their friends and what was going on in their lives. The man had an effete way of speaking. He would become animated about a trivial matter and wildly move his hands in the air. That's when I saw that he had fake nails painted with blue nail polish and silver sparkles. His nails did not at all match his swarthy appearance. How could this girl, who seemed attractive, spend time with such a confused creature? They obviously weren't dating, so I wondered what she getting out of the friendship.

The volume of their conversation gradually increased. I couldn't stay. I left without finishing my tea. Unless I'm prepared to bring my headphones, which allow me to block out conversation with the "White Noise Baby Sleep" app on my phone, there was no point sharing space with strangers.

I went back to my hotel room. On Sunday nights, I usually edited my travel vlog, but I just stared at the computer screen for some time, not wanting to do it. My feeble attempts to rest weren't helping. Earlier at church, I had forgotten the phrase "shipping container" and the day before I had forgotten the word "range" when referring to cell-phone towers. I was obliterating myself. I decided it was time to take Sundays off, no matter how much work I had to do. If God could take a day off after creating the world in six days, I surely could do the same. If certain work couldn't get done because of my day off then so be it, because no work should be more important than treating my body in a way that God had intended.

15

Pride

I left San Diego and went to the border town of Yuma, Arizona to break up my trek to Phoenix. The predominately Hispanic city was an ill-planned sprawl with very few buildings over two stories. It appeared that they had plopped down buildings wherever was cheapest. Nothing was walkable. There was no city center or even a commercial Main Street. Instead, all I saw were repetitive zones of brand-name shops and strip malls. I imagine that Yuma had originally been created as the last vehicle rest stop before entering Mexico, and some people had decided to live there, not by choice but out of economic necessity.

For lunch, I had learned to do a search on my navigation app for "picnic" to locate picnic grounds. Otherwise, I would be stuck making salads and sandwiches in the cramped confines of my car. I found several picnic tables near the center of Yuma and began preparing lunch. Soon, a stream of teenagers with backpacks began walking by. My picnic area was actually part of a high school. Many of the kids sat down near me while waiting for a ride home.

Nearly all of them were Hispanic, though maybe three of them were white. To my right was a group of six boys. They repeatedly called each other "nigga" and other profane terms. Across from me on the left were two overweight girls engrossed in their phones. Beside them was a boy with his guitar. He played a couple of pop tunes and then his friend put on a rap song using a portable speaker. To the right of them was a girl listening to music using headphones. Another girl said goodbye to the boy with the guitar and then he pointed out that she had a hickey, and that he had given it to her. She blushed. This whole scene could be written off as a matter of kids being kids, but it was easy to see that sins were incubating within them, ready to explode once they left home and no longer had to obey parental rules, assuming there were any.

I don't know what it's like to have children, and I may never know, but I'm starting to consider it foolish to send your children off to public school for six to eight hours a day, during which they enter a black box where you know not what goes on. You don't know who they are talking to, what they're being taught, and what they're listening to. You don't know of the porn or gore that is being shown to them at lunchtime. It doesn't help that most teachers are brainwashed servants, ready and willing to indoctrinate your child with the latest advances in globohomo propaganda technology. I don't trust watching a Hollywood movie—now imagine sending your child to watch a Hollywood movie for six hours a day, because that's essentially what public schools are, but at least when it comes to a movie, you can watch it with your child and immediately counter its damaging messages. A God-fearing man who hopes to have children one day must figure out how he and his wife can educate them instead of outsourcing the task to a secular government.

✝

Located in the Arizona desert is St. Anthony's Monastery, perhaps the biggest Orthodox monastery in the United States with over 50 monks. I lodged nearby in Florence, Arizona to prepare for a visit. I wasn't as excited to visit this monastery as I had been when I visited the previous ones, because I didn't feel like I needed to go. My spiritual gas tank was full. I didn't have any pertinent questions to ask and wasn't lacking any information on how to deepen my faith. My plan was simply to attend Vespers, check out the bookstore, and then head to Phoenix.

Founded in the late 1800s, the city of Florence had long passed its glory days. A third of the storefronts on Main Street were empty and another third were closed when I toured it around 6pm. The most active shops were a laundromat and a hardware store, and only three other people were on the sidewalk. There was no hip café, no youths taking selfies. Two blocks away from Main Street, I encountered near-total silence besides what was emanating from the small adobe houses. In Florence, there was no one to display your status to, and if you attempted to, only the dirt would see it. There was no place to meet people for sex or debauchery. I didn't see why anyone would want to live there, and for that reason I wanted to live there. This dusty town was devoid of the sort of people who flock to the big cities for all that Satan can offer. I would much rather stay here and eke out an average—if not impoverished—living. Because of all that it lacked, I didn't see how it would be possible to endure without God's help. And if you chose to forsake God in a place like this, you would become addicted to opioids or other drugs to get you through yet another day. Without God in Florence, you suffer drugs, and without God in the big city, you suffer pleasure, wealth, and attention from the opposite sex, while convincing yourself that all is well, that the satisfactions you're experiencing make it all worthwhile.

After touring the downtown area, I went to the Florence library to work. Recently, someone on my forum had asked what a man should do if he married a woman who turned out to be infertile. All medical intervention has failed and you have a wife who cannot conceive. I knew what the old me would have said. "Divorce her. There is no point staying with a woman who you can't start a family with." The issue was on my mind when, near my table, two Hispanic children, a boy and a girl, started playing hide-and-seek around the book stacks. The girl was extremely overweight—her body was shaped like a teardrop and she already had a double chin, but the strength of youth allowed her to run vigorously after the boy without tiring. They distracted me from my work, and I craned my neck to locate their parents. I endured the noise for a while, hoping that a librarian would inform the kids not to play in the library, but nobody came. I took it upon myself to put a stop to their playtime.

When the girl was near me, I looked to her and said in the gentlest tone I could muster, "This is a library, not a park. It's not a good idea to run here because you may fall and get hurt." The little girl froze in place and looked slightly past me. Then she raised her eyebrows and in the meekest voice possible let out an "Okay." Then she walked to her friend instead of running. I was touched by her sweetness. She responded to my soft discipline with a softness of her own. It's at that moment that I had an answer to the question the man posed on my forum: adopt. My wife and I would have a lot of love to give, and there would be no use wasting it on pets or surrogate hobbies. If there is a child out there who needs a home, even if it's not from my seed, I pray I can give it that home.

✝

St. Anthony's Greek Orthodox Monastery was founded by Elder Ephraim, who established 17 other monasteries in the country after serving on the monastic republic Mount Athos for over a decade. People travel from far and wide to receive his blessing because he is seen as a living saint.

One sign that I am not meant for life in a monastery is that after spending a few hours in one, I don't feel the need to stay. If I were called to be a monk, I imagine that I would hate to leave and would change my plans to remain longer, but that hasn't been the case. After a conversation with a monk, a visit to the bookstore, and a prayer service, I'm ready again for the world. I visited St. Anthony's after doing my day's work, unlike previous visits when I went first thing after waking up.

St. Anthony's was much quieter than I had expected. I saw only a handful of pilgrims. Not long after I entered, Father Nektarios, who had been a monk for 16 years, greeted me. I told him that I would like to attend Vespers as an Armenian Orthodox Christian. He walked me to the church and into the entrance hallway (narthex). Before I could go through an extra set of doors into the nave, he kindly informed me that, since my church was not in communion with the Greeks, I could not worship inside, and I could only watch through the narthex. I was taken aback but did not object. It's their rules and I wouldn't dare question them, but when Vespers started, I could hardly see or hear anything. It was like trying to watch a sports game from the Goodyear blimp. Those LCD screens from the Armenian church in San Diego would have come in handy.

After a few minutes, I got frustrated and exited the church to take a walk through the monastery. My thoughts quickly turned to anger. How could they exclude a fellow Christian like this? I believed in the same things they did, that God is fully human and fully divine—why would they have a policy that seemed intended to embitter someone who believed in the One True God? Were they saying that I wasn't a real Christian? Screw them. If they don't want me to worship in their church, I'll go somewhere else!

Profane words might have entered my inner dialogue that I dare not reproduce here. As furious as I was, I still had the presence of mind to shoot footage for my travelogue. I looked forward to trashing the monastery in my narration, to warn fellow Christians that this wasn't the place where they could worship Christ unless they were part of the "Greek club." I was so consumed with anger that I couldn't even perceive the beauty of their gardens or hear the tranquil sounds of the water fountains. I didn't need their exclusionary monastery—shame on them!

When I was on my way out of the monastery, I saw Father Nektarios walking towards me from the opposite direction. I hoped that he would say something to me so I could voice my displeasure, and sure enough he did.

"Did you enjoy Vespers?" he asked.

"It was hard to through the door and glass," I coolly replied. "I left after a couple of minutes."

"Oh, that's unfortunate, but yes, this monastery is strict with rules. It's established in the Mt. Athonite tradition."

"Yes, but I'm a Christian. I believe in the same things as you. I came here to worship God, but I can't."

"You can worship God," he said, "but just not in that place."

"That's exclusionary! I've been to three other Eastern Orthodox monasteries and they didn't do that."

"Well, each monastery is different, but that is our tradition." He started going into the theological basis of why I had to sit in the narthex, but I didn't want to hear it. Nothing he could say or do would make me feel good about what I had just experienced.

Then something behind Father Nektarios caught my eye. Two monks were slowly approaching. One was exceedingly old and frail, hunched over and making tiny steps. The other monk was holding his right arm. Father Nektarios smiled and said, "That's Elder Ephraim. You may receive a blessing from him."

I approached Elder Ephraim with my head bowed. For a man of his age (92), you would expect a pallor to his skin, but he possessed a bright color between light brown and orange as if an artificial photo filter had been applied to his entire body. He was speaking words softly in Greek that I couldn't understand. I touched the ground, and cupped my hands in front of him, right over left. He put his right hand in mine and gave me a blessing as I kissed his hand.

I stepped back. Father Nektarios started speaking to me, but I couldn't hear his words. I smiled and stared off into the distance. My anger had instantly disappeared; I felt a serene peace. When

Father Nektarios noticed what was happening, he said, "Oh, I'm sorry. I see you're having a moment." After half-a-minute, I came to.

Father Nektorios wanted to continue the theological discussion, but at that point I had lost all interest. I gently changed the subject, asking whether the bookstore was open. He said it wasn't, but that he'd open it for me.

He escorted me into the shop. I wanted him to recommend a book, but he didn't know my life story. I told it to him and he seemed jolted, suggesting that it wasn't a typical conversion story.

"It's hard for me to relate to other people," I said. "They don't understand how I was able to change so quickly. They say I'm faking it."

"Usually, people are graced through small steps. God brings them to Him in stages. Ultimately, He will give you what He knows you need in a dose that you can handle."

He recommended the book *My Elder Joseph the Hesychast* by Elder Ephraim. He apologized that he was recommending a book by the monastery abbot, but it had deeply touched him. I bought the book, along with an icon I had been searching for: The Ladder of Divine Ascent. It depicts the faithful climbing a ladder to heaven. Demons at the bottom try to pull them down while angels at the top try to lift them up. Every day is a struggle to do good and get closer to God, and I wanted to be reminded of that by hanging the icon in my home, if I ever get one.

I left the monastery in good spirits, marveling at God's providence. Although I didn't worship at the church and ended up entering a state of anger where I argued with a monk, God still found a way for me to be blessed by Elder Ephraim, who reposed less than three months later. Though I was disappointed not to attend Vespers, I left the monastery knowing that I had received what I needed.

✝

I drove to Phoenix, a city populated by escaped Californians. I couldn't identify anything distinguishable about it except that the houses had gravel lawns with cacti instead of grass lawns with trees.

One of the men who came to my Friday night dinner was a Catholic who attended the Traditional Latin Mass. Starting in 1962, the Catholic Church instituted reforms during the Second Vatican Council to modernize the church. The result was that the Roman Catholic Mass became more Protestant. Some parishes maintained the pre-Vatican Two Mass, now most commonly called the Latin Mass, and were reluctantly tolerated by the hierarchy. The further the mainline Catholic Church strays, the more the Latin Mass grows. If I meet a Catholic today, the chance that he or she attends the Latin Mass is disproportionately high compared to their relatively small numbers.

After the event dinner, the Catholic offered to give me a ride to my car parked a mile away. He shared some frustrations that he had with the church leadership, but he was determined to remain Catholic. I'm not optimistic the Catholic Church can root out their homosexuals and corrupt Pope, but I did not share these opinions with him, and I certainly did not suggest he should consider changing churches, because through practicing his faith and attending Mass daily, I suspected he was closer to God than I was.

Around the time I visited St. Anthony's, doubts began randomly popping into my mind. I would contemplate God's providence and then a thought would enter: "How do you know this is God's doing? It's just a coincidence." I would pray to Jesus Christ and a different thought would enter: "Jesus was just a man. Are you sure He even existed?" Now that I was finally getting a handle on my sexual temptations, I found myself in the midst of a new style of attack. The doubts were not convincing, and almost childish in nature, but they were distracting. Even before my reversion to the faith, I had deconstructed and discarded most atheistic beliefs, so I was surprised that the demons thought that type of attack could shake my faith. I'd just have to barrel through. When the doubts came, I'd recite the Jesus Prayer until they stopped. I wouldn't get into a debate with the thoughts and open the door for the demons to converse with me. I'd simply pray.

Approximately 25 people came to my Phoenix lecture. The first hour proceeded almost flawlessly. I was smoother than I had ever been, and was thinking about how I could use this talk as the final recording to release on the internet after the tour. Then I stole a glance at my sound recorder on the table to my right and saw that I had forgotten to hit the record button. I went silent in disappointment before regaining my bearings, but the smoothness had gone. I felt tired and started to falter, limping across the finish line.

My guests couldn't tell whether this iteration of the speech was better than the previous ones, but I was competing with myself to improve as time went on. Strangely, I could never predict how a speech would turn out. On some days when I was tired or feeling mildly ill, I delivered a great speech, and on other days where I felt calm or energetic, I ran out of gas around the midway point.

After the speech was over, a man approached me and said he was a lapsed Catholic. He stopped going to Mass because he felt disconnected from it and wasn't sure what to do next. I asked him whether he had been to a Latin Mass. He said he hadn't, and I pointed out the Catholic man I had met the night before. They conversed and it seemed that he would attend the Latin Mass. While I liked to think that my speech gave people a lot of value, meeting just one other like-minded soul during the event could be infinitely more beneficial.

Phoenix had an Armenian church. I attended the Liturgy on

Sunday morning. Just like the church in San Diego, there were karaoke screens beside the altar, but they were projector screens and much easier to ignore. Still, it took away from the worship.

One sign I know a church is holy is if my eyes tear up without cause at some point during the Liturgy. It usually happens close to communion, either before or after confessing my sins, but it has even happened while reciting the Nicene Creed. During this Liturgy, I teared up during two separate periods, suggesting to me that Christ dwelled within the church despite the projectors and my judgment against it. I received communion and then joined the fellowship in the dining hall. The other parishioners were especially friendly and asked what I was doing in Phoenix.

"I'm on a road trip throughout the entire country."

"Are you doing this for research?" one woman asked. "Or maybe you are on a book tour?"

They were on to me!

"Well," I began, "I have always wanted to visit the entire country, so this is a trip I have planned for a while." I hated lying by omission, but there was no point in scandalizing them with my life story and then saying goodbye forever not even an hour later.

I sat at a large table of elderly men and ate a flavorful meal of cucumber-dill yogurt, couscous salad, rice pilaf, hummus, beef kebab, and baklava.

"So what do you do?" one man asked.

"I used to be a microbiologist," I replied.

"You did scientific research?"

"Yes, I did process development in a pharmaceutical company. We created protocols for the manufacturing side of the company to produce certain biological drugs on a large scale. I grew engineered yeast or mammalian cells in large tanks."

"We have a couple of doctors here. Maybe you should talk to them about your research."

"I, uhh, don't do that anymore. I quit that job and lived in Europe for a while. Now I have an internet business." A thirteen-year gap, effortlessly discarded.

"What do you think about combining human DNA with animal DNA?"

"I don't think it's a good idea."

"They're even trying to bring the dinosaurs back. It would be nice if you could pet one."

"I think they made a movie about that," I smiled. The man stared at me blankly, not getting the reference.

Two men at the table started talking about aliens. One expressed how aliens had been found in the Middle East. The other nearly shot out of his seat: "You don't *really* believe that nonsense, do you? Show me the evidence!"

"There are pictures on the internet."

"Pictures? Are you kidding? You have to be narrow-minded to believe in that!"

Then they discussed how many Armenians died in World War II fighting against Hitler. Someone brought up that Hitler may have had an Armenian legion. The topic of the Jews or the Holocaust didn't come up, so I had nothing to contribute, and bade the old men farewell as they eased into another debate.

I needed more footage for my videos, so I drove to the Old Town of Scottsdale. The art shops, wine bars, souvenir stores, and cafés looked mostly new. A lot of the women I saw were in their forties and showcased their plastic surgery and overly gym-toned bodies, suggesting they wanted to compete with females half their age.

Before the advent of air conditioning, women covered themselves from head to toe, but the attention arms race dictates that more and more skin must be revealed. Months or even weeks prior, the sight of all that skin would have sent me into a frenzy, but now I simply turn away.

If an attractive girl is in my field of view, I choose a new field of view that doesn't include her. If I use my free will to choose not to look at her, the temptation is less, and it's for that reason

I've rebuffed ideas that would force women to be modest. Forced modesty is forced grace—an illusion of faith or goodness that would deceive men about the true value of any woman. Of course I would much rather live in a society where women are modest of their own volition, but ultimately, I know that I can't be tempted unless I choose to be, and if a particular area of a city is full of half-naked women, I have the choice to go somewhere else, and if all cities have half-naked women, it's off to the hills. I can bemoan the immodest displays, but I can't use that as an excuse for failing to control myself.

The spiritual doubts remained, still popping up in my mind. I swatted them away with the Jesus Prayer, but they would promptly return. I surmised God was allowing this to happen because He wanted me to learn something new.

16

Prison

After leaving Phoenix, I drove to Las Cruces, New Mexico to rest for the night before heading to White Sands National Park. On my way to the park, I passed several missile test ranges and spacecraft launch sites. Signs sternly warned me to stay off government property. Nearby was Roswell, the city where an alleged UFO landed back in the 1940s. What a coincidence that the location of a UFO landing was not far from where the US government launched experimental aircraft.

It's beneficial for the government to promote the existence of aliens because it reduces faith. If we are just one of many intelligent species in the universe, as Carl Sagan insisted decades ago, are we really the children of God? Perhaps not, and now that lost faith can be replaced with consumerism, feminism, hedonism, and whatever else the social engineers can conjure up.

I arrived at White Sands and drove on the main sand road, eventually parking my car next to huge sand dunes that were two to four stories tall. I climbed the tops, took some pictures, and barreled back down. I squeezed the sand with my hands and admired the utterly barren landscape. Many families were present. Children were sledding on the dunes or playing in the sand with buckets and shovels as if they were on the beach. There were also couples who spent most of their time taking pictures of each other (usually the man taking pictures of the woman). In one case, a woman lay on the sand with her hair splayed in all directions while her man directly above her took a picture. I was confident it received many likes on Instagram.

That night, during my usual prayer, the doubts got louder. "Who are you praying to? There is nobody there." I was tempted to argue back and provide evidence for the existence of God, but decided that would just allow the demons to share more of their disgusting lies. Their first attack on this trip, I believed, was putting worldly fantasies in my mind concerning cabins, homesteads, and motorcycles. The second had been sending me women with whom I could potentially commit fornication. Their latest tactic, their boldest, was attacking the foundational beliefs of my faith to flip me back to atheism in one fell swoop.

I watched a short video from a Greek Orthodox priest that discussed spiritual doubts. He compared them to being on a ship in a violent storm. So much water is crashing onto the deck that you fear the boat will sink, but the boat is stronger than you think. The best you can do is hold on and wait for the storm to pass. You surely can't fight the storm, but you can outlast it.

The next day I went to Carlsbad Caverns, a series of mammoth limestone caves. I put on my newly bought boots and work pants bought from Walmart, ready to do some serious hiking. When I arrived at the visitors center, they asked me whether I wanted to take the elevator down to the caves. Elevator? I opted to walk down. The path to the cave entrance was paved. Handrails had been installed on both sides. The entire structure was well lighted with electric lamps. Emergency stations were posted throughout to "Call a Ranger." I waited for things to get rougher, to justify my purchase of the boots, but the sidewalk never ended. I'm sure I could have done the tour in flip-flops. The only thing missing from the experience was Disney music and dinosaur noises blaring from hidden speakers.

The caves themselves were spectacular to behold, but I didn't have to earn them. The stalagmites, stalactites, towers, mammoth rocks, and drip water ponds were just another excuse to take out my camera and be a tourist like everyone else. There was never a point where I felt the urge to sit down due to exhaustion and appreciate the beauty that was given to me through hard effort. If I liked the Disney tour in Carlsbad, loaded with modern technology and wheelchair-accessible ramps, then maybe I could do something harder with headlamps, ropes, pulleys, and whatnot. Nonetheless, the last place where you'd think to experience First World comfort is in a cave, but that's what the National Park Service had provided.

†

I left New Mexico through oil country and headed into the west of Texas until I reached the town of Odessa. On both sides of the road were oil drills and flaming towers. Various other structures seemed to be either extracting oil or storing it. Many of the drills were moving, although I didn't see anyone manning them. I wondered how the drills worked and how much oil was being pumped out of the earth. The odor around many of these fields was similar to leaving a gas stove on for a while without igniting it.

I became jealous of the oilmen, for they worked with their hands in the outdoors instead of staring at a screen all day. I imagined that they might be jealous of someone like me, who worked in comfort and magically created money from internet content without wearing out his body, though sometimes my lower back feels stiff if I sit down for too long. If either of us swapped jobs, we'd probably hate it even more. They'd be bored to death, and my writer's body wouldn't be able to handle the physical labor.

After Odessa, I made a stop in Abilene, closer to the middle of Texas. The center of the town was dusty and old with shops perfunctorily named "Bakery" and "Monk's Café." There were no parking meters or surveillance cameras. Men wore faded loose jeans and dirt-covered hats. A handful of homeless was lounging on the sidewalk, though not aggressively panhandling. They had long stopped asking me for money because I was starting to look just like them. Abilene felt similar to Cheyenne, Wyoming, or any small town in South Dakota, and I was excited to see that most of Texas could remain this way in the modern era, a throwback to how America used to be.

My excitement faded when I got to Dallas. The name evokes something Southern, charming, dignified, but the reality is what you'd expect from a city its size: strip malls, traffic, and generally unappealing aesthetics that could be confused for any other American city with a population of over one million souls. If you want to learn about Texas, Dallas is the last place you should go.

For the event dinner, I picked a trendy restaurant in the Uptown area. Immediately, I was surrounded by gigantic breasts. Women with blonde hair, sometimes real and sometimes fake, were wearing low-cut tops that revealed their chests, sometimes real and sometimes fake. They wore necklaces with pendants that hung right above their cleavage, as if they had to trick men to take a look. Exaggerated, puffy, high-glossed lips were common. In terms of the type of woman that the average man today craves, this location may be the best I've seen in the United States. The well-to-do Dallas girls are eager to conform to a standard of beauty that would be recognized by most men as actual beauty, and for them to feature life-giving breasts instead of the defecating butt, as was the case most everywhere else, was a welcome change.

A young man came to the event dinner. At first I thought Diego served in the military because of his erect posture and deferent manner, but he had actually been locked up in prison for a few years. He had heard about me when an inmate had given him a tattered copy of one of my books, *Bang*, which I unpublished right before starting the tour. He had got out in the past year and wanted to make up for lost time by sleeping with a lot of women. The tips in the book were helping him to get laid and he wanted to thank me in person, although I was overcome with regret that I had directly enabled yet another man into a life of sin.

I was curious about his time in prison. "Your prison sentence wasn't that long," I started. "I'm guessing you could count down the days and endure it until you were let out, but how about those with long sentences. How did they cope?"

"Either they become religious or gay. Prison is like one big gay party. They do it out in the open. You can hear inmates refer to another man as a 'girl' or his 'girlfriend.' They get into fights when their 'girlfriend' sleeps with another man. Even gifts are exchanged. The rest of those with long sentences become very religious, and they stay friends with only each other."

Didn't that mirror the choices made by those on the outside? Though based on what Diego had told me, it seemed like a higher percentage of people chose God in prison than those who were free. I wondered whether God uses prison and its extreme discomfort to save souls. If Diego hadn't been locked up, he might have ended up dead from a life of crime when he was far from salvation.

"Could I grow a beard in prison?" I asked.

"Yes, but you need to apply for a special religious exemption. If you grow a beard without it, they file what's called a case against you."

"Is it true what they say that you should act tough on the first day so you don't get raped? I'd much rather not be sexually abused."

"No, it's not like that at all," Diego replied. "The people who do the gay stuff in prison already decided to be gay, and then when they get caught by others they say they were raped, but no one believes it. Just don't talk to others who are gay and you'll be fine."

He asked me for game tips, but I had little to offer now that I was out of the game. Instead, I told him how his player career would proceed. "Notches you get today will give a huge rush. You'll feel like a winner, a conqueror. You will be eager to tell your friends the day after a new score, but as time goes on, the reward gets smaller. You will no longer feel like a winner, only relieved you had an orgasm because you were horny, backed up. The satisfaction moves from the egotistical to the bodily. Then you will become more aware of all the little steps it takes to get a notch instead of seeing it as one big fun process like before. The steps will start to appear like their own little mountains. Now it's laborious, and the bodily reward becomes minuscule compared to the labor you have to put in. You'll ask, 'Did I need to sleep with that girl?' You will keep going because sex feels good, even with a woman you don't care about. But soon the sex doesn't feel as good as before. Minor flaws with a girl, perhaps in her attitude or body, start to disturb your arousal. You have to drink more to get in the mood. You're not willing to wait the extra hour or two it takes to lay a girl who is playing hard to get. You start getting angry at them for being the slut you wished they were or for being the slut they really are. You start getting angry at yourself for having to act like a clown for their intimacy. The hunt becomes too draining. Your soul is begging you to stop. When you've extracted all you could from the game, you give up, exhausted, and look in the mirror to see a man you no longer like."

Diego's face froze. He had paid for a dinner to spend time with his favorite game guru and instead he was being warned that it was a dead end. In the same way that prison had turned him away from a life of crime, I hoped that meeting me would turn him away from sexual sin.

✝

The day of the lecture came. I delivered my speech to 30 people. During the Q&A, a married couple spoke. They had been married for 48 years. I asked them how they had met, and it turned out that the wife had prayed to God to send her a good man, and not long after, it happened. Things have surely changed since half-a-century ago, making their rosy story seem more like it had come out of a movie, but God's commandments have not changed. As a Christian, I am called to pick up and carry my cross. I must endure the terrible degradation of a society that makes finding a wife more difficult than ever. I must refuse to commit evil to possibly achieve a good, and that includes the modern notion of dating, of sexually sampling women and falling into lust with the distant aim of one day creating a family. If there's not a single woman left in the world who wants to abstain from premarital sex, who desires to carry her cross, then I'm simply not getting married, because God's instructions are crystal clear. Before I had been given the gift of faith, this would have been an impossible decision. I would follow the secular winds to do all that worldly women demanded of men for them to see me as a long-term partner, but my personal experience showed the result: the woman was elevated as my god, my false idol, my personal savior. No longer. I will wait for the right woman or remain celibate for the rest of my life.

An Orthodox man in the audience had a family question. One of his sons was taking well to the faith, but his oldest teenage son was not. The latter was engaging in sexual banter with girls on Instagram and Snapchat. He had not heeded his father's warnings about where those kinds of activities would lead. The father asked how he should approach the problem.

I said, "If you force your son to cease those activities, and then force him to go to church, a lasting rebellion against God is all but certain. Many parents compel their children into faith, but

I'm sure everyone here knows how that turns out. As soon as the child gets away from his parents, he pursues the temptation wholeheartedly because he never made the *choice* for God—his parents tried to make that choice for him. In essence, they wanted to hijack his free will for his own good, but God gave us all free will for a reason—to choose Him ourselves. Our parents cannot make that choice for us. The best you can do as a parent is give him a proper Christian foundation so that, until he does choose God, he falls only slightly before getting back up. Maybe he'll only fall for five years before recognizing his folly, and revert to the spiritual guidance you gave him when he was younger.

"Oftentimes, we think of the perfect argument against a mistake that someone we know is about to commit, yet when we deliver that argument, not only does it fall on deaf ears, but the person begins to resent us. 'Who is he to stop my pursuit of happiness and the fulfillment of my dreams? He is against me!' Just last week in Phoenix, after four hours of speaking to the audience about the mistakes I had made in life, and how ashamed I was for them, a young man came up to me and asked, 'Roosh, which country is best to meet girls?' My words didn't penetrate him at all because he already made his choice, and when people choose to sin with their hearts, there's nothing you can do. They won't stop trying to bring their fantasy to fruition.

"I know this is not the answer you wanted to hear, because no father wants to see his son fall, but assuming you did the best you could in teaching him the Gospel, which it sounds like you have, you simply have to wait until your son returns. Hopefully, his time rolling in the mud with other pigs will be short, but prepare for a long wait, of watching your son commit acts that are harmful to himself and others. In the meanwhile, pray for him every day. Ask God that He graces your son so that he turns away from evil, and when he's ready, when he's tired of falling, you can help him get back up."

After the Q&A, I mingled with the guests. Diego approached

me. "I went out last night after the dinner," he said. "I hit a bar with friends and pulled two girls back to my place on my own. I entertained them until a buddy could come and wing me. Eventually, he arrived with a few other people, and finally the friend leaves, leaving me all alone with my girl. I told her I wanted to show her something cool in my room. We get there and start kissing, but she wanted to move slow. I stopped and asked myself what I was doing, like what was the point of this, but I kept going. I got her on my bed and we started messing around. She resisted again, though nothing out of the ordinary. I knew it would take more time to seal the deal, but for some reason I was no longer in the mood. The things you said during the dinner were on my mind, about how this would be a dead end. So I asked her to leave. She was surprised, because I guess she expected me to keep trying. I told her again to leave and she did. And now hearing what you said today, I have a lot of thinking to do."

Diego might have hurt other people in the past to necessitate a prison term, but I could tell he had a soul worth saving. He was fornicating more out of ignorance than the desire to commit evil. He had fallen for the sex trap, just like me and most other men in the Western world. He thanked me, but God deserves all the credit.

The next day I woke up early to attend the Liturgy of an Armenian church that was only 15 minutes away from my hotel. The church was in an old building. The nave was small but humble, with no televisions or projectors. The priest appeared young, perhaps younger than me.

I was nearly last to receive communion. I opened my mouth and the priest dropped a small piece of bread that was soaked in wine into my mouth. Then he gave the side of my beard a light caress with the palm of his hand. I couldn't help but smile as I walked back to the pew. In the sermon that followed, he told us not to let social media apps distance ourselves from God. I nodded heartily while looking around to show the flock that I approved of what he was saying.

After the service, Father Ghevond came up to me and asked my name. Then in front of the entire church he introduced me, along with two other visitors. "Daryush [my birth name] is traveling from Washington, DC. He is on a road trip and visiting many Armenian churches. Convince him to stay for our festival next week!" A priest had never done that before, sending the flock to me. And they came. Many sat with me at a picnic table, inquiring as to my journey. They brought me cake, water, pamphlets, and a t-shirt. Armenians, being from the east, can seem initially cold to strangers, but the hospitality here was the best I had received from a church.

I waited around for an hour so that I could be last to talk to Father Ghevond. I told him my life story and the temptations I had been facing.

"Last week, I started getting disturbing doubts while praying, such as 'Who are you praying to? There's no one there' or 'This is all a waste, when you die nothing will happen.' Engaging them in the slightest would just fed them further, so now I simply pray over them."

Father Ghevond clasped his hands together. "C.S. Lewis talked about this in *The Screwtape Letters*. The demons will try to disrupt your prayers, because if they can get you to stop praying, faith can be lost." He went on to explain how the demons had a lot of tricks up their sleeves in order to get me to fall away from God.

"Early on this journey, I was seriously thinking about monastic life. I visited four different monasteries so far, but when I leave them, I'm somewhat relieved, eager to use the knowledge and guidance I received to navigate through the world. And I see how difficult being a parish priest is, with having to deal with so many personalities and minor troubles. So I don't think I'm currently being called to be a monk or a priest. What do you think?"

"Have you considered becoming a deacon? You can stay involved with the Church but not have to make as large of a commitment. St. Nersess Seminary in New York City has a diaconate program that is only a couple of weeks long." St. Nersess is the only Armenian seminary in the United States.

"But I can't sing," I replied.

"You don't have to. There are different roles. You can do the censing or assist in other ways." I hadn't thought of being a deacon before. It seemed to be a reasonable first step before priesthood or monastic life.

"I'm pretty sure my future books will be about the faith, mostly from my personal experiences and other practical things I've learned. I wonder if there is some way I can work with the Armenian Church to produce some writings."

"Yes, certainly. Next time I meet our Primate, I will mention you. Can I give him your contact information?"

I paused. The Primate of the Eastern Diocese was in charge of all the parish churches in the eastern half of the United States. What if he was scandalized by my past? What if he excommunicated me? "Of course," I replied, feigning confidence.

"A lot of your parishioners were asking about my background, such as what I do. I kept it vague because I don't think they would understand, but at the same time I don't want to lie."

"It's okay to withhold details. Unfortunately, some Armenians wouldn't be able to stomach your story, because they are not used to people who…"

"…fell so badly?"

"Yes, exactly. It's… unusual."

The word "unusual" was apt. Why did I have to be so unusual? It seemed I had been on a normal track up to my first corporate job—perhaps just a bit shy and unconfident with women. And then I had found game and opened Pandora's box, and even though I liked to think that box was now closed, most of the world would forever see me as the man I had been while at my worst.

With my spiritual gas tank back to full, I left Father Ghevond's church and went to the Texas State Fair, a gigantic fair with barnyard animals, carnival games, and nauseating rides. I couldn't help but notice vendors selling fried versions of foods I didn't know could be fried, like pecan pie, cheesecake, cheese on a stick, and hard candy. While lively, I wasn't convinced that this was the real Texas.

I caught the performance of black gospel singer Tye Tribbet on the main event stage, who sang about Jesus to aggressive hip hop beats. His audience was almost entirely black. They danced and raised their hands, yelling "Amen!" and "Praise Jesus!" During the Orthodox Liturgy, there is little movement and no dancing. The main movement I make is the sign of the cross. If someone's hand is raised in the air, it's likely they require medical attention, yet there I was witnessing highly participatory worship that involved the body in a somewhat passionate sense. I wondered how these black people would react to a typical Liturgy. They'd surely find it boring, maybe even depressing. Perhaps they'd be turned off by God entirely if forced to participate in it. If that's the case, without their form of worship, could salvation be possible for them? Perhaps God devised an energetic form of worship for the benefit of their souls, because he knew their more passionate character might require livelier music and movements. On the other hand, if you gave that to an Orthodox believer, he might think it was satanic. God must know best how to save the souls of a race of people.

In between songs, the gospel singer preached from the Bible. He told the crowd that God was above race. "No matter how much injustice there is, seek God first. He comes before your race, before your anger." I left the fair confident that if the dancing crowd followed the singer's teachings, they could be saved.

17

Signs

I drove to Waco, a city to the south of Dallas, hoping for a more authentic Texan experience. Instead, I encountered a bland city with enormous six- and eight-lane roads lined with chain stores, junk food restaurants, used tire depots, and check-cashing centers. Like in Yuma, Arizona, there was no real center, just endless sprawl. I was kidding myself to think that I could experience the "real" Texas by traveling so quickly instead of befriending actual Texans. The thing that all travelers want—authenticity—will always just escape them because of the speed at which they have to travel and the shallowness of their approach, and even if I were to stay in a state for many months, I could only upgrade my tourist label to that of a rootless "transplant."

I went to a supermarket in Waco to stock up on items for my mainly salad, bread, and peanut diet. I placed the grocery items in the trunk of my car and got into the driver's seat. This was the point where I would normally press the start button, but I couldn't lift my arm. I couldn't move at all. I sat still for some time and stared off into the distance with the sound of a hundred grackles in the background making their distinct screeching calls. Could I even finish this trip? I still had seven more lectures and thousands of miles to go.

If doubts were entering my head about completing the trip, stemming mostly from fatigue, couldn't my spiritual doubts be caused by fatigue as well? I didn't see why not. The demons knew I was exhausted. They were bombarding me with everything they had, knowing it would shake me that much more than if my mind was at rest. I wanted to write off all the spiritual doubts due to my physical condition, but what if in the future I faced war, imprisonment, plague, or famine? Would the doubts be even stronger, and would I be at risk of losing my faith and even my soul? What's the point of faith if it will be too weak to serve you in tough times? I had to work with the doubts now, address them while I was weak, so that when I was weak again in the future I would know what to do.

I've seen Christians murmur against God in times of crisis instead of looking to Him for help. If you have faith only when things are good, that is not faith. If you look favorably upon God only when you are feeling comfortable and secure, that is not faith. My faith must be preserved when the going gets tough, ten times tougher than what I was experiencing, which was why I had to continue the trip. I had to work through the doubts. I had to lift my arm and push the start button. Either I finished it all, with my faith intact, or I collapsed outright and begged God not to forsake me, but even if I collapsed in the next few weeks, I would not come close to duplicating the worst of what is to come for us in the world.

After Waco, I drove to Fredericksburg, a town to the west of Austin that was founded by German settlers in the late 1800s. It had perfectly preserved its European-style architecture and heritage as shown by the numerous German flags flying on the main street in front of shops that had words in German. I overheard a man in a pickup truck talking to another man in a Southern accent about local politics. I watched two men at a construction site laying concrete. I listened to a farmer in a dusty cap ask a bat expert at the Old Tunnel State Park about controlling the insect population in his yard. And I sat on the patio of my inn at night watching a dozen different types of trucks slowly drive by. If I really tried, I could convince myself that, for a few brief moments, I knew Texas.

Austin was next. Before the event dinner, I walked through downtown to get a feel for the city. It didn't take me long to see a collection of homeless tents under an overpass. Next to a tent, for the first time in my trip, I saw a giant pile of feces. I could understand being down and out, but why defecate right next to where you live? Then I wondered: if the defecator were to suddenly run out of the tent and ask me for help, would I help him? Could I see him as a man deserving of help? Maybe he was mentally ill and didn't know where he should use a toilet. Or maybe it would just be better to give money to a church charity, and let them make the call for me, since I was having trouble making it myself.

A man in his sixties came to the dinner, along with three others. He had a serious heart condition and was about to undergo open-chest surgery. He told me about his plan to go to Ukraine to marry a woman of child-bearing age to start a family.

"Do you speak Russian?" I asked.

"Only a little," he replied. I didn't get the feeling that he understood Ukrainian culture. How could I break it to him that his goal was unreasonable?

"This will be tough, very tough," I said. "Girls in Ukraine have a lot of options now. Foreign men from all over the world are going there, all trying to get the same thing that you want."

"I know of stories of men who have done it. After I heal from my heart surgery, I'm going back to try."

He had made up his mind. I would not interfere. Many people had tried to convince me of my past foolishness, but they had all failed. If anything, they had made me more determined, because my ego wanted to prove them wrong. As I had learned the hard way, so might he.

After dinner, I went for a walk with the guys on Sixth Street, the hub of Austin's nightlife. Police had closed down car traffic to allow for more partying on the street. Numerous homeless men were begging for money, and sometimes the intoxicated party-goers interacted with them in a jovial manner. Tattoos were common, along with obesity and green hair. Profanity was uttered without restraint. One particular block of the area catered to homosexuals, with various signs and stickers stating "Hate Has No Place Here" and that all "hate crimes" would be reported. I didn't need to be reminded that degeneracy and homelessness go hand in hand. Where you see tents, you also see unapologetic sodomites and fornicators. Where you see feces, you also see young people with careers getting drunk. Where you see cardboard signs held by the homeless at traffic lights, you also see college-educated singles looking for a dose of pleasure.

The next day, I held the lecture in an uptown hotel. During the Q&A, I was asked an abundance of spiritual questions. I gave answers that elicited supportive reactions from many of the Orthodox Christians in the audience. I couldn't help but feel a bit proud that my spiritual knowledge was growing so quickly, and just the week before, a lifelong Catholic had said he was impressed with what I had learned in only seven months. I tried not to let the compliments go to my head, but it was impossible not to absorb them in some way. I started to wonder whether I was somehow "special"—whether God had given me extra gifts.

Afterwards, I talked to many of the guests individually. One of them wore a military camouflage outfit. He said he had fought in Iraq for three years and "seen a lot." He then handed me a large copper coin. On one side of the coin was a skull and the text "*Memento mori*," a Latin phrase that translates as "Remember death." I thanked him for the gift and put it in my back pocket.

A married couple handed me a small knitted ring with a coat button attached. "Our daughter made this for your tarantula, Tom. It's a watch." In my travelogue, I had shown a plush tarantula that I bought in Carlsbad Caverns. The young girl figured that my tarantula needed a watch and knitted a little sleeve with a button serving as its watch face. I made sure to feature Tom's watch in future videos so she could see her craftwork.

There was a blonde woman who came to my event alone. She was pretty and had a bubbly demeanor. During the meet-and-greet I had kept a safe distance from her, not wanting to be tempted. Towards the very end, I entered a conversation with her and two other men. The topic of cancer came up and one of the men mentioned that he knew someone who had a terminal case. The blonde woman then blurted out, "*Memento mori*." I jerked my head towards her. I squinted my eyes and stared at her for several seconds. She had not seen the coin that I received an hour before. She could not have possibly heard the private conversation I had with the veteran, and I hadn't seen them talking to each other. Why had she used this exact phrase? I didn't remember ever hearing the phrase used before in conversation, and now I had heard it twice on the same day, in the same room, from two individuals who were strangers to each other.

The blonde asked me to take a picture with her. I put my arm around her and smiled. She was rather thin, with the type of body I preferred, at least in my old days. Three weeks ago, I would have quickly entered a state of arousal, but this time around, I didn't have to expend much willpower to resist lustful thoughts, even though she was more attractive than the woman who had tempted me in San Francisco. When walking out of the conference room, she invited me to go to the hotel bar to drink with a few other guests. I politely declined.

Later that night, I thought further about the phrase *memento mori*. I stared at the copper coin. I simply could not believe that hearing this message twice in one day was a coincidence. With God in charge of the universe, could there even be such a thing as a coincidence? It could potentially be a message from the demons, but *memento mori* was often used in early Christianity to denote the fleeting nature of this world, a reminder to use the time we have here wisely. I ruled out demonic influence. So this must be a message from God. Did my behavior need to be corrected in some way? Was He warning me about something? I wracked my brain all night but couldn't figure it out.

On Sunday, I went to St. John Orthodox Church after receiving an invite from a man who had come to my lecture. I don't know whether I was tired or moody, but I was quick to judge the church. The inner room had the feel of a library. The priest was a boomer. There were off-notes in the singing. I concluded that this church was obviously not as good as the others I had been to.

Towards the end of the Liturgy, my eyes fixated on the large icon of Jesus Christ to the right of the altar. I quickly had the feeling that Jesus was looking directly at me. I stared at the icon for what seemed like minutes, and then two words popped into my head: *memento mori*. Tears began to well in my eyes as memories flashed before me: getting into an argument with a monk, being overly pleased with myself at answering spiritual questions, enjoying compliments about my faith, and judging different styles of Christian worship, sometimes harshly. I continued to stare at Jesus, no longer even hearing the words of the Liturgy, and was finally able to decode the message I had received the night before through the copper coin and the pretty woman: *Remember that you will die in this world. Do not become full of pride.* It was my pride. The spiritual doubts had come because I was developing pride. The problem was self-inflicted.

During the fellowship, I met several men who knew of my work. One was about my age and had gotten into game at nearly the same time I did, but had failed miserably at it. He could hardly get dates, and the whole sleeping around thing just hadn't come naturally to him. Without a woman, and without the means to get one, he turned to God while still in his mid-twenties, at the age when my success at pickup had been on the upswing. Within two years, he had met his wife and went on to have five children with her. While I was happy for him, I couldn't help but feel sorry for myself. If only I had been bad at game! It was my success at fornication that had kept me in it for so long. Otherwise I might have turned to Christ sooner. Perhaps I would have had a daughter who knitted little things for our stuffed animals or who drew crayon pictures of us holding hands under a happy sun. Instead, I had wished for sin and I had got it.

18

Megachurch

I drove to San Antonio, where the Tex meets the Mex, or more like where the Mex is taking over the Tex. The Hispanics I saw spoke fluent English, suggesting that they were not new arrivals.

A trend I have noticed over the years is mothers dressing their young daughters in inappropriate clothing. If a mother wears yoga pants all day because "it's comfortable," she's going to dress her daughter similarly. In a San Antonio supermarket called HEB, there were several cases of mothers doing this. I have absolutely no desire to know the shape of a pre-pubescent girl's body, so why were there mothers putting this on display? During a time when the normalization of pedophilia does appear to be a real phenomenon, I was disturbed that mothers, whose main job is to protect their children, were doing the opposite.

I ate a dinner of supermarket sushi in my hotel room and went to bed. Two hours later, I woke up scratching my stomach and arm. I looked in the mirror and could see huge red welts. Could this be bed bugs? Bed bugs wouldn't be very successful at survival if you could feel the effects of their bites so quickly, and it didn't look like my rash of suspected scabies, which I still had on my thighs. Was it from a fire ant? A real tarantula? Then I remembered my sushi dinner. I'm not allergic to tuna, but perhaps it had been prepared on a surface with other exotic foods. Yet another road mystery. I took allergy medicine and went back to bed. I was barely limping along, so even small blows like this were disheartening.

San Antonio has several missions that were started by Catholic Spaniards in the eighteenth century, the most famous being the Alamo. The purpose of the missions, which served as a self-encapsulated village with a church, was to spread Christianity, at least from the perspective of the Catholic priests.

I visited one of the missions called San Jose. I toured the large church where the natives and Catholics had worshipped together and walked alongside the long stone wall that had protected them from raids and other threats. I asked myself whether the missionary work had saved souls that would otherwise have been condemned to hell. The Orthodox Church does teach that it's possible to go to Heaven even if you haven't heard the Gospel, assuming you follow your God-given conscience, but it seems obvious to me that the path to Heaven is a lot easier if you hear the Gospel directly. I must conclude that missionary work of the Catholic sort, while initially difficult to adapt for the natives, ultimately saved more souls than it condemned. I can't help but think of the same question when it comes to slavery in the United States. Black slavery is looked upon as one of the saddest stories in human history, but many slaves took up Christianity and were saved because of it, and their descendants continue to worship Christ exuberantly in modern America. How many black people would not have been saved if they stayed in Africa and adopted various voodoo, shamanistic, or cannibalistic practices? Was the benefit of eternal salvation for a few worth the many who had been chained as slaves? I don't know, but I do know that God's plan is perfectly made to save as many souls as possible without removing our free will and forcing us to be His slaves.

After San Jose, I visited downtown San Antonio. The streets were free of trash and garbage, a stark contrast to Austin. I walked by the Alamo and then went down some stairs to the River Walk, a canal lined with shops and restaurants. I didn't need to read an architectural book to know that the Spaniards had created this—the distinguished stone construction and romantic winding paths are things you simply don't see created by Americans. One can think of the failings of the Europeans, but city planning is not one of them, and I suspect that is because they've had to work with limited land space. Americans had no constraints, so they'd just plop down some buildings in a new town, build outwards before building upwards, construct a subway, jam in some bike lanes, and call it a day. It hasn't worked, because any American city with over one million people is inherently unlivable. Contrast this to European cities, even ones in Eastern Europe that were dominated by communism for 50 years. They are pleasant, if not beautiful—an extension of nature itself. I lived in the Polish city of Poznań for five years without a car and never experienced urban frustration, but the same cannot be said about a city in America of the same size. Americans have to live with design problems created by people whose bones long ago faded to dust.

While on the River Walk, I passed an elderly man who was begging for money. His back was bent and he seemed genuinely homeless. When I was in Holy Cross Monastery, I told a monk that I didn't like giving money directly to homeless people because they would just use it to buy alcohol or drugs. He suggested I give them a gift card instead.

I reached into my pocket and found a $10 McDonald's gift card I had bought a couple of states over for this very purpose. I approached the homeless man and said, "I have a gift card for $10 at McDonald's."

"Ten dollars?"

"Yes."

He reached out his hand and took the card.

I know McDonald's is not exactly healthy food, but the gambit seemed a good compromise of helping someone in need while knowing he wouldn't spend it on booze. Of course, he could always attempt to sell the gift card for a lesser amount in cash, but I imagined no one would trust him that the card had value.

The next day I left San Antonio for Houston. I made a stop in a highway gas station to use the bathroom. As I parked my car, a black man and woman with their child walked past me. I used the bathroom, came back out, and saw the black man pushing their compact SUV towards the end of the gas station. Their rear left tire was flat. What help could I give them with my sports car? I had no experience with changing tires and definitely couldn't tow them. I was ready to get back on the highway, but something told me to offer help. Maybe they just needed to use a cell phone.

I pulled up next to them. A woman was in the driver's seat. "Do you need any help?" I asked.

"What?" she replied brusquely.

"Do you need any help?"

Her face relaxed. "We're trying to get up there." She pointed to a small hill that led to a motel then glanced at my car. "I don't want to mess up your nice car with a push."

The hill was somewhat steep. Trying to push it with my car, which had an angular front bumper, would likely end in disaster. I said, "I can get out of my car and help you try to push it up."

"Thanks, but we'll just wait for someone who has a truck to help." I wished them luck and drove off.

The fact that I had debated whether or not to help, even under God's grace, meant the old me would not have offered to help them. What benefit would it have given me? It would have taken time and perhaps some of my resources. The exception would have been if the driver was an attractive woman and there was at least a 1% prospect of sleeping with her.

In the past several weeks, for the first time in my life, I had felt a desire to treat others with excessive kindness. I was sure this could lead to temptation if I took things too far and got pleasure from it, or if I helped others just so I could broadcast it and feel proud, so I made sure not to tell anyone about the

McDonald's gift card or the black family. I even debated not including the anecdotes here, but in the end decided that it was useful to show how God can change a man from the inside out.

I received a second wind upon arriving in Houston. I can't say it's a beautiful city, and it resembled a gigantic strip mall more than anything else, but at least it wasn't California.

At the dinner event, the four guests were livelier than usual and brought up many questions that kept us engaged for several hours. There was one man, who, based on what he said about his business and material life goals, I surmised was living in accordance with his ego. My speech included a part where I remarked how a man was enslaved to his ego if he asked me this question: "Roosh, how many girls have you been with?" Sure enough, this man asked that question. I smirked and said, "You have unwittingly become a participant in my speech tomorrow." Then a thought immediately came to mind: "He won't come tomorrow." He seemed to have missed my conversion, and became quiet when the dinner conversation turned to spiritual matters. If Satan is leading you by the nose to a state of material excess, he will ensure that you flee from anyone who stands against that. I had already seen it in my forum, where the most diehard fornicators became infuriated when I changed the rules to forbid the discussion of sexual sin. The next day, sure enough, the businessman did not come to the lecture, and I doubt he could have accurately explained to himself why.

There was another man at the dinner whose mother had died a year prior. When it happened, he had felt unbridled wrath. He had wanted to join the military and kill the enemies of America, but before he could do so, he came to God. As grace entered him, the wrath had subsided. How else could it have subsided? A heavy loss cannot be endured without God, only managed through intoxication, fornication, despair, or anger. You look to whatever was giving you happiness or solace before your loss and then turn the dial up to its maximum setting to erase the pain. Not only does the pain remain, masked by your amplification of worldly pursuits, but you soon have to deal with the repercussions from a new batch of sins. It will be that much harder to recover from the inevitable crash.

The Houston lecture proceeded without issue. The Q&A was almost entirely devoted to spiritual matters, thanks to the large proportion of practicing Christians in the audience, mostly Catholic. I was humbler than I had been the previous week when discussing other denominations and made it abundantly clear that I was a spiritual baby. When one man told me details of his intimate relationship with a single mother, I told him that I could not advise him to stay or leave, because I had no foreknowledge whether or not God had sent that woman to him to aid in his salvation, or vice versa.

At the end of the event, a Baptist approached me and said, "Roosh, can I lay my hands upon you and pray?"

"Do I have to do anything?" I asked nervously.

"No, nothing."

I consented. He faced me and squeezed my upper arms. He asked God to help me resist temptation and continue working through me to lead others to salvation. I thanked him for his prayer and then a Catholic man asked whether I could pray for his family, who, unlike him, had not yet come to Christ. Then I remembered the novice I had met in St. Herman's Monastery who carried around a notepad to write down the names of those for whom he should pray. I felt that it was now time for me to start praying for others.

There was an Armenian church in Houston, but I skipped it to attend Joel Osteen's Lakewood megachurch. I felt uneasy about going because I knew my pride could be involved—I wanted to identify all the wrong things about Joel and his church so that I could share them with others, but I convinced myself that I was going with an "open mind," as if I would convert to Osteen's flavor of Christianity if it impressed me enough.

Arriving at the church felt like attending a sporting event due to the large number of parking attendants directing the slow-moving traffic. I walked inside the church, which used to be an arena for the Houston basketball team, and was warmly greeted by two ushers. Another usher directed me to the nosebleed section. I shook hands with my seatmate, a young black man, and enjoyed the opening act, a woman in a leather jacket singing about Jesus. She was an exceptional singer, but the music was too loud, as if I were at a concert. If God had wanted to speak to me during her singing, I wouldn't have heard Him.

Members of the audience shouted "Amen" during the parts of the service they liked. Some would launch out of their seats and raise their hands with palms facing the sky to—I assume—receive the Holy Spirit. Besides the occasional cases of inappropriately dressed women, which you can also find in an Orthodox church, I genuinely felt that these people were practicing Christians.

The church itself, however, did not indicate that it was Christian. There were no crosses, icons, or paintings depicting Jesus. There was no imagery depicting scenes from the Bible. The only pictures were of Joel and his wife. If an alien attended the service, it would assume that Joel was god and people came to the gigantic building to worship him. If someone wanted to create a Holy Altar in a hurry, they could find more useful items in my travel bag (two icons and two crosses) than in Joel's stadium.

After a series of songs, Joel came on the stage and delivered an impromptu prayer. I was so far from him that I had to watch on the Jumbotron screen. He asked God to bless everyone in the stadium and those watching from home. Then the pitch came. Joel had a problem: he needed more money. You see, his program was currently shown on 20 television markets, but now there was an opportunity to be on 40 markets, and they wouldn't put him on in the dead of night like usual but right after the nightly news. He would go on during primetime! He had already paid $4 million to take advantage of this opportunity, but he needed $10 million more.

Surely the crowd would be turned off by him discussing money matters before the sermon, on the Lord's Day no less, but they clapped loudly, cheering him on. Joel exclaimed that his opportunity was their own, because if he was able to expand his reach and save more people through television, God would bless the entire congregation with good health and financial stability. But those blessings could come only if they donated more by "stretching your faith," as Joel put it, a euphemism for "stretching your wallet." His wife and two other speakers came on to stress how they must take advantage of the television opportunity, because it was a way for everyone to get closer to God. The parishioners agreed. When dozens of large plastic buckets circulated throughout the stadium, they gave generously indeed.

I thought of the man who hadn't attended my speech the previous day because he was too enslaved to his ego to hear about God, obsessed over numbers concerning sales and money, and here was the leader of one of the biggest churches in America obsessing over numbers concerning TV viewership and money. Instead of focusing on his existing congregation, and ensuring the flock in the stadium was on the path to salvation, Joel wanted to save those to whom he would never minister directly. Or maybe I was wrong. Was it possible that if people watched Joel on television and bought his books, they would have a higher chance of being saved than if they did not? Couldn't his seeming praise of God lead people to God? As if Joel had sensed my question, the Jumbotron displayed recorded testimonials of individuals who had accidentally tuned into Joel's TV program at three in the morning and been delivered from bad health or what have you through Joel's inspirational preaching. In theory, I would say yes, it is certainly possible to be saved by watching TV, as God can save people in any way He wishes, but the god that Joel talks about wants you to be "not mediocre" and focused on having a successful life like Joel with material health and abundance. Is being a materialistic Christian, firmly attached to the world, enough to save your soul? At the risk of elevating my pride, I'll just have to not answer that question.

By the time of Joel's final sermon, I gathered that the service was aimed at keeping me in an excited, happy state. Two or three gloomy moments of the show were expertly managed to make the audience briefly feel sad, only to be lifted back up again into hope and positivity, in a more exuberant state than they had been before. Then the grand finale arrived. Joel got back on stage. The topic of his sermon was "Outlast the opposition." When the going gets tough, he said, hold onto your faith and just hang in there, because things will turn around and doors will open again. He threw in a few Bible quotes from the Old Testament to justify what he was saying, but the quotes were so truncated that all context was lost.

Joel reiterated how maintaining the faith would open the doors to material blessings in this world. He said that when he had started pastoring, he felt insecure and scared and... the face on the Jumbotron was suddenly enveloped in sorrow. He turned his back on the congregation and began sobbing. The crowd stood up and cheered him on, encouraging him to continue. "You can do it, Joel!" If he had been crying about the loss of a family member, I could understand his sobbing, but fear of public speaking? Color me skeptical. After a minute, he turned around. His face was pink and wet. He mentioned that he never knew when the tears would come, and while I am the first to confirm that, I had a feeling he knew that the tears would come at the absolute climax of his sermon.

There was no doubt that his sermon had been motivational. It even made me feel good in the moment, that I could conquer any difficulty, but it had no meat for me to grab onto, no spiritual weapon for when I was tempted by the demons, when I had difficulty praying, or when I felt that God had gone quiet on me.

He provided no lessons from the Church Fathers or saints. It was true that the words "God" and "Jesus" had come out of his mouth dozens of times, but who was God? Who was Jesus? According to Joel, they were inside a vending machine that he owned. Insert money, push the code for the holy candy bar you want, and you will receive a snack that makes you feel happy and blessed. The congregation didn't seem to mind Joel's style of vending machine Christianity. For him to accomplish his immense size and reach, they have put many millions into his coin slot, and will certainly give many millions more. Joel's trick was to link his commercial success to their personal lives—if Joel was doing well, so would they.

Thirty minutes after Joel's sermon, after enduring a traffic nightmare to get out of the stadium parking lot, my emotional high faded. I wished I had gone to the Armenian church instead.

19

Race

I left Houston on Monday and had to be in Miami in three and a half days, a distance of 1,200 miles, in addition to whatever sightseeing I could scrounge. Normally, I would welcome the challenge, but this late in the tour I just wanted to get it over with already.

My first stop was in Lafayette, Louisiana. I parked my car and a young woman who happened to be walking by gave me a big smile. I entered a small diner and ordered the local favorite, a fried shrimp po' boy sandwich. The female clerk was particularly chatty and friendly. In only a few minutes, the women in Louisiana had been nicer to me than what I had experienced in three weeks in Texas.

Late that night, I rolled into the French Quarter of New Orleans. I was struck by the beautiful architecture that persisted for several blocks. Many buildings had spacious balconies on multiple floors. For a second, I could imagine that I was walking in a Western European city. If something is beautiful for the sake of beauty alone, that is considered a waste in America. Only traditional Europeans could construct an abomination to capitalistic utility.

After checking in to my hotel, I walked to Bourbon Street. The wonderful architecture remained, but it was taken over by cheesy bars, strip clubs, junk food shops, and the obnoxious flashing lights that promoted them. It was only Monday but the street was full of partygoers wearing beads and holding alcoholic beverages in oversized plastic containers. People even older than me staggered drunk, unable to control their faculties. Others in various states of intoxication huddled in doorways. The Hustler strip club—I didn't even know there was such a thing—posted semi-nude magazine covers on its storefront for everyone to see. Many could argue that Bourbon Street partying is a "tradition," but it says a lot that we take the most beautiful architecture in the South, and perhaps in America, and turn it into a den of decadence.

A sense of disgust began to overwhelm me as I walked among the inebriated tourists and seedy underclass, because it reminded me that I used to seek this out with all my soul. I could easily have been among them searching for a lay or two. Everyone seemed so happy and entertained, debating with themselves which bar to hit next to continue their once-in-a-lifetime party experience. They eagerly chose Bourbon Street to be the bearer of their deliverance.

I left New Orleans and drove by Pass Christian, Mississippi, just so that I could say on video that I was a Christian passing through Pass Christian, and then entered Alabama. I drove through Mobile and had lunch in Fairhope. I expected hillbillies and rednecks to approach me aggressively and ask whether I was an A-rab or something, but instead I found yuppies and women in yoga pants. How could a Southern state like Alabama have what is commonly found up and down the East and West coasts?

Panama City, Florida was next. There were hardly any tourists around, a far cry from when I had visited with a friend in the spring of 2002, the year after I graduated university. The plan back then had been to go as a "wiser" man better able to finagle sex with numerous girls. I did not sleep with a single girl on that trip. How much better off would I have been if I had given up then! But I was stubborn, and kept going until I had crafted a game system that fit my more cerebral nature. And then I had presented that system to the world, to false profits and glory, and there went 18 years of my life.

I wasn't too impressed driving down the western panhandle of Florida. It was rural, which I liked, but without the beauty of the Mountain West or the desert lands of the Southwest. It was an endless landscape of tall grass and plain trees. The culture appeared neither Southern nor Eastern but a hybrid that I had not encountered before. The people were rather loose in their demeanor, to the point of insolence, and as much as I would hate to use the word "uneducated," that was what I perceived.

I stopped in Saint Petersburg. On the surface, it was a perfect city—manicured, organized, clean, quiet, and safe. It felt more suburban than urban. I could even recommend that you retire there, like the Jewish elderly do, but despite all its benefits, would this city, like so many others that seemed ideal on the surface, bring me closer to God or take me away from Him? It would take far more than a two-hour stay to find out.

Four hours later and I was in Miami, a city I had originally been to in 2001 during my senior year in university, one year before the failure in Panama City. The goal of the trip had been to lose my virginity. I failed in that, too, but I did my first cold approach on a girl waiting in line outside a club. She would be the first of many thousands of girls I would talk to.

I held the Miami dinner in a quiet South Beach restaurant. Three white men joined me. One was a practicing Christian while the other two were not. The latter two saw the usefulness of Christianity when applied to society, and wanted to receive the benefits of living in that society, but did not want to submit to Christ themselves. I was reminded of women who want to feel "spiritual" by doing things like yoga or meditation without ever having to hear a "no" from God, the source of all good.

During the dinner, I couldn't help but notice three beautiful women at the bar. They appeared Eastern European, probably Russian, and seemed to know many of the staff.

"It doesn't look like they are here for love," I jokingly told the guys.

"They are probably working," one said, suggesting that they were prostitutes. I had that suspicion, too. They would surely sleep with a guy for "free" if he was attractive enough, but if the price was right, the nature of the interaction could change. From the perspective of a secular woman living in Miami, she might even find it rational to monetize her body until the "right" man came along, but sins have a way of blocking out the good, and it wouldn't take many years before the beautiful women asked, "Where are all the good men?" At the same time, the men who prowled the bars for years would ask, "Where are all the good women?" Certainly not in restaurants and hotels, in bars and clubs, or on sugar daddy websites. You can't roll in the mud for years and expect not to repel those who haven't.

Later in the night, the topic of race came up. One man, Bobby, said that he preferred to live next to people of his race, a fair statement. I posed a hypothetical scenario to him. "You have a choice to live next to one of two families. The first family is Mexican. They hardly speak English but are devoutly Catholic and place religious statues in their front yard. Ten of them will live in the house, which means many work trucks leaving at six in the morning. The second 'family' is white, but they are homosexual. Two men live there and throw all sorts of sex parties, and they have a huge gay pride flag outside. Which would you rather live near?"

"The white gays," he said without hesitation.

"Really? Even though you know the evil that is taking place? You would let your kids feel comfortable playing around that house?"

"Yes, because I think race should be at the top."

"I can't agree. God is at the top."

"What is the name of your church?" he asked.

"Orthodox."

"Before the word Orthodox."

"Armenian."

"Exactly!"

"But we don't worship Armenia in the church, and besides, a person of any race can join. Even you can join if you want." I remembered a Mexican man who was an acolyte in the Armenian church I had visited in Dallas.

"Race comes first, and then God."

"I'm pretty sure that is not in the Bible."

He replied that Bible translations were not 100% accurate, which was my cue to bow out of the debate.

We walked around South Beach. The women were perhaps the most beautiful I had seen in the United States, perhaps because a substantial number of them came from South America and Eastern Europe. Numerous exotic cars were on the road, including Bentleys. In these parts, a BMW might as well be on a tier right above poverty. One man was walking with a Hispanic woman whose minuscule dress left nothing to the imagination, looking more like lingerie than streetwear, yet even if you did land such a woman in Miami, the high standard of beauty all around wouldn't make you feel secure in your choice, particularly if you were trying to sate your lust. And if your intention was to establish a family with the Hispanic woman in the minidress or the Russian women in the restaurant, you would feel paranoid about her being desired by so many other men who have the financial means, gym bodies, and Casanova banter to at least get their foot in the door. I don't see how you can win in such a town.

I noticed another worldly benefit of Miami: men were dating up. If a man was good-looking, he was dating a good-looking woman, unlike most other parts of the country where men often had to date down, but this benefit has a downside. You will enjoy dating beautiful women for a time, screening them mostly for their appearance instead of their faith and values, and then many years later, you will realize that all you've done is sleep with beautiful women. Measuring your dating success on beauty alone will lead to failure. It satisfies you just enough to close your eyes to the type of woman you should really be with. Look at the people who are good at dating—and I include myself in this category—and you are sure to find someone who doesn't have any children, or maybe one child out of wedlock. Ironically, those who are bad at dating tend to hang on to the first decent match that comes along, without much of an urge to land someone who is "better."

Could it be that I'm simply jealous of men who are dating up? I'm not rich, and no longer possess the will or desire to pursue superficially beautiful women, so it could just be sour grapes. I can't cut it in a materialistic game where you will never reach the top no matter how hard you try, and any increase you experience will immediately be met with the desire for further increases. Thinking that I can find contentment, peace, and everlasting life with God must be a coping mechanism instead of striving to win in business, fame, and sex. That wouldn't be a bad argument if I hadn't been in that world for two decades, and while I wasn't a "big fish" in the United States, I did find smaller European cities where I was exotic enough to be in demand. I look back at my sexual peak, in 2011, when I slept with a lot of European women in their prime, and instead of today feeling like a winner, I feel disgusted. I look back at all the prideful things I did to get in the news in multiple countries, and feel ashamed. So no, I would say that it's not jealousy. Let the worldly people have their worldly things. I won't get in their way, but when they fail at the game they are playing, I will be more than happy to share with them the reasons why, and where they have to turn to next.

On the day of my Miami speech, Kanye West released an album called *Jesus Is King*. I gave it a listen. The music was a bit too modern for my taste, but the song *God Is* caught my attention, where he mentioned how he couldn't keep quiet about how God had saved him. I felt the same. I had been graced by God and embarked on a nationwide trip to tell everybody what had happened, grateful for His power to lift me from the pit of darkness. I watched a few interviews of Kanye promoting the album, and he couldn't help but praise Christ at every opportunity. I had been trying to manage how I presented my conversion to the public so they wouldn't be shocked, but maybe they needed to be shocked. Maybe they needed to see how God could quickly change a man.

At the beginning of my speech in Miami, the audience was the coldest yet. They didn't laugh at my jokes, like the guests in other cities, but after half an hour, they began to warm up and I received the expected responses. I had long ago learned simply to barrel through regardless of the audience's reaction.

After the speech was over, I talked to a woman who came with her boyfriend. She had been praying to God for some time, but felt like she wasn't receiving anything back.

"Are you currently intimate with your boyfriend?" I asked.

"Yes, for two years."

"I have read that God may withhold grace if you are active in sin, especially if you know what you're doing is sin. I can't tell you for sure, but I've encountered the idea multiple times. If this is something you want to pursue, you can tell your boyfriend that Roosh said, 'We can't have sex anymore until marriage.'"

She laughed and said, "We did plan on getting married within a few months."

"So then abstaining won't be that difficult. It may be worth a try, but you can talk to your boyfriend about it."

I spoke to another woman who had moved to Miami to find a husband. Based on what I had seen of Miami so far, I was extremely skeptical of her plan, and told her that I didn't think it would work. I assumed that she had no spiritual life, but it turned out that she was quite devout. I reminded myself that I was still too spiritually immature to guide others, especially based on a short conversation where I discovered only a tiny slice of their lives.

An Armenian man came to my speech and we agreed to attend a service the next day at the Armenian church north of Miami. I arrived there before Narek and took my seat in a front pew. We were both last to receive communion.

After the Liturgy, we went to a pancake house. As it was now the end of October, the restaurant had a Halloween theme. Most of the staff dressed up in costumes that leaned towards the gory end of the spectrum. When it was time to order our meals, I looked up at our waitress and noticed she was wearing a pentagram around her neck. Initially, I reasoned that she had just picked it from a store shelf as part of her costume and was not satanic. Personally, I would be extra diligent not to wear any satanic symbol—it simply couldn't happen that I would accidentally put one on just for the sake of having a fun costume. I proceeded to place my order, but my conscience wouldn't stop bothering me. I didn't want someone who was proud to wear a pentagram serving me food. God had given me a new conscience when he graced me. To stay out of trouble, all I have to do is listen to it, even if it causes me discomfort or inconvenience.

20

Exorcism

I was close to Everglades National Park but had no interest in visiting a swamp and being devoured by mosquitos. Instead, I took a half-hour airboat ride on a swampy-enough river near Miami to gawk at the occasional alligator and turtle. A handful of other tourists were on the boat with me, mostly from Europe, including a young Russian couple. The female was rather attractive and sat right in front of me wearing a spaghetti-strap top. As the boat ride progressed, her right strap started to come undone. She was practically undressing in front of me. I couldn't even take a boat ride in a swamp without being tempted in some way, and if you think that I'm too weak when it comes to matters of the flesh, you are absolutely correct. A man doesn't dive headfirst into fornication as I did if he is strong in that particular area. Temptations unrelated to women will surely come, but at least they won't remind me of my past failures.

I made it up to Cocoa Beach near Cape Canaveral, often called the Space Coast. To relax, I rented a kayak on Banana River. The river was wide like a lake and had few places to stop, so I did more exercising than relaxing. I took my paddle strokes seriously, shouting "dig" each time the end of the paddle went in the water, and at the end when I was getting closer to shore, I changed the "dig" to "glory," as in "glory to God."

Afterwards, I went to the beach. I stood in the water at waist height and stared at the waves. Sometimes, I'd go under them, sometimes over, and if the wave was big enough, I'd try to catch it with my body. After an hour of this, I got tired. The waves would never stop. I imagined at that moment if I declared myself superior to the waves. I could defeat the waves and outlast them! They must conform to me! Obviously, that would make me delusional. I wasn't more powerful than the ocean, and if I didn't respect its power, I would find myself at its bottom. And yet, at the height of my life of sin, that was exactly what I had been doing. I had exclaimed to God that he was not my God, that I was stronger than Him and could figure things out using my intellect and power. I could outlast all the waves of this world and come out the victor. Rebelling against water is futile, and that's only water. Rebelling against God, my Creator, had been the height of insanity. I had legitimately been mentally ill, swallowed whole by pride and arrogance to think I could go swimming in the vast ocean without Him and survive. How loving God must be to have stayed with me despite my error, to make me whole again as if I had just been born.

†

I drove to Orlando on Halloween and met Jay Dyer for dinner. Jay has a large internet presence that focuses on Orthodox theology and world politics. I was first introduced to his talks on esotericism in Hollywood, and since we were both minor "internet celebs," it was only natural that we should meet.

"Most of the Protestants and Catholics were corrupted starting in the 1960s," he said. "Now they are working on doing the same to the Orthodox Churches."

"How do they corrupt them?"

"They start in the seminaries. The government and NGOs give them a ton of money in exchange for installing specific priests as teachers. These priests are gay and share false teachings. The corruption spreads from them to the new priests, who become installed in the parishes, and then on to the parishioners. John Courtney Murray shared how they did that to the Catholic Church in the book *The American Proposition.*"

"Which branch of Orthodoxy are they doing that to now?" I asked.

"The Greek Orthodox Church. There are many suspected gay priests in leadership positions. The goal is to move things more ecumenical, to a one-world type of faith that is watered down and doesn't lead to salvation."

"And you believe the CIA is behind this?"

"Yes, they are at the center."

"And they also corrupt us through other institutions?"

"Correct."

"So their goal is just to put people in a weakened state so that they can be easily steered, led, and controlled. I understand that, but at the same time I don't."

"Because you're not a psychopath," he replied. "You don't want to enslave people."

"But how about the men at the bottom of the plan, like a CIA field agent. He must think he's serving the country. Or maybe he's just doing it for the steady paycheck."

"The higher you go, the more sinister it gets."

"It's like that meme where the fat American is chasing after the cheeseburger on a string held by someone behind him, who is chasing after another reward held by someone behind him, and on and on it goes until the last person in control is actually an alien."

"But it's really Satan."

"So Satan is doing all of this to spite God. By having a soul condemned for eternity, he feels powerful, like a god, and there has to be a group of human beings who are in direct communion with Satan. What are they getting out of it? I imagine they are beyond the stage of accumulating only wealth or pleasure."

"Eternal life in this world," Jay answered. "They are transhumanists. They want to live forever, to merge with technology."

"And then if you go further down the ladder from them, the motivation could just be the material benefits of money, or sex with teenagers or children."

"This is why homosexuals are elevated to the top of movements. They are easily controlled because they are a slave to their lusts, so their handlers provide them with their desires as long as they remain a loyal soldier."

We finished dinner and went outside for a walk. The streets were filled with revelers in Halloween costumes. Women had insisted on adding "sexy" to their costumes. Sexy prison inmate. Sexy cat. Sexy nun. Or just a sexy outfit. The men's outfits were less sexy, unless the man had big muscles, in which case he would be dressed up as a lifeguard or Tarzan. With hundreds of people out, partying and drinking, it felt like an open-air brothel. Lust was in the air, and in the case of costumes outfitted with occult symbols or darkened angel wings, so was evil.

Jay and I found a quiet place to sit and resume our conversation. We agreed that most human phenomena that can be labeled a trend or norm are psychological operations to weaken and enslave us, with the ultimate aim of keeping us away from God. I had been a victim of the sexual liberation psyop. I had bought the lie that sleeping around and divorcing reproduction from sex would lead to happiness. If I had died while living that lie, I would have certainly lost my soul. Satan wins, I lose. But why would humans who are pushing degeneracy voluntarily serve the devil? Don't they know that, by following him, it must automatically be true that an all-loving God was above him? For the answer, we only have to look at one-third of the angels, who voluntarily chose to fall out of Heaven to follow Satan. Those angels worshipped right beside God, and then through their own free will, decided that they did not want to be a part of His plan any longer. So I shouldn't be surprised that a human being would make the same choice.

"What do you think of psychedelic drugs?" I asked. "I have

heard that they have figured out precise cocktails to speak with demons. Even normal people who take drugs like DMT see weird things like elves."

"Some kind of portal is opened. I believe those elves are demons."

"The elves seem almost polite. If they were demons, wouldn't they be angry or scary?"

"No, because Satan wants us to feel good," Jay replied. "He wants to give us pleasure wrapped in lies so that we forget about God. This is why those who see elves don't describe it as a negative experience, but then their outlook changes into something pantheistic or evolutionary based on vague notions of love—'We are all connected' and things like that. People who have those experiences never start preaching about following God's commandments, for instance."

"So the drug experience commits them to a form of one-world unity or globalism, which happens to be the same agenda as the oligarchs on top of our current society. What a coincidence that human rulers and the demons seem to have the exact same plan."

It's hard not to feel a measure of despair when you know what we're up against in this world, but is that the correct emotion? We're born into a fallen world, and surprise—it's fallen—and, as the Book of Revelation makes clear, it will get more evil until we reach the end of times. I wanted to ask Jay how to face such evil, but I already knew the answer.

"It seems like the best thing we could do," I started, "is turn to Christ. I can't think of any other way to spite Satan than to preserve our souls. And if we manage to save our soul then maybe we can help save a sibling, a parent, or a friend, but other than that, I don't think that defeating evil in this world," I pointed at the partygoers before us, "is part of God's plan for us. This life is a test, and if we follow Christ until the end, we pass. I get it, but it can all be hard to endure at times."

We continued to talk about politics and God. There was still much I had to learn, but I can safely say that, on that Halloween night, I had all the spiritual and secular information I needed for my salvation. If you locked me in a dungeon, I don't believe I'd be missing anything to save myself. Of course, I would continue to learn more about my faith, but after meeting with Jay, I lacked nothing intellectual that was blocking me from God. My spiritual foundation had been laid.

†

A young woman came to my Orlando dinner, along with three men. I was initially nervous when I saw Chloe's name because I thought it would be yet another sexual temptation, but she was modestly attired. She was interested in marriage and didn't want to date intimately.

"Guys don't approach me," she said.

"Generally, you don't want to be approached by strange men," I replied.

"But even in church the men never say anything to me."

"And you stick around for coffee hour after the service?"

"Yes, but still nothing. I would like a Christian man who is simply masculine and red-pilled, but I can't seem to find them. I'm not sure what to do."

If she had wanted to date and have casual sex, there would be unlimited options for her. All she'd have to do is upload a couple of sexy photos on Tinder, hit the bars on the weekend, and wait for men intoxicated on alcohol and lust to come pounding down her door for a sexual encounter. She would experience the illusion of having a multitude of men to choose from, but in reality she would encounter only one or two reasonable prospects a year who would get lost in the sea of men's photos, lewd text messages, and disingenuous pickup lines. By not wanting to use the apps and the bars, she was doing it the right way, and you'd think it would be easy for her in church, but the men there are too weak. Many churches in America give Christianity a bad name by preaching false concepts that amount to spiritual feminism. Men are taught to worship womankind (and Israel) as much as Jesus. They call themselves Christian while believing in the lies of the sexes and society. The men who attend these churches cannot properly protect and provide for their families because their worldview is based more on the egalitarianism of secular humanism than on the teachings of Christ.

Nevertheless, Chloe had more options than a man in her situation, and perhaps she had concealed from me how choosy she really was, but her short laundry list shouldn't be seen as unreasonable. For a woman planning to be a stay-at-home wife, she should be choosy. If she chooses the wrong man, she would be emotionally and financially miserable, because she would have given up a corporate career to dedicate her life to the family home. Even worse, the wrong man might put her salvation at risk. So if men want women to be feminine, stay-at-home mothers, they better have the skills, maturity, and masculinity to allow women to do just that, but most men refuse to wait until marriage to have sex, and actually prefer a woman to have a career to help with household finances, and then when they marry that type of woman, they blame all womankind for her inevitable rebellion, cheating, and demand for divorce.

For the longest time, I had thought that being a player was the definition of masculinity, but it was immature masculinity. It had been about simulating the behavior of a strong man to fulfill the desires of a half-grown man who had no self-control over his impulses due to a lack of faith. A reformed man who once fell for the tricks of casual sex can retain his masculine behavior in his dealings with women, but he must gain control of his pride and bodily impulses in a way that is required for the subsequent formation of a family under God's rule. At that point, a Christian woman will see both the material rewards and the spiritual rewards of being with such a man, and strive to be pleasing to him. Just as a woman will often adopt the hobbies and interests of a man she's attracted to, she will do the same for the Christian "alpha male provider" with whom she can create a family. But if this type of man is lacking in her community, she will simply take the path of least resistance and date endlessly to get cheap validation while dedicating herself to an office job.

Even if being a mature, masculine man doesn't get me a wife and lead to the creation of a family, I still have God. He will help me to bear the cross of remaining alone for the rest of my life. That would be impossible without God. To secure the sexual pleasure I would so desperately need, I would have to spend an hour a day in the gym, take steroids, get a hair transplant, inject my forehead creases with Botox, and travel to Southeast Asia, merely to have fleeting sexual encounters that won't save me in the end.

†

The Saturday lecture, my twentieth event, went off without a hitch. Delivering my speech, answering questions, and having small talk with the guests had become so automatic that I could do it for six or seven hours without having to think. Only three more events were left.

I found an Armenian church only 20 minutes away from my hotel. I woke up on Sunday morning, prayed, got dressed, and drove there only to realize that I was one hour early because I had forgotten to adjust my clock to account for daylight savings time. Instead of sitting in my car for an hour, I headed over to a nearby Starbucks where I could read a book.

I bought a bottle of water and found a table outside. I left the water untouched, as I'm supposed to abstain from food or drink before receiving communion. The sun was too strong, so I went back inside, but now the music was too loud. I couldn't read, so I put on my headphones and listened to Orthodox hymns while observing the people around me. Most were in stylish gym clothes, a fashion segment I learned is called "athleisure," where you want to be comfortable outside of the gym but are ready to exercise at a moment's notice.

The Starbucks was something of a hot spot, near an upper-middle-class neighborhood. Many of the women were attractive. I sat by the door and had a front-row seat witnessing the parade of flesh before me. I thought that I was strong enough to resist glancing at the shapely butts, but three or four butts in, I realized that I was not. Looking at the butts reminded me of the butts of women I had been with in the past, providing a straight-line path to temptation. So I kept my head down, staring at my phone. If the world is becoming an open-air brothel, and you're trying to heal yourself from being addicted to what the brothel provides, you don't have much choice but to remove yourself from it completely.

I arrived at the church a few minutes early and encountered the priest. After introducing myself, he asked me whether I would like to participate in the Liturgy.

"Yes, I would like to receive communion."

"No, I mean do you want to serve as an acolyte by the Holy Altar," he replied.

I have no singing ability and I didn't know how to serve as an acolyte. I had spoken in front of hundreds of people on my tour, but the thought of standing in church before 25 or so people, unsure of what to do or how to do it, put me in a mild panic. I politely declined.

During the Liturgy, I noticed there was an iPad on the altar. I thought this piece of technology was inappropriate, though I could easily position myself not to see it. After the Liturgy, I engaged in small talk with the parishioners. One woman had two sons who went to my church in Washington, DC, and I recognized them from the pictures she showed me. The priest joined the fellowship and made the rounds, cracking several jokes. I couldn't have guessed it from the solemn Liturgy he had just performed, but he was something of a comedian. I didn't know priests were allowed to be funny. I waited for most people to leave and then asked him whether I could talk with him in private.

I told him my story. "A part of me wants to suffer for my sins," I said. "I know that Jesus Christ died for me, and there is nothing I have to do except give myself to Him, but I want to go through some extra pain to fully atone."

"That would be like the Catholics who whip themselves," he replied. "What did St. Paul say? That your body is a holy temple. Trying to abuse yourself or remove your sins through pain is fanaticism. Jesus Christ already suffered for our sins."

I then eased into the topic of what had been bothering me lately: my mother. I'd become concerned about her salvation since her faith appeared to be noticeably weaker than mine. She had shown signs of being a cafeteria Christian, of picking and choosing certain beliefs and rituals that suited her.

I began to detail my mother's sins to the priest, as if I was building a case against her so that he could advise me to perform a much-needed intervention for the salvation of her soul, but before I could finish, he yelled at me. "Stop! That's enough! You *cannot* judge her. Only God can judge her. Only He sees the full picture, while you see just a tiny part. Your judgment of her is more a reflection of *your* sins than hers."

Taken aback, I thought he might have misunderstood me. "But I'm concerned about her."

"Her salvation is between her and God. Be an example to her, without this pride. Let her follow you if she chooses. Pray for her. Maybe give a few words if you think it can help, but no more."

I sat silent for a moment, digesting the truth he had just shared with me. "I thought I could offer her more direct help, but I see it was just pride." I remembered how I had judged him for using an iPad during the Liturgy. "Father, my pride is killing me. I knock it down in one area and it just comes back in another. I'm paranoid that there are demons everywhere, trying to pull me down."

"If you think there are demons everywhere, then you will become a fanatic. You will be obsessed with them. Walking with Christ is not easy, but remember that you always have Him. Stay focused on Christ, not on evil. Share the love of Christ with your mother, without accusing her. Let God help her." He smiled at me and said, "You'll be okay."

He stood up, put his hands on top of my head, and prayed for me. I hugged him and left the church. I entered my car and began to feel a tight pressure in my chest. I started coughing violently. My eyes sealed shut to brace against the pressure that moved upwards into my throat. I tried to speak, but nothing came out. I couldn't open my eyes or even move my arms. I sobbed without knowing why—I wasn't thinking of anything sad, but the tears wouldn't stop. I felt as if something inside me was dying and being removed. After a few minutes, the tears and coughing abated. I sat in the seat, staring at my Jesus icon hanging from the rearview mirror, exhausted.

21

Country

I drove north from Orlando and stopped at a random park for a picnic. I prepared lunch and put on a YouTube video that would be my entertainment. Then an older man on a Harley-Davidson motorcycle rode up and parked nearby. He got off the bike and walked directly towards me. He said hello and I replied the same, but I didn't turn to face him because I preferred to watch my video. Then I remembered Metropolitan Philaret's prayer that I recite every morning, that all who I come across are sent by God. I softened my demeanor and said, "You from around here?"

"Yup, spent most of my life here. I'm retired now." He looked to be about the same age as my dad.

"I'm on a road trip," I said, glancing at his trucker hat. "This is the first time I've been here. I'm not even sure what the name of this town is."

"White Springs. Did you drive by Main Street?"

"I think so. I saw a few old storefronts."

"That would be the town."

He spoke slowly and calmly with a slight Southern drawl, always keeping his eyes on the river, as if a great beast was about to jump out of it.

"The river is low," he said. "I reckon my boat can't get through those rocks over there. It's only good for a canoe."

A heavyset man walked up. In a familiar tone, my new friend asked him how he was doing.

"I just had back surgery, so I'm taking it easy."

"I had back surgery in May. They may have to go in again soon."

"It's a pain." The heavyset man stared at the river. "Boy, the river is really low. Let me go see if I can get my boat in it." He walked to the boat ramp and came back, confirming that it was too low for his boat. He said goodbye and left.

"Do you own land here?" I asked.

"I live on about 15 acres, and I also have 100 acres across from me. Not sure what to do with it. But we have chickens and goats. Me and the old lady get by."

"In the Washington, DC suburbs, developers build massive houses on quarter-acre plots that are only a few feet away from their neighbor, and then people buy them for half-a-million dollars or more."

He shook his head. "A lot of those types sell their house and come here. They can buy a big plot of land and a house for a good price, and then they retire."

"It feels like a slower pace of life here," I said. He was still staring at the river.

"I reckon maybe 12 cars drive by my house every day."

"And how is the spiritual life here? Do people go to church?"

"Oh, there's a lot of churches. I go once in a while."

I told him I was an Armenian Orthodox Christian, but he didn't know what that meant.

"I'm headed towards Georgia and then maybe Alabama after this," I said. "I'm trying to get an authentic Southern experience, because I was in Fairhope, Alabama, and it was mostly yuppies."

"Go to the north of Alabama and you'll get it." He looked at me carefully. "But they won't have anything to do with you. They keep to themselves."

After a few more minutes of small talk, he got on his motor-cycle and left. From this random interaction, I learned that my attention span might very well be broken. I was about to have lunch in front of a river, and instead of staring at it, instead of listening to the birds, I was about to put on electronic entertainment. The man in the hat took it easy, I pretended to take it easy. He talked to talk, I talked to gain information, a new perspective, or fodder for my writing. Was the wiring of my brain permanently screwed up from living in the city for so long? Though I was on my way out of the city, I was still saddled with its habits, teachings, and culture. Does the modern city make us so unhuman that we essentially need a miracle or revelation from God to be human again? And speaking of God, how much of Him did the man in the hat need? Did he need to seek guidance from the monks in the monasteries? Did he need to read the Desert Fathers to learn how the demons were tempting him? I imagined that one simple prayer a week for him was equivalent to ten of mine.

It looks like the remainder of my life in this world will be an attempt to heal from city life, and while evil exists everywhere, including in the countryside, as the obesity and opioid epidemics show, you simply don't have as many opportunities for the sins of lust, greed, and pride. Who will you lust over in your tiny town? How will you accumulate wealth? And even if you do get rich or gain status, there won't be many people who will be impressed by it.

I left White Springs and drove into Thomasville, Georgia. The downtown area had a roughly equal white and black population against a backdrop of Southern architecture and huge oak trees. The people walked much slower than in other cities, and even talked slower. It was pleasing to hear the melodious quality of authentic Southern accents. It's too bad that so many Southerners feel ashamed that their accent makes them sound "dumb" and try to diminish it through training.

While I was walking on a street in downtown Thomasville, a black man asked me how I was doing. Ten seconds later, I saw another black man walking in my direction. I told myself that if this black man also spoke to me, then the black people here definitely were different. Sure enough, he also said hello. I can say that the blacks in Georgia were rather polite. They were more likely to be in work clothes than in hip hop gear with their pants hanging low. Even the white people were nicer. In the supermarket, a white woman shopper in her late twenties referred to me as "Sir." That would never happen in a big city.

I went into a coffee shop to finish the book Father Damascene had given me at St. Herman's Monastery. The first soft chair I sat in was too low and would make my lower back ache. The second chair was next to the air-conditioning vent and would make me too cold. The other chairs had some kind of minor defect, so I moved to a table, but it was dirty. I poured some of my hot tea on the table and used a napkin to wipe it clean. The temperature of the café was just right; I felt neither hot nor cold. No one near me was loud. I opened my book and began to read, but the music was just audible enough to disturb my reading. I took out my headphones, connected them to my smartphone, and fired up my white noise app. I selected the pleasing waterfall sound. I could now read. Unless the furniture, temperature, and noise are just right, I'm unable to focus.

The café had a lot of young white kids who seemed to be in high school. Up to this point on my trip, most young whites I had observed were heavily influenced by pop culture. They had dyed hair, piercings, and shirts with secular or vulgar sayings. These white kids had normal haircuts and wore clothes that could be suitable for church. They weren't disruptive or taking selfies. Their general mannerisms were even more proper than mine. Whether white or black, people raised in the South seemed to have more class than people in other parts of the country. I could get used to them real fast.

I visited Pebble Hill Plantation outside Thomasville. It was founded right before the Civil War by Thomas Jefferson Johnson when he was around 30 years of age, at a time when what would become the city of Thomasville was mostly open land. He also started the county (Thomas County), so I presumed the city was named after him too. After the Civil War, the plantation turned into a resort for rich Northerners and Midwesterners, until finally it was bequeathed to a foundation. I admired the architecture of the buildings, constructed with numerous balconies and tasteful columns to block the sun, counteracting the oppressive Southern summer. Today, thanks to the easy availability of cheap heating and cooling, most houses look like uninspired Lego blocks meant to serve as a super-sized dwelling instead of matching their environs through architectural beauty.

I was curious: did Johnson own slaves? The foundation's published materials didn't mention anything, so I had to go online, where I found that he owned about 20 slaves before the Civil War. As an American, how should I feel about that? If I were black, perhaps I'd feel a mix of indignation and sorrow. If I were a white person whose ancestors were in the United States during the slavery era, or a Jewish person whose ancestors traded slaves across the Atlantic, perhaps I'd feel guilt or regret. But my parents had come to the country in the 1970s, and, as far as I knew, their ancestors had not dealt in slaves, so I view American slavery more as a historical event disconnected from my biography. I should be pleased that slavery is over in America, but is it really? Back then, slaves labored under a master, but they were fed and sheltered. They were allowed to keep close ties with their community (to an extent) and were encouraged to worship the Gospel. Today, "free" men do not labor for themselves. They eat plastic food, have become addicted to sedentary comfort, and can hardly afford to pay for basic health care when they get sick. They are atomized, having few friends, and many won't even create a family. The Gospel is concealed from them and instead they receive unlimited pornography, entertainment, and news that make them depressed, anxious and, in many cases, mentally deranged. Even worse is the financial debt. Student loan, credit card, car, and mortgage debt ensure that all these "free men" will be beholden to the banks for the rest of their lives. I would rather be a slave under a man who followed Christ than for one who didn't. You could argue that a man of Christ would never own slaves, though maybe God had a plan with American slavery. Maybe the Africans who came to America as slaves were more likely to be saved, and the ones who died in slavery did so as martyrs. I cannot possibly know that for sure, but I do know that people today seem to be suffering as badly as the slaves of old, just in a different way.

I traveled north to Americus, Georgia. Its founder, John Americus Smith, bought some land and started a cotton plantation. The ensuing economic success helped to create the town. I imagine that many cities and counties were started by men who took a chance and made it work. It strikes me that these men started entire towns when they had been younger than me, whereas I have barely been able to start my own life. Here I was, at 40, without a permanent home or family of my own. Sure, I have thousands of people who read me online, many of whom want to hear me talk in person, but where has the time gone? I already know the answer to that question, and am ashamed to think about it, and when I look at my rootless peers, many are in the same boat. We never matured. We remained like children, crying out for our daily dose of candy in the form of fun, cars, sex, status, or toys. While thinking that we were free, we were slaves to pleasure, and instead of harnessing our will to create for the common good, we harnessed it to sleep with more women, to lift weights to become more sexually attractive, or to work in jobs for money that steeped us further into sin.

I'm not a man—I'm a child. I'm a child who is finally growing up and ready to put aside his toys to become an adult, but I'm still far from establishing my own city, or even establishing my own family. Slavery aside, how much more maturity did the men of the South have to possess to do what they did, to have the ability to delay their most immediate desires to aid their families and communities with grand plans and responsibilities?

†

I drove to Atlanta. I started my tour of the city by walking through midtown near the Georgia Tech campus. I saw more gay flags in an hour than I had seen in the days spent in Thomasville and Americus, and even the crosswalks were painted in the rainbow color. To protest, I decided not to walk over the rainbow crosswalk. I refused to legitimize it. I greatly threatened the homosexual lobby through my brave action.

The event dinner was attended by three men, including Adam, who had attended my Minneapolis dinner to regale me with all manner of conspiracy theories, many of which I already believed. Adam considered himself Orthodox Jewish but had been impacted by my speech enough to begin praying to Christ. He had made considerable progress since I had last seen him, and he told me stories that suggested grace was entering his life, such as the sudden urge to be excessively polite to strangers, something I had also experienced, but Satan was plying him with even more offerings of pleasure than before. His problem was above my meager qualifications, so I advised him to seek guidance from a priest or monk. I can help those with a lack of faith who are starting from a blank slate, more or less, but not those with spiritual problems. It's questionable if I should even advise those with no faith. After all, Jesus was silent for 30 years before he began to teach, and he was fully God. I'd been a Christian for only eight months and I had already spoken to hundreds about the faith, though mostly centered on my testimony.

I woke up the next day feeling unwell. My neck ached and my left leg was numb. I was dizzy and had several new itchy spots. My body was shutting down. For the first time on a lecture day, I didn't want to perform. I wanted to cancel the entire event and stay in the hotel, but I could do no such thing, especially now that I was so close to finishing the tour. Either I completed the speech or I fainted in front of my audience.

As had happened many times before, I gained energy once I met my guests in the hotel conference room. I delivered the talk, but my brain felt slower to remember key parts of the speech. I even left out a couple of my best jokes, but in a two-hour speech, they were minor omissions.

During the Q&A, I realized that a huge chunk of the audience was between 18 and 23, representatives of the zoomer generation. Their questions were sharper than what I would have asked at their age, and a recurring theme was the burgeoning "Groyper" movement, led by dissident Nick Fuentes, who had attended my talk in Chicago. They had been challenging establishment conservatives on topics such as legal immigration and aid to Israel.

It was tempting for me to look down on these men solely because of their youth and lack of life experience, but how could I when I had lived like a degenerate for two decades? I took the ideas of free love and sexual liberation from the boomers and, alongside fellow Generation Xers, wasted my birthright to perfect the achievement of seamless casual sex. It was Generation X that created game, along with other vain lifestyles that threw away all notions of nationalism and Christianity. I had been partially responsible for fueling the meme of traveling around the world to get better sex. The millennials, I could argue, were even worse than my generation. They had taken our sexual liberation and applied it to various homosexual and transsexual lifestyles, and it is the millennial parents who are injecting their kids with sex-changing hormones. They control Silicon Valley and have brought Soviet-era censorship and deplatforming to America. And now these preceding generations are going to advise the zoomers?

I told the young men in the room not to listen to those who had come before them. "If we were so smart, the country wouldn't be in the shape that it's in. Your solutions can't be worse than the ones tried already, and if you ever feel that it's hopeless, that too many of your fellow zoomers are addicted to smartphones or too woke for their own good, just remember that it takes only 10% or so of you to completely change the country."

There was no Armenian church in Atlanta. Instead, I toured East Atlanta Village. It was a standard hipster neighborhood with tattoo parlors and dive bars featuring advertisements for Pabst Blue Ribbon, the type of place where financially successful white people appreciate living near destitute minorities to prove they're not racist.

I vegetated for the rest of the day in my hotel room. After I got tired of YouTube and Twitter, I turned on the television and stumbled on *90 Day Fiancé*, a show about Americans who found a love interest abroad, usually through the internet. The relationship proceeds before the camera, and when the foreign partner comes to America on a special fiancé visa, the couple has 90 days to decide whether or not to get married.

All the relationships on the show had an identical pattern: the American almost always found a partner who was more attractive than someone they could have found locally. It was not about finding someone who was more family-oriented or spiritual, for how family-oriented could the foreigner be if they were ready to leave their own family to come to America? The American women, often older, found the type of good-looking men in Africa or the Middle East they couldn't date in the States. The American men invariably found a young and sexy woman. In one case, a man in his forties found a Brazilian model who was in her early twenties. He spent over $100,000 on her during their courtship. She even bought a car in Brazil on his credit card, although he didn't seem to mind.

Lying was common. In each relationship, at least one partner exaggerated their wealth or concealed damaging information that was revealed only after the other partner had become heavily invested. The foreigners did what was necessary to come to America for a better life, and the Americans kept their heads in the sand and believed that this person, whose physical qualities were higher than those they could expect to get in the States, really did love them for themselves. The lies were smoothed over or simply ignored.

What I saw were perfect matches—one person in lust meeting another person in lust. One lusted after looks and the other lusted after money or novelty, and they were so blinded by their lusts that not only did they lie to themselves, but they accepted the lies they were told to them so they could hold onto the fantasy that this person would permanently satisfy their cravings. In one case, an American woman sought a Russian man in Russia. She ignored that he was on his third marriage, having left two previous women—with whom he had children—in the lurch. He had now impregnated her, and she was optimistic that everything would work out. Lust separates us from God, and since all truth is from God, it separates us from the truth as well.

I had behaved in much the same way as those on the show. I had been caught up in intense lust and went abroad to fulfill it with foreign women, particularly in Eastern Europe. The pattern of all my short relationships had been the same: we lied to each other and withheld information about our past or future intentions to carry on a sexual dalliance that satisfied our most immediate desires. And all of those lust-based relationships had failed— every single one of them.

Sure, you may "love" these girls because of their beauty and what they can give you, and they "love" you because of the novelty, wealth, comfort, or opportunity you can offer, but because there is no spiritual relationship, there will be no relationship. One will get tired of the other person's beauty, their money will soon not be enough, boredom sets in, a brand-new desire demands to be sated, and so on. Unless I can look at the next girl I meet and see her soul and not her lips or breasts, I will fail, and the only way I can examine a woman's soul correctly is if I first examine mine.

22

Apostasy

I went to a hand car wash, hoping that they could scrub off all the dead bugs stuck to my hood from thousands of miles of highway driving. I asked the Hispanic attendant how much the car wash cost, but he didn't understand. I dusted off my Spanish.

"¿Cuánto cuesta por el servicio todo?" *How much for full service?*

"Veinte," he replied. *Twenty (dollars).*

I sat in the car while he hand-scrubbed my vehicle. Six cars were in front of mine getting detailed. The workers had to wash all these cars for at least an eight-hour shift. I wondered how much they were getting paid.

I pulled my car up and another Hispanic man continued to work on it. Besides a power vacuum, the cleaning was done all by hand. I studied these men for some time and wondered, why them? And wait, why me? I could complain about my trip and how difficult it was, but many people would see my road experience as a dream. I could travel across the country and speak in front of crowds of people who respect me without worrying much about money. Soon my trip would end and I could relax for a long time, and then leisurely decide on my next project, but these Hispanic men had no choice in the matter. What did they do with their paltry earnings? Did they send the money home? Maybe they have children. Maybe their small income prevented them from committing misdeeds, from extending their adolescence with a tour of carnality through Europe. So they drank their beers at night and woke up the next day to get back to the car wash and scrub and scrub. Maybe I was worse off, and a life of hard labor would have prevented me from attempting to fulfill my bestial desires. My car was ready. It was spotless.

I went back westward into Northern Alabama, yearning for an authentic hillbilly experience. I wanted to walk into an establishment and feel intimated by a group of local men in camouflage gear. I started in a small Alabama town called Oxford. I ate lunch at a chain bakery. Multiple women stared at me, including a mother and daughter team who laughed at me, though I didn't know why.

I spent one night in a cheap motel and woke up the next day with multiple red welts that looked like big mosquito bites. *This* was definitely bed bugs.

After another day of travel in Alabama, the hillbilly experience eluded me. I looked at the map and saw a town named Arab. Could I encounter some action there? I drove to the town and parked my car on the main street. I popped into a coffee shop and asked the barista how to pronounce the name of the town. She replied, "A-rab." I guessed that was how they pronounced the word "Arab" as well, as in: "Hey, you with the big beard... we don't want any A-rabs in these parts, so git on outta here." I sat down near the entrance of the coffee shop, waiting for a confrontation. Many men came in and ignored me, not even making eye contact. One young man in a camouflage jacket came in with a holstered gun. Yes, this would be it! He had a physiognomy that suggested his name was C-Bass or Knuckles. He'd walk up to me and nonchalantly stroke his gun while saying he didn't want to see my kind around here. I'd ask him what his problem was, acting all tough, but quickly fold when it became clear he meant business. But no, he didn't make eye contact either. Like the Floridian man in White Springs said, they didn't want to have anything to do with me.

Next I visited the university town of Athens, Alabama. The odds of encountering C-Bass were now zero. I rested for two days before traveling to Nashville.

✝

The number one attraction in Nashville is Broadway, a downtown street with numerous honky-tonk bars that helped to develop Nashville's reputation as Music City. Each bar had a live band playing country music and rock 'n' roll covers, and even early in the evening, at 6pm, most were full of white Southerners drinking and dancing. The music was enjoyable, but it was inexorably paired with intoxication and its big brother, fornication.

With its music scene and Southern charm, Nashville is what I expected Austin to be. What happened to Austin to lose all of that? If you broadcast your city as a center of music, intoxication, and, by implication, fornication, you will attract sinners. And if you attract enough sinners, you also attract those who sinners enable: the homeless, the drug-addled, and the criminal. This happened to Austin, and it will happen to Nashville now that it's becoming a hot spot for people in Chicago and New York City to move to because of its lively nightlife, light traffic, and low cost of living. They will come here and turn Nashville into the same cesspool they left. Unless someone changes their ways—or even better, repents—before moving from one city to the next, they will simply bring their existing way of life with them, just as I had taken my fixation with sex abroad and helped to enable foreign women of weak faith to fall in a way that would have been harder if I had not made it so easy for them. Ironically, after spending years in a place like Poland, I had the audacity to complain that the girls had become "slutty" and "low quality," a situation I had personally helped to create.

The event dinner was held in Woolworth on Fifth, a classic diner that was the source of desegregation protests during the Civil Rights era. I was joined by two men and a mother and her daughter. The daughter, married and pregnant, was in her early twenties.

"My oldest daughter has gone in another direction," the mother said, glancing at her daughter beside her.

"So let me guess—she has a career that she highly values."

"Yes."

"And she values her strength and independence."

"Yes."

"And she is in some kind of rebellion against God."

"Yes."

The I'm-rebelling-against-God starter pack for a woman includes an office job that is at the center of her life, an apartment in a gentrifying area near the highest-rated restaurants, the scars of various "jerks" who used her for sex, a handful of "meaningful" tattoos, a subtle hatred of men for not meeting all her unreasonable standards, and a futile attempt to satisfy her spiritual needs by practicing yoga or New Age instead of following Jesus Christ.

"I have tried to talk to her…"

"…and she resisted," I interrupted.

"Exactly. We got into an argument and she didn't want to hear it."

"We can be aware of the exact problem someone is having, and choose to deliver the solution in a loving tone, but they will still resist, sometimes with great force. From my own experience and what I've learned from the Orthodox Church, words hardly help. Even the perfect piece of advice falls on deaf ears. All we really can do is pray for the person, because we have to consider how we ourselves came to Christ. If you listen to a hundred testimonies, none of them include, 'My parents browbeat me with Christ and then I felt grace.' What happened was no one told them to follow Christ, and then they followed Christ! It's funny that we come to Christ on our own, and then as soon as we do, we want to instruct others to just start praying or going to church, as if that is all they need to counter a lifetime of secular obsessions. They end up resenting you instead."

But what consolation could my words bring to a mother who saw a daughter harming herself? Okay, she would pray for her, but the years would drag on, and her daughter might never create her own family. In some cases, with older family members, it will come down to the deathbed, but if God can wait that long for someone to repent, then as parents, siblings, and friends we can wait for those we love to join the Body of Christ, no matter how much it pains us to see them hurt themselves for so many years or even decades.

The two men present were my age and still single. They peppered me with questions about how to find a suitable wife in a degrading society, and besides the suggestion to try church, I had nothing substantial to offer. In Nashville, many churches featured excellent rock bands in order to fill the pews (or stadium seats). Would it be a good idea to find a woman in one of those churches? I couldn't say. I would need more time to start putting theories and ideas into practice, but I did give them two pieces of advice.

"I can tell you what I'm doing. First, I'm accepting that I may never find a wife and create a family due to a combination of my past and the modern environment where faithful women are scarce, but if your salvation is dependent on a woman, you will be sent a woman. Based on how women behave these days, however, your salvation may be compromised through marriage with the wrong one. Right now, I'm under the assumption that I will go it alone. I have my mother to watch over, and I have God to serve, and that's that. I'm sure God will give me a productive way to serve Him for the remainder of my days in case I don't get married.

"The second thing I'm doing is fixing myself. Step by step, I'm addressing my lust, anger, and pride. Not only will fixing myself allow me to judge a woman more properly, since broken could only attract broken, but this ensures I don't bring any evil into a future relationship. Give me a girl today and there is a chance I will accidentally wreck it, but if I wait a year or two, that relationship has a better chance of surviving.

"Once I have these two parts worked out, it's just a matter of pursuing the faith and treating others as I would want to be treated. If God wills it, a girl will come across my path, and I can use what I know as a man to pursue a courtship. I would start with a stable church community and proceed from there. Whatever the case, your search for a wife starts and ends with Christ. There will be no tricks or hacks."

When asking for advice, most people want practical action items. Go to this place, say this line, and take a woman on these kinds of dates—all materialistic actions that lead to a materialistic result, but finding a good wife, at least one who is spiritual, is a spiritual action, so you need to approach it spiritually. If you're not on the spiritual path then you're back in the dating casino where you pick a random girl without God's guidance and hope for the best. Most men lose that game.

Towards the end of our meal, I noticed something queer about our waitress. She wore large triangle earrings with a lone eye inside them. I knew what it was—the Eye of Horus, an occult symbol from ancient Egypt that is involved in pagan worship and witchcraft. I became curious about how the waitress would explain the earrings, so after the dinner was over and there was no more food to come, I asked her what her earrings meant.

"It's a symbol that comes from ancient Egypt," she replied. "It was usually hidden in those times, but I want to bring it to the surface so it's more visible." In other words, she hoped to promote a symbol of evil so that dark powers could assert more control over this world. I wouldn't be surprised if she also owned a pentagram necklace.

The next day, I gave my speech in front of a mostly Southern audience. Many people came from Florida, Mississippi, and Alabama, in addition to various parts of Tennessee. The Q&A followed and the first question was from a man who asked what could be done about black people, insinuating that the solution must involve violence against them.

I replied, "The problem with trying to fix the world, and you have proposed a solution to a problem that you perceive, is that if you are not close to God, there is still evil coursing through you, and any attempt to heal the world will actually cause more damage. How can evil fix evil? When I was fornicating, my grand solution to fix women was to admonish them for not wearing high heels. I would heal the rift between men and women by making women more sexually appealing to me! So the main problem is not against the blacks or any other group, but first ridding yourself of whatever anger and pride you have. There is always a time for political activism, but violence should not be the first solution on your list."

I thought my answer was lukewarm enough for it not to embarrass him in front of the audience, but he grabbed his girlfriend and left the room anyway.

Towards the end, a man asked me whether I was planning a future tour. "I don't plan on doing a tour for a long time," I answered. "This is my second-to-last stop, and I'm amazed I even got this far without a great mishap. I have to tell you all that I have a weird feeling this is the last year I could attempt such a tour. Earlier this year, we saw a couple of big shootings in El Paso and Dayton, and many of you know I was shut down by two credit card processors a few months ago. Maybe the United States will be too dangerous for a public event, or maybe it will just be impossible for a dissident like myself to organize them. I guess we'll see."

After the Q&A, I talked to most of the attendees, including a large group of young men under 25 who were curious about the Groyper movement. Their faces shined with eagerness. They wanted to disrupt the plans of fake conservatives so that a true conservative movement could replace it. They understood that existing conservatives were moderates in disguise who acted like the Washington Generals basketball team playing against the Harlem Globetrotters. The Globetrotter is spinning the ball right in front of you—just take it from him! Now they are bringing ladders onto the court to dunk on you—a flagrant violation! And yet all the Generals can do is act dumb and lose on purpose, just to continue getting their paychecks. I hope the Groypers can put an end to this rigged game.

Two zoomers invited me to worship the next day at Nashville's Greek Orthodox Church. I hesitated because of my experience at St. Anthony's Monastery in Arizona but eventually agreed. To decrease the chance of a bad experience, I decided not to talk to anyone there, not even the priest.

I parked my car at the church and walked to the main entrance. Before I could make it inside, a woman stopped in her tracks and stared at me intently. "Are you... Roosh?" She introduced herself and said that she had enjoyed the episode of my video travelogue where I went to St. Anthony's Monastery. A minute later, I walked inside the church and found the two young men who had invited me. I joined them in worship.

The Liturgy was half in English and half in Greek, and it was plenty holy, but I was distracted by the numerous attractive women of child-bearing age in the congregation. It wouldn't be much longer until I went back to my Armenian church, where the average age of a female parishioner was around 60. I kept my eyes on the altar.

After the Liturgy, an Asian man recognized me and said he enjoyed my work (the church had many non-Greek converts). Then another young man recognized me, also referring to my visit to St. Anthony's. The Orthodox world in the United States must be small, because my video on St. Anthony's had less than 25,000 views. Then an older man with a Greek physiognomy approached me.

"I saw your video about St. Anthony's and how you were angry about not being allowed in the church nave. I hope you understand that these rules exist for a reason, to prevent the faith from being corrupted."

"I understand," I solemnly replied. "I do not want to change the rules."

"Do you remember the glow you spoke of concerning Elder Ephraim?" he asked.

"Yes, of course."

"Could that have happened if his faith wasn't pure?"

He then provided multiple bullet points about how the Greek Orthodox Church produces the holiest of saints, and referred to it as "*the* Orthodox Church," presupposing the exclusion of others, including my own. His tone got stronger and his speech became more rapid as he worked himself up into an excited agitation. I knew he was reaching the climax of a pitch that aimed to convince me to apostatize from my church. Right before he was about to bring down the hammer, I interrupted him.

"I have to be honest... I feel like you're trying to convince me of something. Earlier you were just sharing your thoughts, but now you have the air of a salesman. My heart closes to salesmen. I didn't come to this nice church to be persuaded by another man who knows me only through the internet."

Without hesitating, he tried to continue the pitch right where he had left off. "Really," I insisted, "I don't want to hear your arguments for why I should leave my church. I'm glad you like your church, but I like mine, too."

"I have to tell you this because it's something that God would want me to do."

"If God wills me to leave the Armenian Church, I will do so, since I obey Him, but He has given me no definitive sign that it's something I should do."

"How do you know He didn't give you a sign?"

"Look, if you believe I'm in the wrong church, then pray for me that God will put me in the right one instead of having a debate that is sure to turn ugly."

I didn't want to justify myself to him. If he were a priest or a monk, I would indulge his line of questioning out of respect, but he was just a random parishioner who was giving unsolicited spiritual guidance based on watching a video that showed only a tiny part of an already short visit to a Greek monastery. And yet he wouldn't give up! He argued that since he was speaking to me, it was the sign that God wanted me to convert. Many non-Christians try to "convert" me every day to a life of sin. The media and even the National Park Service tries to convince me that science is god and should wholly determine how I see the world. If I repeatedly hear the argument of apostasy, does that mean God wants me to apostatize? If a thousand people tell me to sleep with a prostitute, does that mean I should sleep with her? Without discernment, we would just be followers of trends dictated by the most persistent and well-funded voices. If God wanted me to leave the Armenian Church, it wouldn't only be through a chorus of voices telling me to do so, because there will always be a chorus that drives you away from God, but a simultaneous closing of doors to the Armenian Church and an opening of doors to another.

My experiences in the Greek Orthodox world have involved more drama than I would have preferred. Of the other Orthodox churches I've been to—Russian Orthodox, Antiochian, and Orthodox Church in America—I have not encountered anything I could remotely describe as drama. Could I be blamed if I did my best to avoid Greek Orthodox places of worship in the future?

After the fellowship period had ended, I went to have pancakes with the two young men who originally invited me to the church. They were around 23, ready to start their lives. They both lamented that they had to live in a big city to find work. I launched into a monologue.

"That is the big scam of life in the United States. First, you're pushed into university to get a degree that saddles you with a high amount of debt but which gives you only a narrow range of skills. After you graduate, who is going to employ you for those skills? A corporation in the city, and that city will have a metropolitan population of one million or more. Then you go into the city with your new job, ready to start your new life, but you'll succumb to temptation. You'll drink, fornicate, experiment with drugs, and to alleviate the drudgery of your job and commute, you become addicted to entertainment or anything else in this world that can provide you with temporary joy. You're not saving as much money as you thought you would, and the interest on your student loans is so high that it will take you more than ten years to pay it off. A decade passes. More of your money must be spent on things that give you pleasure. Now you're addicted to the city, barely able to save, with a host of addictions that you didn't have before.

"If you're lucky, and I mean really lucky, you'll find a suitable woman to marry, but she's going to be your reflection—a woman attached to the city and its pleasures. Both of you will covet your careers as much as the lustful love you have for each other. Then the first child comes. You can't raise it in the city, so off to the suburbs you go for a $450,000 house where you're not allowed to have chickens. The debt continues to pile on. Both of you have to continue working, the diversity trainings and self-censorship beat you down, and on top of that you have a child to raise, but you can't raise it, because mommy and daddy need to work to keep up with the mortgage, car payments, and student loan payments, so add daycare to the mix, where your child is tended to by a stranger barely making above minimum wage, and that doesn't get better in the public schools, which these days seem hell-bent on making every child gay, or at least confused as to what gender they are. How can you possibly win that game? You're enslaved the whole way throughout, and because you can't properly raise your child, at least in the way that children used to be raised, it becomes enslaved as well, only to repeat your exact life of university education, career in the city, and then something that looks even less like family than what you had. This is the trap that faces most Americans, and I see only two ways out of it.

"The first is not to go to university. Stay in the smaller towns to be a tradesman, which is harder on the body and offers less financial stability, unless you have the knack of a businessman who can start a firm, but you avoid the most sinful aspects of the city and the debt slavery. The second way to win is to make most of your money on the internet, allowing you to buy land in the countryside. Most commonly this will involve computer programming or internet work. If a man falls for the meme of university, he can still take this route by living frugally and moving his skillset online, but that could take many years. I'm on the internet path and can become a mountain man after my tour is done, but look how much I damaged myself in the process. It would have been better if I never went to university in the first place and became an electrician, or just started writing books immediately upon graduating.

"Both of you are currently in the early stages of the trap, but if you know how the trap works, you can get out of it. Try to specialize in work that exists outside of cities, pay down your debts as fast as you can, and ask Christ to help you resist temptations that are sure to come. It will be hard, but you should be on firm ground by the time you're 30."

If only someone had given me that sermon when I was 23. Perhaps a part of my path was to live wrongly for an extended period so that I could serve as an example for others.

23

Home

From Nashville I drove to Gatlinburg, a city on the western border of the Great Smoky Mountains. I wasn't in the mood to explore a gigantic national park, but I figured it would be worth checking out in case I wanted to do an excursion from my future home base in the Washington, DC area.

Now that it was mid-November, the tourist horde had thinned out enough that everyone in the park was cheery and said hello as I passed, unlike in crowded Yellowstone. I was able to enjoy two trails in relative peace, and soak in the brisk air and autumn coloration of orange, red, and brown, all without having to time my walking pace to keep distance from others.

The next day I drove deeper into the park to enjoy rolling mountain views and snow-covered trees. It felt like forever since I had seen park beauty like this (perhaps a few weeks), and I uttered a handful of doxologies to praise God for His creation. The views weren't as stunning as those in the Rocky Mountains, but they were cozier, and all I needed to complete them was a warm blanket and small campfire.

On one of the steep trails I saw a sign for the Appalachian Trail. If you're from the East Coast, you've surely heard of this trail, one of the oldest in the country that spans 2,180 miles from Georgia to Maine. Hiking the entire Appalachian Trail is growing in popularity. Tired of city life or just looking for meaning, many people take a sabbatical and walk the entire thing to "feel close to nature" or just to have an impressive feat notched on their belt, but such a trail can only provide meaning temporarily, and then as soon as your journey is complete, the meaning is gone, and all you have left are memories that diminish with time. I'd be the first to agree that walking the Appalachian Trail is healthier than sleeping with a hundred girls, or having a goal to buy a huge house, but it still keeps you firmly rooted in the material world, of thinking that there is something here on earth that will yield satisfaction and purpose. Satan does not at all mind if you desire to climb Mount Everest—and would actually help you succeed—because it gives you something to be proud of. I desire to feel no pride, for pride is not of God. If I did a truly good thing then the reward will come not from my feelings but solely from God.

Before leaving the park, I ate lunch in my car. It was a fasting week so that meant no dairy or animal products. I made a kale salad with blueberries, raisins, and tomato, an English muffin with hummus, an apple, an orange, and a handful of peanuts. Then I broke off a chunk of 85% dark chocolate and placed it on the paper plate in the middle of my car console. Usually, I broke the chocolate into small pieces, but this time I decided to stab them with a knife. After I had done so, I looked underneath the paper plate and saw that I had made a dozen small cuts into the console covering. I ate the chocolate, thinking of the unnecessary damage I had done to my car, and wondered why I had used a knife to cut the chocolate into pieces. Then I thought, "Is dark chocolate safe to eat during the fast?" I grabbed the packaging and saw under the ingredients "cocoa butter," which comes from cocoa beans, a non-dairy product. Then I looked at the ingredients of the English muffins I had been eating. "Contains: milk." Damaging my car made me realize that I was not properly keeping the fast.

†

I spent one night in Asheville, North Carolina, a city that is notorious for being overrun by liberals. Four years ago, it was revealed that two men who owned the Waking Life Espresso coffee shop produced a secret podcast in which they bragged about using pickup tactics to sleep with local women. The feminists picketed in front of their coffee shop and, with the help of the media, forced the coffee shop to permanently close down. You must understand that if the coffee shop wasn't shut down, it would pose a danger to the community because it fostered "hate," and women who might have wanted to sleep with the proprietors wouldn't know that they possessed "misogynistic" thoughts, so in the end the sin of fornication was avenged by the sin of wrath.

The first place I attempted to visit in Asheville was a coffee shop that did not pose a danger to the community, because when I reached for the door handle, I noticed a gay pride sticker. Many times on my tour, I had visited an establishment that was pro-gay, and by now I was sick of supporting Satan's business interests. I went to the homeless shelter instead, more commonly known as the library.

As was the case with many other leftist-infested cities, the Asheville library was more than half-filled with homeless people who spent inordinate amounts of time in the bathroom, but even the non-homeless appeared lost and confused. I saw aging gays and hippies, the progenitors of the Asheville problem, nonplussed by the degradation of their library, alongside college students with green hair and displeasing tattoos. They all enabled each other and so they deserved each other. If you want cutesy cafés, yoga studios, and esoteric candle shops, you must also have homeless people who sleep on benches, set up encampments in parks, shoot up drugs in public, defecate on the streets, and foul the library bathrooms. In the early part of my tour, I could at least tolerate such a scene, and be gleeful that I had something to film for my travelogue, but I had run out of tolerance. I didn't want to see them anymore. I didn't want to drink alcohol, party, get laid, or buy stuff. I just wanted to worship Christ and be around other people who desired the same. Perhaps this had been possible in the cities of old, but today's American cities were not constructed to encourage the worship of God. Instead, they were developed in such a way that He was the last thing you'd think about when living in one.

With only a week left of my tour, I started researching homes to rent in West Virginia and western Virginia. On paper, West Virginia was a better bet—more gun freedom, fewer liberals, a Republican-controlled state legislature, and more local resistance against degenerate inventions like Drag Queen Story Time, but it had its share of problems—the highest rate of opioid deaths in the country, mass poverty, and higher costs when it comes to car and health insurance. I could move to West Virginia and not have to worry about new laws that limited my freedom, but what would be the point if my neighbors were meth addicts with whom I couldn't even have a conversation? My example was hyperbolic, but I had no idea what it was like to live there, and I might be trying to trade the cross of having to live in a liberal-infested trash heap for another cross that may be harder to bear.

After analyzing both states for some time, and trying to pre-dict the future trajectory of the country, I realized what I was doing wrong: I was trying to save myself. I was doing research to find heaven in the United States, to live in a place where I could limit the amount of evil that would come my way. Was I afraid that God would leave me? Did I think that I couldn't glorify Him when surrounded by demon worshippers? I knew from firsthand experience that I was more eager to pray when I was surrounded by sin, so paradoxically, by trying to live in a good area where I didn't need God's help, I might be hurting my faith. If everything was comfortable on my five-acre plot of land in a perfectly conservative town, would I become so complacent that I feel I don't need God? I knew the answer wasn't to move to Portland or San Francisco, but I must not proceed as if God didn't exist by attempting to save myself from a country that seemed to be getting worse by the week. If Washington, DC was my cross to bear then so be it.

✝

I arrived in Charlotte, North Carolina for my final event. My brain was still processing the travel data from several cities ago, so I couldn't analyze Charlotte beyond saying that it felt Southern but with a lot of transplants from the North. Besides, I didn't see how it could be that different from the 22 other major cities I had visited on the tour. I might feel some regret for not visiting a specific park, such as the Grand Canyon, but when it came to cities, I regretted that I had scheduled all my events in them.

Two men who attended the event dinner were Protestants, one a Presbyterian and the other a Reformed Baptist. I initially wanted to put them in the same box as the other lapsed Protestants I had met who grew up in a church and stopped going as an adult, but these two were far more spiritually advanced than me. They were walking the walk when it came to marriage—one did not have sex with his wife before they married and the other was taking the same approach with his fiancée. In the past, I would have deemed such behavior as "no longer in existence," but now that I had decided on the same path, examples of it were popping up everywhere, showing me that it definitely could be done regardless of the poisoned state of the modern world.

The two men reminded me that I must not judge the faith of others, including denominations that have beliefs my church would deem heretical, because even in the most heretical church, some were sure to be higher than me in the eyes of God. If someone tells me they are a brother in Christ, I will treat them as such and resist the temptation to proclaim my faith as superior.

The day of the final talk arrived. Thirty people attended. I wanted to get excited that the end was so near, but I restrained myself. The speech wasn't easy. Several times, I went completely blank. Silence filled the room and I couldn't recall where I was in my speech. Staring at the audience didn't help, since they didn't know what was supposed to come next. I had to refer to my notes and triangulate my position before starting again. I had gone blank before, but not as many times in one speech. Maybe my guests thought I was being especially dramatic.

I barreled through the speech and then the Q&A. Many of the questions were similar to the ones I'd been asked before, so I recited the answers from memory. The meet-and-greet followed. I took selfies with the attendees, offered advice, and in the case of spiritual problems, I urged them to consult a priest. And that was it. I was done. All the events of my nationwide tour had been successfully completed.

I packed all my equipment and began walking to my car when I experienced a deep pain in my legs and lower back, enough to give me a limp. I heaved my things into the trunk and then collapsed into the driver's seat. I believe the sudden mental and physical degradation was God's way of enlightening me on how little innate human power I possessed. During my last speech, He had begun turning off "God power" to let me know what my physical state would be without His help.

I sat in my car and stared at my Jesus icon for a while. I believe it was He who had helped me to accomplish the feat of traveling 17,000 miles for five months to talk to nearly 900 people in 23 cities while visiting almost 100 more. Why had Christ given me such strength to accomplish this? Why had He lifted me from the pit in such a mighty way? When people saw what had happened to me, it was as if God were telling them, "Look what I did to Roosh. Imagine what I can do for you." To whom much is given, much is expected, so I choose to exhaust myself for the Lord, and use the power He has given me to fix the damage I caused to the world by my own stupid will.

I didn't want to imagine the next project He had in store for me, because it would certainly be harder than the one I had just completed, but I would graciously accept it. What I had achieved didn't deserve a pat on the back or a victory lap. There was no need for a reward from other humans when I could receive a reward from God.

✝

I visited Charlotte's Armenian church the next day. During the Liturgy, I noticed a mentally handicapped man sitting two rows in front of me. He had trouble controlling his body—his head shook back and forth and he looked around the church instead of focusing on the altar. I wondered what was going through his mind.

After the Liturgy, I stuck around for the fellowship. When I don't know anyone in a church, I simply stand by the tea station and wait for someone to make a friendly overture. After a few minutes, a nice lady greeted me with a smile and introduced me to an elder. Then the priest came to speak with me. He seemed like the youngest I had met. Then a deacon approached me and asked me about my background. I told him that I used to be a world champion fornicator and had recently come to Christ. "I want you to meet someone," he replied, and he introduced me to another deacon who was a few years older than me.

The deacon was rather popular. Five, six, seven people went up to him to exchange greetings before we could start our conversation. I took it that he was the social connector of the church and probably organized many of its events and activities. I shared my story with him, as I had done dozens of times on this trip, and he shared his.

"I've been involved in this church since I was 12 or 13," he started. "As I got older, I felt that I knew the Gospel and was a true follower of Christ. I got married, had children, and started a business that was doing very well. I moved my family into a big house and had cars and everything else you would expect. I saw all of these as a blessing from God. Then my business suddenly went bust. Everything went upside down. We lived on savings for a while but that eventually ran out. I was in bad shape. I became stressed and then scared of what would happen to my children. I asked myself why God would put me through this trial. Wasn't I good in His eyes? Was I not serving Him as He wanted? Or did I miss something?

"I went back and read the Bible carefully, line by line. I encountered Matthew chapter 6, verse 33: 'But seek first the kingdom of God and His righteousness, and all these things shall be added to you.' There was one word I had missed, and immediately felt enlightened as to what I did wrong. The word is 'first.' I had prioritized everything else of this world before God. It hit me that I wasn't following Christ as faithfully as I thought I was. Everything changed after that. I started to pray to Him for help, and was accepting of whatever He gave, always putting Him above things that I used to think were important. Since then, things have been up and down when it comes to money, but my family is stronger than ever, and we added one more child."

I remember how worried I had been when I unpublished 11 of my books. I knew my income would go down, and maybe I wouldn't be able to live as comfortably as before, but it hadn't declined as much as I thought it would, and countless Christians in multiple states have offered me help in the form of shelter or money. If you count all the aid that I have been offered, my "income" has increased since unpublishing half of my book catalog.

"I have a question about fasting," I said to the deacon. "I maintain the normal fasting days of Wednesday and Friday, and also the fasting weeks, but on those days I'm essentially stuffing myself with bagels. I'm not eating meat or dairy, sure, but otherwise I think I'm getting the same number of calories."

"Because that's not fasting. The Church Fathers said you should be half full when you fast."

"Half?!"

"Yes. It should be much less food than you normally eat or you're just doing a dietary restriction, not a fast. There will be no spiritual benefit."

For the five months I had been "fasting," it turned out that I hadn't really been fasting at all.

"I have another question," I said. "How do I pray for someone? Usually I say, 'Lord Jesus Christ, have mercy on...' and then I say a bunch of names."

"That is a bit too fast. I would say the whole prayer for each name. And you have the right idea in asking the Lord to have mercy on them. Many people will ask me to pray that they get hired for a certain job or that their illness goes away, but how do we know that their current difficulty is not what God prescribed for them? I'm sure it's easy to see in your own life how negative events brought you closer to God, so the success that people think they should receive may actually hurt them. This is why when you start to pray for someone, their lives may take a turn for the worse. God's mercy is based on saving their soul for eternity, and that comes with suffering in this world. The Church Fathers say that if nothing bad has happened to you for a while, God has forsaken you. Many people in this situation may in fact pray for suffering to deepen their faith, because without it, we will remain distant from God."

"I've met many men who pray to find a good wife. Do you think that is the right approach?"

"They should instead pray on becoming a good husband. If you become a good husband, who is suitable to start a family in a way that won't impede the salvation of a woman, God will match you up with one who is capable of being a good wife. So in your case, I would pray to God to help heal your past wounds and become a man who can properly lead a household. If you arrive at that point, God will give you a suitable wife."

An old man walked by with a prayer rope. "He is a holy

man," the deacon said. "He was here when the church started." The old man sat at our table. Then the other deacon I had spoken to earlier also sat, along with the mentally handicapped man I had noticed during the Liturgy. They were the old man's sons.

The handicapped man sat right next to me. I put out my hand and he shook it gently. He said a few words about something to do with telephones. His manner was gentle and sweet. I looked at him intently. Most of society would ignore him, and many couples would abort him if the doctor told them that their future child would be handicapped, but when I stared at him, I saw only a beautiful man created by God, with an innocence and kindness that most "healthy" people didn't have. If I were a father, and was informed by a doctor that the baby in my wife's womb was like him, I would not insist on an abortion. If my wife did, I like to believe that I would tell her to have the baby and then feel free to leave me so I could raise him on my own.

On a homestead, I would make such a handicapped child useful when it came to gardening or taking care of the animals. With his gentle manner, I imagine it wouldn't be a problem for him to feed the chickens and goats. We'd have a bountiful supply of food. This fantasy aside, it was looking more like the cross I would have to bear is the single life, but I would bear it without complaint, because in God's infinite wisdom, such a life would sanctify me, and if God did give me a wife, even a difficult one, I would bear her as well.

I left the church feeling blessed. All my plans for the tour had been realized without being set back even by a day. The worst thing to have happened was the annoying rash I caught in Indiana that flared up every now and then. I had forgotten my toiletry bag in a Boston guesthouse and had to backtrack one hour to get it. In Oregon, I took a park road that turned into rocks and had to backtrack 90 minutes, costing me three hours. My sensitive stomach had acted up many times, but it always did so when I traveled. I think another time I had forgotten my shampoo bottle in a hotel. I hadn't caught a single cold. I hadn't been pulled over by a policeman for speeding, which I had done quite often. I hadn't been a victim of theft or violence. Not a single dollar bill had been lost from my pocket. I had been exhausted many times, particularly during the second half of the trip, and I was nearly always in a state of mild irritability, but I don't know who wouldn't be. How could things have gone so smoothly? How could I not have suffered some mild catastrophe in an endeavor that involved a thousand moving parts? The only times I had felt anxiety were when hotel staff took an extra couple of days to confirm my conference room bookings, but they all came through in the end. I had booked venues with my full name and none of them canceled on me. Was there a logical explanation for not experiencing a single major issue on a trip of this magnitude?

The last time I had undertaken a similar journey was in South America, when I focused entirely on sightseeing, intoxication, and sex, without doing any events. My daily work consisted solely of maintaining a diary. So many mishaps occurred that I was able to fill a book called *A Dead Bat In Paraguay* with them. Maybe someone out there will respond that I had "good luck" on my tour. After several years of enduring slander by the media, having my books banned, watching my reputation permanently maligned as a rapist, being hoodwinked by the woman I thought I would marry, and losing my dear sister, my "luck" had suddenly turned and now I would be materially successful or something. As a Christian, I do not accept this explanation. I see my trip as nothing short of a gift from God. He cleared the highways and byways for me, the mountain paths and ocean boulevards, because for the first time in my life, I voluntarily served His will. I testified to 900 people and, based on the emails I was receiving, inspired others to start their journey of faith. I don't expect my life to be all roses from this point on, since suffering is necessary to preserve one's salvation, but at least in the task of traveling throughout the entire country, God had been with me every step of the way.

✝

I began my journey home. I drove north from Charlotte and stopped for one night in Reidsville, North Carolina. People were friendlier than in Charlotte and pickup trucks seemed to be the sole means of transportation. Many restaurants advertised country-fried steak and biscuits with gravy. I wondered what this town would do when all the city slickers flocking to Charlotte turned the entire state blue and started grabbing guns and raising taxes. It's already happening in the West Coast. Californians are fleeing to Texas, Idaho, Utah, Colorado, and Montana, while the conservatives that remain accept being maltreated. Wouldn't the same thing happen in a place like North Carolina? Maybe not, because they aren't a rootless people like the Californians, many of whom have been in that state for only a generation or two, flush with cash from real estate and tech ventures. They can orchestrate a big move across the country, because it's not like they have big families to take with them. The folks of Reidsville don't have money to move, and since they are rooted to the land, they wouldn't move even if they could. I imagine they're the type who wouldn't complain much if they were financially hurting, but once the top-down directive comes to remove the rights they believe are their birthright, to tear down the statues of their ancestors, I expect them to resist, maybe not in an ultra-violent way, but more than the fleeing Californians.

Transplants are not rooted to the land, and when you're not rooted, you're rootless. The rootless don't fight because they have nothing to fight for. They see their current home as a place where they can maximize their extraction of money and pleasure, and when that scheme dries up because of bad traffic, high taxes, homelessness, or violence, it's no problem to move somewhere else and continue extracting while still voting for the same type of politicians who created the hellhole they left behind. The spirit of the gold rush never died. The gold miners go to one place for tech jobs, and once the biggest nuggets have been mined and they have taken more value out of the land than they gave, they get up and move somewhere else. For the longest time, the gold miners would flock to the West, the Northeast, and Florida, but now they are invading the Southern and Midwestern states where the culture is different. The future of America will be shaped by how those states react to the invaders.

The last stop on my trip was Charlottesville, Virginia, a Southern town dominated by the University of Virginia. If you go to the Walmart, you may see hillbillies, but if you stroll by the campus not far down the road, you may see a tranny or two. Maybe I'm too optimistic that there will be a reaction after all, and slowly but surely the rooted will let the rootless take over their lands and country. We won't have to wait long to find out.

On my last day before heading home, I reflected on the trip. I had seen beautiful parks and lands that foreigners from as far away as China come to venerate, but I had also experienced the ugliness and stench of the major cities, which seemed closer to hell than heaven. I learned that my faith could be deepened in these little hells, because you need to call upon God's name for mercy as you see the homeless encampments, the throngs of young people aching to fornicate, the lost souls staring at their smartphones with dead eyes hoping that the virtual world can give them the sort of meaning that only God can provide. And I learned it's a lie that you can't have a family during these times, that all women are cheaters and sluts who will divorce you and take half of your money.

My trip ended on November 28, 2019. I could go on at length about the best cities (Havre de Grace, Maryland; Clifton Forge, Virginia; Cheyenne, Wyoming; Weimar, Texas) or the worst (Yuma, Arizona; Portland, Oregon; Los Angeles, California), the best park (Rocky Mountains) or the worst (Black Hills), just like how in the past I discussed the best countries to meet women, but I see no use in it. This world is no longer my world. All that I have seen and touched will soon fade away. It's only here to test our souls, to build up our virtue so that we get closer to our Creator, but if you worship these things in and of themselves, whether the cities or nature, you have missed the point of existence.

I had imagined that the road trip would give me a stronger American identity. I would not only act like an American but *feel* like an American, but I didn't feel any more American than before despite talking to hundreds of other Americans who came to see me and participating in hundreds of short interactions with hotel staff, waiters, shopkeepers, and rambling strangers. Maybe the act of seeing the entire country would give me an identity? I drove from one coast to the other and back again, saw thousands of storefronts and American flags. Did I feel more like an American now? Still not. But I did learn more about another identity, one that goes deeper than the physical environment or the people or the buildings. It goes deeper than your style, accent, and choice of slang words, foods, or trends. It is the Christian identity. On this trip I embraced the one and only identity that matters. I am a Christian, because I believe Jesus Christ is my Lord and Savior. My entire identity has become wrapped around this ultimate truth of reality.

I saw a lot, and am grateful for it, but I'm no more an American than when I first started my journey. Only my faith in God will feed and nourish me, and while this doesn't mean turning my back on my country or wishing it harm, I see America as a place God picked for me and my soul to deepen faith, and He picked it at this exact time in human history, with all the evils that seem to be growing around me, because He knows that I will be able to endure it as long as I lean on Him. I am an American because God has deemed it so, but I am a Christian first, and I pray that the Lord helps me to remain faithful until my time here is done and I can finally go back home.

Epilogue

I wanted to take a long break. I wanted to read dozens of books, go for long walks through the park, and maybe experiment with making YouTube tutorial videos. I even considered learning a new hobby, such as electricity. I knew I would write a book about the tour, but that could wait a while.

My mother welcomed me back to her apartment in the Washington, DC suburbs. I could stay with her until I found a place to live in the Blue Ridge Mountains of Virginia or West Virginia, not more than two hours away. For the first two days, I vegetated on the internet, consuming podcasts and videos, but my mind kept interrupting me: "There is no time." I perceived it more as a deep-seated feeling than plain words, yet it still made no sense to me because I had all the time in the world. Taking at least one month off surely wouldn't be considered a delay.

On the third day, the same feeling entered me: "There is no time." During my next prayer, I stared at my icon of Jesus Christ, asking Him what this meant. How could there be no time? I was tired—I wanted to take a break! "There is no time," it repeated. Was something going to happen? Would God dictate that I should immediately get back to work because He knew a seismic event was about to occur? After praying about it for a day, I discerned that, yes, this was a message from God to get back to work immediately. I obeyed. Less than one week after the end of my trip, I began writing articles for my blog with titles such as *How I Turned to God*, *How to Control Your Lust*, and *How I Pray*.

The most momentous article was *I Have Unpublished Game and the Rest of My Pickup Books*. It turned out that unpublishing my older pickup books like *Bang* several months previously had been only an intermediate step. God had sensed how difficult it would be for me to banish all my books in one go, so He allowed me to unpublish the lesser works first, gain further spiritual strength, and then unpublish the rest, including *Game*, my newest pickup book that provided more than 50% of my income. Even if it was 100%, I could not continue profiting from sin and smut. I had a modest savings and would simply live off that until I could figure out how to earn a living again.

In spite of no longer having a consistent monthly income, I strongly desired to move to the mountains, and I was sure that this was not simply a worldly desire. By doing so, I would remove myself from the temptations of the city and suburbs. I would physically separate myself from those who were serving the will of Satan. Most importantly, I would pray more. I imagined that I would pray twice as much in a quiet mountain home than anywhere else. While there was a material component to my desire, for who wouldn't want to live in the mountains with the fresh air and singing birds, I reasoned that my motivations were mainly spiritual. I began seeking out a rental. If things went well in the next year or two, I could buy an exceedingly modest cabin from my savings and call it a life.

I found a house for rent in Martinsburg, West Virginia, in the state's Eastern Panhandle. I performed the public library test and, sure enough, it was packed with homeless people who were likely being affected by the state's opioid epidemic. When I drove up to the house, the long driveway was uneven gravel. My Dodge Challenger struggled to make it. The house itself was pleasant—a two-bedroom rancher on two acres of land—but I couldn't move to the mountain without first securing a mountain vehicle.

Buying an old used truck in good condition was not easy, especially since it was the middle of winter. I had to look at 12 trucks until I finally found a 1999 Toyota 4Runner with 218,000 miles. I bought it for $2,900. Besides a minor brake problem and a ticking noise from the engine that I didn't discover until later, I was exceedingly pleased with my purchase. Now I could move into a mountain home.

I looked at two more rentals. One was near Front Royal, Virginia, in the middle of national parkland. To get to the house, I had to drive three miles on a rough, non-state road. This wouldn't be a problem for my truck, but it would destroy my Challenger. Another downside was that it took 30 minutes to drive from the house to the nearest supermarket. The house was quite lovely, and felt more like a cabin thanks to its brick walls and fireplace, but it was too much of a jump for me to go from the city to living in the middle of nowhere.

The second house was in Harpers Ferry, West Virginia, located only an hour and 15 minutes from my parents. It lacked a fireplace but was on one acre of land, the perfect size for a mountain beginner. It was even built right on a small mountain. When I inspected the home with the showing agent, who worked for the property management company that represented the house's owner, I detected a sharp, chemical smell. The agent pointed out an ozone machine in the kitchen that was there to deodorize the home. I had never seen one before, but assumed that this was the standard protocol for the company when they changed tenants. Everything else about the house checked out. I applied for a one-year lease and was approved.

On Saturday, February 1, 2020, a little over two months after I had finished my tour, I moved to the mountain with the help of my father and two brothers. As soon as we walked into the house, we were hit with an incredible stench. "It smells like animal urine," one of my brothers said. Mostly pungent in the living room, it smelled like a combination of animal urine and body odor, and the peculiar thing was that it was spread over wide areas, not localized in places as you would expect if a dog had urinated in his favorite corner. Whatever the case, I had essentially moved into an animal toilet.

I contacted the landlord on Monday about the odor and they quickly sent a carpet-cleaning company, but even after a steam cleaning, the odor remained. I tried using boxes of baking soda to deodorize it, but it didn't help. The odor seemed to be off-gassing—it built up to an intolerable level if I shut the windows and left the house for a couple of hours. I had never encountered anything like it before, and I had lived in dozens of apartments throughout Europe.

Now that the problem involved more than a steam cleaner, the property management company dragged its heels. They sent one flooring contractor to get an estimate, and then waited one week to send another. To deal with the odor until it was fixed, I bought packages of plastic tarp to cover the carpet. Despite that, the odor still found a way to seep through (plastic is porous). I decided to be patient. I had never experienced a case where a landlord refused to make a necessary repair, even in Third World countries. It would be resolved eventually.

In the meantime, I enjoyed mountain living. For the first time in years, I could sleep without using a white-noise machine to drown out cars and loud neighbors. The air was so clean that I didn't have to cough up gray mucus from my lungs every other day. I had marathon conversations with one of my neighbors, talking to him for longer than I had talked to all the previous neighbors in my life combined. I picked up my first hitchhiker, a young local man who filled me in on details about the community. Best of all, I put out two bird feeders and officially became a bird-watcher.

Since my house was on the edge of a forest, it took only a day for the birds to flock to my feeders. I was soon able to identify 17 species, from the adorable Carolina chickadee to the goofy-looking pileated woodpecker. I'd wake up, look out the window, and watch the birds. I'd eat lunch and watch the birds. When the weather warmed enough, I'd sit outside and watch the birds. The woods were my free television set and the birds my entertainment, and I didn't tire of it. My favorite bird was the northern cardinal, a red-colored bird with a black mask for a face. A male and a female made the property their home. I named the male Carl and learned his songs. Often, I would hear Carl but was unable to see him, as bright as his foliage was. "Carl, where are you?" I'd say aloud. If a day went by without seeing Carl, I'd get concerned, but eventually he would make a grand appearance. As beautiful as he was, I perceived him to be humble and even stoic. He was content to rest on the branches and never got into fights with the other birds, unlike the more aggressive blue jay. I started to learn about the birds' personalities and their preferred foods. I thought I'd move to the mountain to become something like a mountain man, to work the land, do woodworking, and repair my cars, but I simply watched the birds.

By the second week of moving into the house, I began having bad dreams. They came almost every night. Many were of the sexual variety where I'd participate in acts I would never have consented to in real life. I'd wake up from these dreams and feel sullied, even though I knew I did not possess my normal will while in a dream state. Other dreams were terrifying nightmares.

I was invited to live in the house of two Ivy League professors. They had a boy of about eight and a newborn baby. I was encouraged to take a look at the baby, and when I did, I saw that it was a demon. Its face was leathery and wrinkled, its eyes black and sinister. At the next opportunity, I escaped the house with the older boy and drove far away. One day we stopped to eat at a diner. While seated at the table, I could see his parents walking towards us with the baby demon who had grown up quickly and could now walk on its own. It sat next to me and forcibly scooted me down the seat as if to say "I got you." I felt a burning on the side of the leg that the demon touched and then I woke up, my heart pounding out of my chest.

I had so many of these nightmares, the likes of which I had never experienced before, that I started going to bed with a wooden cross on my nightstand. Immediately before closing my eyes to sleep, I'd say a special prayer, asking God to help me endure these terrible dreams, and when I woke up from one, I'd grab my cross and pray myself back to sleep. Many times I would wake up in the morning with the cross in a random spot on the bed.

In another nightmare, I was a witness to two men fighting inside a dark house. One of the men commanded a demon to attack the other man. At the moment the demon was harnessed, I was placed within the perspective of the man being attacked, seeing and feeling as he could, though I knew it was not me who was the target. The effect was no less frightening. The demon, similar in appearance to the one from the previous nightmare, was rather short and displayed a wicked smile, excited to proceed with the strike. The demon ran towards me (i.e., the man), and right before we collided, I woke up.

At the time of these nightmares, I was reading *The Desert Fathers*. In the book, many monks discussed how they had been attacked by demons upon moving to the caves to worship Christ. Were they also coming after me because my salvation was more secure in the mountains? Did they have to adopt more direct interventions to unravel my faith, unlike in the city where I was steadily faced with human temptations? I wasn't sure, but I knew something was going on, because I went from having one or two mildly sexual dreams a month to having one or two outrageously sexual dreams a week, and from having one nightmare a year—if that—to three or more a week. It was so bad that I started to dread going to bed, but I began to see it as a test that must be passed.

One of my neighbors stopped by in the afternoon. After a few minutes of small talk, she said, "This house was empty for a while after the police arrested the previous tenant."

"Police?" I inquired.

"He was selling drugs. At least half a dozen cops came with a warrant and took him to jail." That was news to me.

I wondered whether the house's use as a drug den was in some way connected to the odor, which had still not been resolved by the landlord even though I had been living there for a month. I told them that the wait was unacceptable, and would give them one more month to complete all the necessary repairs or else I would terminate the lease. I was assured that the repairs would be made, and they were just waiting on the owner to make a final authorization to one of the estimates. But the days went by and no one came to fix the problem.

One afternoon by the house I saw the hitchhiker I had given a ride to. He recognized me and said, "I had been meaning to find you. I wanted to tell you something."

"I'm ready," I replied.

"This house was used as a crack house. About eight or ten niggers would come to the house, smoke crack, and then all pass out on the floor. I'm telling you the truth."

"A crack house?"

"Yes, and it wasn't only crack. They were doing all sorts of drugs up here. They got busted good, though."

"It's funny because the house has a really bad odor. If they were passing out on the floor, that would explain why the carpet smells."

"Oh man, who knows what they did to the house!"

I had moved into a crack house. My mountain dream had become a nightmare in more ways than one. Who knew what kinds of evil those addicts had committed? Intoxication, for sure, and probably fornication, day after day, strengthening the powers of evil on the mountain. What had the neighborhood demon thought when he found out that a man of repentance and prayer would be moving in? He formulated a plan to trip me up by sending me the most vile of dreams. Perhaps he had also influenced my landlord with the property management company and the house's owner not to make necessary repairs, to make me stew in the animal toilet and send me packing to a city of sin.

Before moving in, I had imagined that I would pray twice as much, but my prayers did not increase. I still attended church every Sunday, but there were fewer opportunities to help others since I was usually isolated at home. Instead of perhaps volunteering at the local food bank, I ended up using the internet far more than usual, and the constant isolation started to take a toll on me. I didn't know that all the meaningless interactions I had with people every day in random shops and cafés played a role in fulfilling my social needs. Now that I was home most days, with only Carl and his feathered friends to keep me company, I sought out more trivial social interactions on the internet. The barrier to developing relationships in my immediate area seemed so great when I had all that I needed—my church, friends, and family—one hour away. If the evil presence and the foul odor left by the crackheads were taken away, there would still be difficult adjustments, and the things I thought would happen, like additional prayer, would not be automatic, which told me that the mountain life might have been a fantasy, like so many of my fantasies before it.

Two more weeks passed. I was still optimistic that the landlord would fix the flooring because they answered most of my calls and emails, apologizing profusely. I reasoned that it would all work out in the end and deemed it safe to prepare for the growing season. I bought the book *Square Foot Gardening* and took notes on it. I bought vermiculite, peat moss, and five different kinds of compost as the book recommended. I bought a wheelbarrow and shovels. The property was on sloping land, making the construction of a raised bed difficult, so I decided to go with big garden bags instead, which would be mobile in case I moved after my one-year lease ended.

Then I received good news from the landlord: the owner had

authorized the contractor's estimate and the entire flooring would be replaced. I would just have to wait until the contractor called me to begin work. I had known that my patience would pay off. To celebrate, I went to the store to buy some more gardening supplies, including several bags of seeds—tomatoes, spinach, carrots, and lettuce. At around this time, the coronavirus pandemic was making its way from China to the United States. At least I would be prepared from a food standpoint. Everything was going to fall into place.

It took nearly another week for the contractor to call me. He said that he was waiting for the owner to authorize the repair plan. But hadn't the landlord told me that it had already been authorized. Had she lied to me? I contacted the landlord and she assured me that the repair was about to take place. By now, my emotions were exhausted from being whipped up and down, of being hopeful and then having that hope squashed. The deadline I had imposed for the job to be completed, April 1, was fast approaching. The carpet had been cleaned six weeks prior, and since then no work had been done. It was hard for me to accept that I was being played. The owner of the house had no intention of carrying out the repair, and the landlord simply stalled and lied, since their hands were tied. Maybe they thought I would just get used to the smell.

Several more days went by and nothing happened. I told my mother that I'd be moving back in. I bought cardboard boxes and started packing, though a small part of me still hoped that the contractor would call me at any moment and say he was on his way to begin the repair. That call never came. The day before I moved out, I sent an email to the landlord unilaterally terminating the lease. She implored me not to give up, since the contractor would contact me the very next day to start work. I didn't believe her.

Because I had so many more possessions than when I moved in, I had to rent a truck instead of only using my 4Runner. My father came to help me, making jokes about my failed stint in the mountains. I froze when it was time to take down my two bird feeders. I loved watching the birds every day, and now they were being taken away from me. Why had God rebuked me? Why didn't He want me to live in peace in the mountains so that I could worship Him without being surrounded by temptation? I failed to make sense of what was happening as I dumped the birdseed on the ground.

I had been able to conduct a massive road trip, completing dozens of events along the way without a single major setback, but when I had tried to be a normal man living in a normal home, I was stymied. I knew that God's will would become clear to me in the future, and I would be able to look back and think, "Aha, so that's why He didn't want me to live in that house!" But understanding that was of no consolation when I bade farewell to my mountain home.

As expected, the contractor did not call me on the day I moved, or ever again. Looking back, so many mistakes had to be made for this fiasco to occur. First, I failed to inspect the house properly by not connecting the deodorizer machine to a serious problem. At the very least, I should have visited the house again after the machine had been removed to verify everything was okay. Second, the agent who initially showed me the house lied that any odor would be gone after the deodorizer machine had been removed. Third, my landlord at the property management company lied to me several times about the timetable of the repair and its approval. Last, the owner of the house refused to complete a repair required by West Virginia law to make the home "fit and habitable." So many things had gone wrong, on so many levels, by all parties involved, that I couldn't help but see my dislodgment as ordained by God. I just wanted to know *why*, but even if the answer had been given to me immediately, I doubt I would have understood. My ability to see the complete course of my salvation is too limited.

Once settled in at my mom's house, the coronavirus pandemic started in earnest. There was no way I'd sign another lease until the real estate market stabilized, which meant that I would have to learn how to live with my mother for an extended time in a multicultural suburb, the type of place that I have spent many pages of this book criticizing. Immediately, I entered a depression. I had had the mountain and the birds and now I had hip hop music, traffic, and police sirens.

A few days after moving back into my mother's, I swore I heard Carl singing. It couldn't be—I had lived in the suburbs for decades and had never seen a northern cardinal. I would stare at the window, looking for Carl, but saw only sparrows, crows, and American robins. I must be hearing things, or perhaps there was another bird with a song similar to Carl's.

I went for a short walk on a grassy path by the trees. I saw a European starling and a blue jay. Then a flash of red streaked across my vision. A beautiful song filled my ears. I turned to the trees and there, only a few feet away, was a northern cardinal in full glory singing to the heavens. He was not afraid of me, and continued singing as if I were the only person in the world who could hear it. "Glory to God," I exclaimed, and crossed myself. God had not forsaken me. Very quickly after moving back to the suburbs, He sent my favorite creature to me. As the days went on, I saw families of cardinals, far more in number than I had seen in the mountains.

I wondered why the birds who lived near my mother's apartment didn't move to the mountains. The air is cleaner and the views more spectacular, and I would assume food is more plentiful or at least less tainted by human refuse. Yet the birds in the suburbs seem content to live near people, among the rubbish and the concrete. They don't complain, and continue to live and sing as do their brothers and sisters in the mountains. Maybe I should accept that my mother's house is good enough for me and live and sing just like the birds. What do I have to complain about as long as I can continue to live and work in the name of God?

I know I cannot live in my mother's apartment forever, which I'll add is only one-bedroom (I sleep on a foam mattress on the floor and have turned the corner of her living room into a live stream studio), but I must move for the right reasons. I made an idol out of the mountains, and went there because I wanted to experience a shade of heaven on earth. As light as the cross I have to bear has become, I didn't want to carry it, and wanted to extend the bliss I had experienced in the Rocky Mountains. God showed me what a mistake that plan was, just like all the other plans I had devised through my own will.

The fact that my spiritual development didn't deepen in the mountains was all the proof I needed that the decision to move there had been worldly. I will move there one day because I need a place to live where I can continue serving God, not because I want to devise a new "mountain man" identity, experience pleasure from the beautiful views, or even watch the birds. With this frame of mind, if I move to the mountains in the future and experience hardship, I know it will be spiritually useful, if not necessary. I'd welcome the increased weight of my cross instead of lamenting that my plan to experience heaven had failed, but as the country descended further into chaos with the violent Black Lives Matter protests of the summer, I would be lying if I said that I didn't long for the mountain.

Many questions remain. Will I remain single and celibate for the rest of my life? Should I remove myself from the world, especially online, and pursue monasticism? Should I leave the Armenian Church and join the main branch of Eastern Orthodoxy? Will I be able to endure the trials and tribulations of living in a country that is in rapid decline? I don't have the answers to these questions, but I know that if I orient my heart and soul towards Jesus Christ, I will do what is most necessary for my salvation and the salvation of those around me. May God show me the way and have mercy on me as I embark on this new life.

Appendix
What I've Learned About Life Speech

The following is a transcript of the speech I gave in Nashville, Tennessee on November 16, 2019. It was my long goodbye to the secular life I had lived. (Note: It contains sexual content.)

I've been in Nashville for a couple days, and one thing I can tell you is that Nashville is what I thought Austin was going to be, with a cool Southern charm and the live bands. When I went to Austin, it was about a month ago, and it was the first time in the United States I saw a pile of feces on the street, so I don't think Austin is good anymore.

Now I hope you don't mind the trash can I'm speaking on. Usually, the hotel gives me a podium, but I feel that this is some kind of garbage can.

It is good to be here, I have never seen so many cowboy hats. Nashville is more Southern than I thought. It turns out that the South is not just one culture—it's a lot of individual cultures, so I'm glad that I can learn more about the country that I'm from.

One thing I've learned on this tour is that a lot of who we are and how we turn out as men or women is based on where we are from and where we grew up, so I wanted to start my story way back in 1986. Now is there anyone here who wasn't born in 1986? So more than half of the room. I was seven years old and I hate to admit it, but I was something of a momma's boy. My dad was hands-off. He would bring home the bacon and make sure we had food and shelter, but he wasn't too involved in the day-to-day concerns of his boy. I was in the third grade at that time, and the way my school—the elementary school I was in—worked is that in the morning we would line up on the blacktop according to our grade. I had to pass the big kids before finding the line to my third-grade class.

It was wintertime, and I remember my mom made me wear this woolen ethnic hat that was not cool. It was very ugly. And what started happening was that on the walk to the blacktop, the big kids would run up to me, pull my hat off and throw it down and laugh in front of dozens of kids. Now this was a very traumatizing thing for a boy in the third grade. I didn't know how to fix it, because when you're in the third grade, the fifth graders look like giants. My dad wasn't involved with that kind of thing, so I went to my mom. I said, "Mom, these big kids are taking off that really ugly hat you make me wear every day." She was in the principal's office within an hour, saying, "These boys are hurting my son." And I can tell you that those boys never bothered me again after that.

So what did I learn? I learned that if you have a problem, mom is going to bail you out. Just a couple of years later, I was in the neighborhood feeling especially cocky. Me, cocky? And I started talking trash to a kid who was bigger than me. And there are two men in this room who are six foot six, so imagine I was talking trash to them. This kid on the playground didn't have to take that garbage, so what did he do? When I got close to him, he punched me in the face. And what did I do? I went home crying to mom.

I said, "Mom, this big kid punched me in the face... for no reason at all!" And what is she going to do about it? She came out and said, "Scotty, it's not a good idea to punch innocent little boys in the face." Here I started to reinforce the idea that if I have a problem in life, go to mother for help and not my dad.

The first thing I learned in life before I knew that I learned it is that men need fathers who are hands-on. It's not enough to just work and bring home the bacon and pay the mortgage, because too much mom makes you a girl. It makes you seek your mommy for any kind of help that you have in life, and unfortunately, a lot of the dads that are older, some of the boomer dads—and no offense to boomers—they were hands-off. They were so hands-off that when men needed advice on how to meet girls, they went on the internet and sought my guidance.

Have people in this room heard of what's called Drag Queen Story Time? It's when a man dresses up as a woman then gets hired by the local government at the library to read to young kids, and I see this as a grooming program, as a way to remove the disgust instinct from children for people who are really dangerous to them.

My job is to understand what's going on in the culture, so I look at the photos from these events, and one thing I noticed: where are the fathers? If you look at the pictures from Drag Queen Story Time, it's almost all moms with the intention of creating open-minded children who aren't bigots. This is what happens when we start to remove the role of fathers.

I grew up and attended the University of Maryland. I studied microbiology. It was a tough major, so it was helpful if you had a study buddy, and mine was a very attractive girl. She was curvy. I was sexually interested in her, but I didn't know how to date her, how to put the moves on her. Who did I go to for help? Don't all yell it out at the same time! I went to my mom. I said, "Mom, there's this good-looking girl in class and I want to date her." Of course, I said it in nicer terms, since I wanted to do more than just date.

My mom was so excited. "Yes, finally I can teach my boy how to interact with girls!" What is the advice that my mom gave? She said to hold the door open for her at every opportunity I get. Whenever I go into a restaurant or a coffee shop with her, make sure I pay the bill every single time. Don't let that poor girl open her purse at all. Be nice to her.

My mom taught me to be a clown, but in the wrong way, to hide my real intentions and put on this mask of being a doormat to get the girl and have this amazing love and relationship. I did that for months and months. I was holding the door open for her, paying for coffee and tea, going out for pizza. I would pay and pay, but nothing happened.

After one long afternoon studying with her, she needed a ride home. I gave her a ride home and then she invited me inside. I went into her home that she shared with a couple of people. Then she invited me to her room and sat me on her bed, and then she sat down about three feet away. My mom never told me about this. What did I do? Nothing! I didn't do anything, and she got impatient and said, "Well, I have some chores to do." The next day I told my friends, "She invited me to her room. She sat me on her bed. Do you think she liked me?" This is how clueless I was.

The second thing I learned is that whatever is gifted to you in life by Mother Nature, the universe, or God, you have to—as men—reach out and take it. Things will only be placed in front of you but no closer. You have to bridge that gap, that last step, with your strength, your knowledge, and your effort. If you are a woman, you don't have to do that, because there will oftentimes be a lot of men willing to give you what you want. For a woman, it sometimes seems like, "Wow, things keep happening to me. These wonderful coincidences and gifts keep coming to me." Some women get so tired of all the attention they receive, but you men probably don't have that problem.

Today, women are being trained to take, to be ambitious go-getters, to be strong and independent. A woman is being trained to have a career that she values and dedicates herself to. At the same time, men are being trained to be their allies, to atone for thousands of years of patriarchy and toxic masculinity, to just step aside and let women have their time in the spotlight earning the big bucks in the city so that on Friday and Saturday nights they can go to Broadway in the honky-tonk bars and get trashed. Unfortunately, if you're a man and you buy the lie that you have to step aside, you don't get anything, not even the leftovers.

After I graduated from university, the next step was to get a job. I got a job in Maryland at a pharmaceutical company as an industrial microbiologist. One thing I noticed at work is that there were so many butt-kissers. Everyone was trying so hard to impress others. To me it seemed fake, like when you are in a Lyft or Uber and you are fake nice to the driver because you want a good rating. They were always trying to impress upon the management that they care.

I remember the department head sent an email saying, "I need someone to inventory and organize the stockroom." The stockroom? I'm a microbiologist. I didn't go to university for four years to organize a stockroom. No, no—I'm not going to volunteer, and I watched a lot of people who did. I just came here to do my job in the scientific field.

Not long after that, it was time for performance reviews. Has anyone here been through one of these? It's when someone you don't like evaluates all your strengths and weaknesses. I was expecting to get the standard 3% raise. They sat me down and said, "Roosh, your performance this time around was under the curve, below the standard. Your raise is zero, and one more thing: we're putting you on 90 days' probation."

"I'm going to jail?" I asked.

"No, you're not going to jail, but if your performance doesn't increase after the 90 days, we have to let you go."

Whoa. That was a wake-up call. This one company, if I didn't do what they wanted, could have me out on my butt. My sole source of income, gone. So what was I going to do? Since this company was squeezing me out, I decided to change jobs. I found a recruiter online and she helped me land another job down the street making $10,000 a year more. My title jumped from industrial microbiologist to associate scientist. I would show my old company.

Now that I knew how things worked, so guess who raised his hand the highest when the boss needed help on something dumb? That would be me. I made it seem like work at this company was so integral to my happiness that if the company made money, I was happy and pleased with my life, that I was dedicating myself to them. I actually brought inventory-organizing techniques from my old company to the new one.

My boss at the time, Dr. Wang, a Taiwanese man who I could hardly understand, was saying, "Roosh, look at our stockroom. We are so happy that we hired you. Since you're such an integral team player, we want to pay for your master's degree at Johns Hopkins University." I had no plans to do that—I did not want to go back and study for three more years, but I said, "Yes, Dr. Wang, I plan on doing just that. I'm considering which field of study I want to focus on, but thank you so much for this offer. I look forward to being an important member of this company for years and years."

I guess you can say that he was a little bit surprised when, one year into the job, I got him into a meeting and said, "Dr. Wang, I need to quit to travel the world and bang a lot of girls."

He said, "What? But you love it here? You were going to get your master's degree and our stockroom is so tidy. What do you want? Is it the money? Do you want some more? We'll give it to you."

I replied, "But Dr. Wang... I really need to bang."

So I left that company in 2007. During the one year I worked there, I lived like a pauper and saved a lot of money to do what I really wanted to do.

The third thing I learned in life is to either play to win or don't play at all. Every human sphere, group, organization, or bureaucracy has a set of rules built in where if you play by those rules then you will win within that specific game. At my first company, I didn't play by the rules, and if you're not playing by the rules then you are getting played. I got played. I was under a lot of stress that I would lose my job and not be able to pay my rent, but at the second company I was armed with the rules, so Dr. Wang got played instead.

You may not like the idea of playing people, and I can understand that, so it's better to be careful about which game you choose to play, because every game has rules, and even if you want to play the *game* game, the game of picking up girls, you're going to have to play the women you meet (or the men) in order to get what you want from them before they get what they want from you. Now I'm extremely choosy about which game I play, to minimize the number of games that I'm in.

I left my corporate job. I was free—I didn't have to go to work every day and be stuck in traffic, and traffic in Nashville is worse than I thought it would be. No way will I get stuck in Nashville traffic. So what am I going to do? At the time, I saw myself as a conqueror, an explorer. I wanted to be like the *conquistadores* of old, of going to South America, the Third World. And what am I going to do there? Hmm… visit every country on the continent! What else is there to do? That's what I'm going to do—a random goal that spoke to me. This is now who I am. I had never really traveled much before, but my identity became "traveler." I picked a new identity.

I can say this: Hollywood makes travel to the Third World much more romantic and pleasing than it actually is. I started the trip and stayed in grungy hostels where you have bunk beds of two or three stocked with mostly Australian people, because they have this concept called the gap year where they graduate and for one year they try to bang as many people as they can. I would hang out with Australians at night and go to bars. It wasn't much of an exotic experience. It didn't help that there was no comfort there. I got used to a lot of the First World comforts that we have in the USA as we slowly degrade into Third World status. I was used to air conditioning, having my own car, phones that work, cleanliness, and so on.

In the hostels I stayed at, they had bed bugs, scabies, and lice. You would wake up with a rash on your body. Food preparers wouldn't wash their hands before making you a meal, so I contracted parasite after parasite. If you want, I can go into the details of all the times I spent on the toilet bowls in South America. Does anyone want me to...? Okay, no. I also didn't have a big fat check being deposited in my checking account every two weeks. Suddenly, money was a bit tight. I also got homesick. There was one hostel where 33 of us were stacked on triple bunk beds, so that was probably the most uncomfortable way to get a night's sleep. I missed home.

All that I realized only one month into my grand tour, but I had told people back home that I was going to be gone for a long time. "I don't know when I am coming back," I said. Online, I told the world that I was going to conquer and travel throughout the entire continent, but here I was on my second country, already tired. I couldn't go back, because my ego was invested. If I went back before I conquered, I would be seen as a weak man. I would be someone who wasn't as strong as he had thought. Maybe how I saw myself was different than who I really was. I didn't want that image to clash, so I stayed in South America.

I started my trip in the capital of Ecuador. By bus, I traveled through Peru, Bolivia, Chile, Argentina, Paraguay, Uruguay, and Brazil, the land of big butts. I thought that Brazil was going to fulfill all the fantasies that I had as a man who was starting to dive deeper into game. I wasn't just going to pick up girls in the United States—I was going to be some kind of international Casanova, known all across the world for his sexual prowess.

I went to Brazil and the city of Rio de Janeiro, the tropical paradise. At this time, I found some of my Australian friends and went to a nightclub. I looked more homeless than I do now, but it's getting a little close. There was a good-looking girl making undeniable eye contact with me. I didn't need my mom's help anymore. I knew what to do. I walked up to her and things went well. We started to touch, kiss, grope, and then after that she invited me to her apartment where we had a night of passion.

After this night, I thought, "Yes, this is why I came here, to have an experience like this one." I must tell you that she was the most beautiful girl I had ever been with. All the sufferings I had experienced during the trip were worth it because I believed at the time that, as long as I had the most beautiful girl in the world, I could be living in a refrigerator cardboard box out on the streets, like many people in this city, and be totally happy.

Although she was the most beautiful girl I had ever been with, and that she was calm, sweet, loving, and way more affectionate than girls I had dated here in the States, everything else was all messed up. My money was not so great, I was tired, my stomach was sick, and I didn't want to stay in dirty hostels anymore. I wanted to go back home. It had been six months since I started the trip, the longest trip I had ever taken, so I couldn't really enjoy the pleasure that I had sought.

After one month of dating, if that's what you want to call it, I had to leave. I told her, "I'm sorry, but I'm a wreck. I need to heal my body and raise my income, but I'm coming back." I saw her as something like the true love that I had always wanted, and I can tell you when I left her, all these romantic love songs on the radio suddenly had a meaning to it. "Yes, I'm a part of this now because I fell in love with a beautiful exotic girl who gave me immense pleasure."

I went back to the USA and got my money right. I healed up as much as I could, and after some time decided that it was time to go back, time to reunite with the only love of my life, but first I had to go to Colombia for six months to bang some girls there. It's because I have to get it out of my system! I knew she was the one… I just needed a little bit more fun, and then I'd be ready.

After six months in Colombia, I was ready to reunite with her, but first there was a groupie in Brazil I had to sleep with, and then I was really done. I went back to the girl in Rio, one-and-a-half years after leaving her. She was not as excited to see me as I thought she would be. She said, "You didn't even send me a postcard." That's true, I was busy with all those other girls. She broke up with me, but I used my high-octane game to weasel in one more night in her apartment, and then it was over for good.

The fourth thing I learned in life is when you're gaining in life, you're also losing, and when you're losing in life, you're also gaining. What do I mean? I gained the most beautiful girl I had ever been with, but I had to lose my health in the process. It wasn't an even exchange. At the same time, I lost the income I was used to earning and the comfort of living in the suburbs of Washington, DC, but I had gained the strength to do the type of trip that I'm doing now, and this trip is way harder than the first trip I took.

I hope a lot of you here, if you haven't already, meet a great woman and decide to marry her. What an amazing addition to your life, a woman you are compatible with, but if you marry her, you also lose the freedom to do whatever you want. You can't go out on Saturday night anymore to party and get drunk. Now you have to make a sacrifice for the love of your wife.

Some of you here are young and may be losing hope in the USA, to find a woman, so now your mind is thinking of going somewhere else, to Asia, to Europe. You want to gain the freedom to travel, to experience the novelty of dating women with different accents, but at the same time you have to understand that you lose time with your family and friends. You hurt the existing bonds you have to pursue novelty somewhere else.

Lastly, you may get a little black-pilled. You see what's going on in the world outside and start to lose hope in the material world to solve the problems of the day and give you what you need, but that sets the stage for you to gain hope in the spiritual world.

We live in a very goal-oriented culture. A lot of questions people have for you is, "What is your goal?" We're defined by the goals and projects that we have, and think that if we have a goal and achieve it, accomplish it, it will be a pure gain in life, a profit, but you have to consider what you are losing at the same time, and whenever you gain at life, you're also losing, no exceptions. Now I'm a little bit careful about which goals that I set out to do.

After I got tired in South America—because that's how novelty works, you just get tired and need something new, some new lights and action—I went to Europe. This was in 2011. I went to Iceland for two months and Denmark for two months. I became a media sensation in both of those countries. In Denmark, I got a tip: "Hey, Roosh, you should go to Poland." I said, "Poland, is that a city in Germany?"

"No, dummy, it is a country of 40 million people. It's cheap, it's safe, and the girls are beautiful."

I was there, because at this point I had readjusted my life totally to just pursue sex. If you told me in this time, there is a land, a magical land, a paradise even, where the women are sexy and they'll sleep with you quickly, I would pack my bags and get on an airplane, because I was the conqueror. This was my identity, and I was getting very heavily invested into it.

I went to Poland in 2011 and, sure enough, the Polish girls at that time had a type of man they wanted to be intimate with, and that type was me. They had a salsa craze and all these women were asking me, "Are you Spanish?"

"No, but I could be."

I played up the foreigner angle and 2011 was my highest notch-count year. I was going out five nights each week to either chase after girls or to go on dates. I remember I didn't have a laundry machine in my apartment, so I had to go to the laundromat constantly with sheets, bedsheets and bedsheets. I felt great. This is it. This is what I wanted the first time I went to South

America in 2007. Four years later, it happened. I was a rock star. I was a king. Of course, I would go online to share all my exploits, put them into books, share all the sexual details.

There is a meme, and it goes something like this: every year has to be better than the previous one. Has anyone ever heard of that? That you have to keep growing and growing without hitting a ceiling? I bought it. I thought I would be 80 years old and in that year, I would bang one thousand girls. Every year has to be better, but how can I top 2011 when pursuing the flesh was a full-time job? How am I going to top that in 2012?

I was traveling through Eastern Europe, and in 2012 I was in Croatia. There was one girl I met. We exchanged phone numbers, but nothing happened. One thing I learned in Europe is that if you have a beard, the hipster bars are very good. So I did the only thing that a man with a beard would do: I found an apartment right next to the city's biggest hipster bar.

I went to this hipster bar on a weekend night. I started talking to a girl and she said, "You have a great beard." I knew that when a girl compliments your beard in a bar, she wants to sleep with you. I didn't learn that from my mom. The girl gave me a look of passion.

There was a move I had been perfecting. The move was to look at the girl and say, "This bar is kind of loud and smelly. How about we go for a short walk outside where it's quieter and the air is fresh?" She said, "I want to, but I'm here with four of my friends."

I replied, "It's only going to be a 15-minute walk. We'll be right back." She agreed.

We went for a walk and, about two or three minutes into the walk, wouldn't you believe that we were right in front of my apartment building. What are the odds? I looked at her and said, "Wow, this is actually where I live. Since we're here... I just bought a bottle of very fine Italian wine. This wine won an award on the internet for the best vintage of 2010." I really poured it on.

"My Italian friend said it's the best wine he's ever tasted. Would you like to come upstairs and have a glass of wine with me?" She didn't even hesitate to say yes. It was the cheapest bottle I could find in the supermarket.

We went upstairs, and I don't think we even opened the bottle of wine. I slept with her, and her friends started calling and texting. She left. What a great thing—I got to experience a dose of pleasure. I can tell you, man to man, for the men in this room, that I was no longer horny at all. I was content. I just wanted to sit in front of the laptop in the afterglow of another episode of conquering, but 2012 had to be better than 2011. I had to keep growing.

I contacted the other girl that I knew, asked her where she was, and after two to three hours of work, I brought her back on the same night and slept with her too. I was so proud of what I did that I announced on my blog that I slept with two girls in one night. What a "king" I was.

I have to tell you what was going through my mind to do this, to pursue sex when there was no physical need for it. I believed that sex alone, sex with anybody, was the peak of male existence. If you listened to any rap song at the time, about getting laid and getting paid, I would think, "This is it! This black man raised in a broken home figured it out! He figured out the secret to life and now I'm going to do it too!" And I was doing it—I was getting laid and writing the sex stories for everyone, writing the game tips, and then I would get paid. I was living the dream, this was the peak. I'd made it.

The reality—and it didn't hit me at the time—was the only peak I had achieved by doing this, of sleeping with these two girls who I didn't care about, of having the most intimacy with another human being that you could, really it was a peak of how broken I was. I knew I couldn't top this, because my body didn't want to go along with the meme of "keep going" and "keep achieving," but my whole life was entwined in it. All the attention and adoration and compliments I received online came from what I was doing. Men were writing to me every day: "Roosh, you changed my life because now I can sleep with a woman I met in a bar." They were buying my books. How could I stop? How could I admit to myself that maybe this wasn't the path?

So I hung on. I kept going. I had to continue to pick up girls in Eastern Europe, continue to write the *Bang* guides. In some ways, I was sleeping with women I didn't care about for the attention and financial benefit, and who also does that? A prostitute.

The fifth thing I learned is that your ego will enslave you if you let it. Your ego loves numbers. It needs the numbers, because how else can it compare itself with other people? It's going to be obsessed with the number of girls you've been with, how much your salary is, how much your car is worth, how much you can bench press and deadlift. For any pursuit that can be quantified with a number, there is a very good chance that your ego is attached to it, because what the ego needs to do is prove that it is better than him, and him, and him.

Without a number, how can I compare myself to you? What am I going to use? Some men even use height. If there is a number, I can get my ego involved and prove I am better.

How do I know if a man is highly likely to be enslaved by his ego? What question does he ask me? Does anyone want to take a guess? If a guy asks me, "So Roosh, how many girls have you been with?", then I know numbers are very important to him. If I say a number that is higher than his, the insecure ego will make him think, "But my girls are hotter than Roosh's!" And if I say a number that is lower than his, it's going to think, "Yeah, that's right, I knew I was better than Roosh. I should be writing all those *Bang* guides." This is how the ego works.

What happens when you stop chasing after the numbers? When you release yourself from the bondage of the ego, especially in the city where you see guys with their fancy cars or hot girls, what happens after that is you start to pursue your physical needs. "I need to work to make money for food and shelter... I am going to sleep with that girl because I am horny right now." I thought that was it—pursuing a physical need was healthy. Problem is your physical needs can be manipulated. A little bit of porn, a little bit of racy Instagram photos, and the girls in the yoga pants can make you think that your physical need is higher than it really is. You can then transcend your physical needs, and begin to serve your spiritual needs after that.

I was still in Europe for a couple of years, kind of hanging on. Then 2015 came, and that year was a bit rough. I had my first-ever tour through six cities. I spoke in Berlin, Germany, then London, England, a country I would be banned from. I did two talks in the US—one in Washington, DC and one in New York City. Then I thought, "Let me do two more talks in Canada."

One week before I went to Canada, the people there lost their minds. The mayor's office, the local media, and the feminist organizations connected to the universities all rose up at the same time—by coincidence I'm sure—to look at me and say, "Roosh is a bad man. We cannot let him speak here because of all the sexist, misogynistic, pickup artist stuff that he's been putting out. His work has been hurting women."

I thought, "I have a right to speak there. Who are these people to stop me? No, I'm going to do my talks anyway." The two talks I had planned were in Montreal and Toronto. I went to Montreal first. You're probably thinking, "Why doesn't Roosh have a check-in girl here? Why is he doing everything? Is he cheap or something?" I'll tell you why: the check-in girl I hired for Montreal, three days before the event, leaked the venue to the media. She stabbed me in the back. Why would a woman do that? She wanted to be a hero—"I saved Montreal from a bad person!"

I wasn't going to give up. I scrambled and found an alternate venue, but I can tell you that this was a viral story. This was the top story in Montreal for a couple of days. People wanted to get me, and it wasn't my home country. I wondered what they could do to me. Could they kick me out of the country? So what I had to do was implement counter-terrorist techniques. Instead of everyone meeting in the room, we met in a park. I vetted everyone. People turned off their phones. We walked to the venue in secret.

Everyone here seems pretty calm, but for that talk men were tense. Half of them were staring at the door waiting for some blue-haired freaks to come barreling in. I don't even know if they heard half of the things that I said, but the talk was done. I did it! I conquered Canada! Which isn't hard to do actually—I'm sure all of you here can conquer Canada as well.

I wanted to party with the guys in the bars. We went to the nightlife area and I was feeling good. "Yes, I did it again! I can't be stopped!" I saw a group of girls on the street. I approached them and asked if they wanted to join me and maybe 12 other guys in the bar. They agreed and we went in. I started talking to one girl by a table. It's kind of weird that when I was talking to her, she was texting a lot. Now I'm sure a lot of you men here have been on dates with a girl who texted, so what I did was use that as an opportunity to stroke her legs, because I was not only going to conquer Canada, but get laid too.

One thing I didn't know was that there were roaming bands of Antifa looking for me. Then she said, "I have to go to my friends real quick." She was playing hard to get, but that's okay, because I wrote the book on game—I knew how to overcome that. She didn't come back until a while after, and when she did, there was a large group of people standing behind her. "That's weird," I thought. She had a beer in her hand and she looked at me and said, "How dare you come to Montreal and bring your filth and hate speech! Hate speech has no home here! You get out!" I thought, "I guess I'm not getting laid tonight." Then she threw her whole beer at me.

I was younger and faster then, so I turned my head before the moment of impact. The beer hit the side of my head. I didn't tell you but I wore a disguise at the time that I bought at a costume shop. It was called the "rock star wig." I was wearing an insanely long wig that went down to the small of my back. I had thought, "I may get laid in this wig. Should I tell her about it? No, Roosh, just go with it."

I took the wig off and, to get these clowns wet, I started to spin the wig in the air. They were yelling at me, and you can watch this on YouTube today by searching for "Roosh beer." At the time, Buzzfeed came out with a story: "We got him, girls! We got Roosh! He got soaked in beer!"

I'm glad she did text her goons, because how about if I did sleep with her? What would she do after that?

After Montreal, I went to Toronto. I successfully held the event there. I did it, Canada conquered. It's part of the United States now. But the enemy was still seething: "We gotta get this Roosh guy!" What they did was start a petition online to get all of my Amazon books banned, and 400,000 people signed it. You would think Jeff Bozo would ban it, but he did not. Yet three years after that, when I put out a book called *Game* with a photo of a man and a woman sitting underneath a tree, he banned that.

These things I could deal with, but then the bad news came towards the end of that year. My sister, who is seven years younger than me, was diagnosed with breast cancer. This came out of the blue. An older brother never expects to get that kind of news. There isn't any way to prepare yourself, but, as a scientist, one way I did prepare was dive into the medical books and articles to ensure she would get the best care, and during that care there was no way I would let her go through it without me, so one of the first things I did was book a flight home.

I was in Poland at the time, and when I got the news and bought a ticket, my flight was slated to leave one week after. During this week, I was starting to come to terms with what was happening, looking at cancer survivability numbers, and on and on. I pared down my life in Poland. I told my landlord I would be leaving. I began giving away my stuff. I didn't know when I was coming back, because cancer treatment can take a long time.

Three days before the flight, my friends decided to throw me a farewell party at my favorite bar. This was a bar where we would go to pick up Polish girls, the bar they were most receptive to a foreigner. I went to that bar, and I wasn't in any mood to pick up girls, but by this point in my life, the only strategy or technique I had to get over hard times, bad news, or grief was to meet a girl in a bar and bring her back home. It was the only way I reliably knew how to experience any kind of human joy.

In this bar, after a couple of hours, once I started to drink to take away the pain from my sister's diagnosis, I wanted to feel pleasure. I didn't want to be in pain. I saw a good-looking girl. I approached her and she took a liking to me. After one hour, we went to a nightclub, one that I had spent a lot of time in. I had the moves—I took her to the dance floor and we danced, if that's what you want to call it, though it was more like dirty dancing. We kissed. I felt good. The problems I had were gone. With a beautiful girl in front of me while under the influence of alcohol, nothing was wrong.

She told me that she has a rule, and her rule is that she doesn't sleep with a man the first time she meets him. I didn't think of it at the time, but if she had to make a rule about that, imagine how many times she slept with a guy the first time she met him. Guys, I have a rule: I do not drink more than 20 beers in a single night. In that case, I probably have an alcohol problem.

I used her rule as a way to build comfort, a game tactic to strengthen the connection to set up sex for next time. The day before I was set to fly back home, we had a first date. I took her to a cheeseburger shack called Fat Bob's, and after we ate, I brought her back to my apartment. I slept with her. No alcohol was involved. I was happy. I didn't ask her about her previous sexual history or partners, yet she volunteered it. She said,

"You're the second guy that I have ever been with." And do you know what I did in response? I made her a girlfriend. I decided that this girl would be the one.

You're probably thinking, "Roosh, are you crazy?" The answer is that at the time the only way I knew how to get through a difficult phase of life was to have the companionship, intimacy, and support of a beautiful girl, so that is what I did.

The sixth thing that I learned in life is that love is a matter of will, a decision that you make. Attraction is different; it's not a choice. You don't know who you're going to be physically or emotionally attracted to, but you can definitely pick and choose who you enter a relationship with, so I used my will to get into a relationship with this beautiful girl, and when you decide to love someone, the beauty flows. Suddenly, you see all of the good things about her. All the red flags that should be blaring at you, like the neon lights on Broadway, become more like yellow lights that are not so bad. I actually thought it was my game that got her in bed quickly. It was my cheeseburger game. I made her feel really happy with the grease.

One thing I can ask you: do you think I paid the price for making a girl like this my girlfriend? We're going to find out soon.

I went back to the US and started to meet with the doctors. They came up with a treatment plan for my sister, which came in phases. The first phase was chemotherapy, a chemical treatment meant to kill the cancer cells right before it kills the person, but a lot of times, the chemo does kill the person. Then there would be surgery to remove the tumor and finally the radiation to zap the site of where the tumor was so that it doesn't grow back.

She had some world-class doctors, perhaps the best on the East Coast. I confirmed that her treatment plan was up to the modern standard, but one thing I noticed is that the side effects of the chemotherapy and radiation were cancer, but she already had cancer, so how can the cure cause the same disease you're trying to cure? But what else could I do? You can go online, do a Google search for cancer cures and you're going to find a lot of stuff—baking soda, lemon juice. Am I going to tell my sister not to do the medical standard for an alternative juice thing that Steve Jobs did? This treatment was her best option.

She started the chemo and had severe side effects. I would take her to the infusion center and watch them infuse her with this toxic stuff, but we did it because the doctors were so encouraging: "You are young. We're going to give you the hardest treatment to beat this." They used a military type of analogy, and I liked that, because I read a lot of war books. Yes, we have to hit it hard, we have to go on the offense. So she had to endure a lot.

When her chemo was almost done, I had some free time. I thought it would be a great idea for me to hold a happy hour, but then my ego got involved and instead of doing one happy hour in Washington, DC, I thought, "Why don't I do 150 happy hours at the same time? What could go wrong?"

I planned it all out. The happy hours would happen not only in the USA but in dozens of other countries as well. One week before the happy hours, about the same amount of time before the outrage of the Canada talks started, the Australian media said, "Roosh, a sexist, is coming to Australia to hold some kind of happy hour." I wasn't going there, so as a joke I said that I was. "Here is my flight ticket, I'm going to show up!" Then the border control official had to do a news interview, because there was some kind of panic that I was going to enter the country, and he said, "We are monitoring the border right now. This Roosh individual will not be allowed in." Then I made a meme of me holding a stack of cash saying, "I will get in by boat." It was all just a big joke.

As the days went by, media outlets in almost every single country where I was doing a happy hour suddenly rose up and said that this Roosh fellow must be stopped. And why? The narrative that they spun was that the happy hour is going to take place with some guys in a bar and they're going to talk about girls and sports and things like that, and then they're going to drink, and then after they get a little bit drunk, they're going to go out on the streets and… rape. I'm not joking. They called all the men who were going to the happy hour "pro-rape terrorists." Hundreds of articles… "pro-rape terrorists." The same phrase showed up everywhere. Coincidence? One article called me the "king of rape." I hope a lot of you are happy to be hearing the king of rape speak in Music Town.

They started to attack my sites, to take them down, and then they doxed—I was staying with my dad at the time—they doxed my dad's address. They had articles saying that I was a rape king, leading gangs of rapists across the world, and now here is his address. On Facebook alone the dox was viewed one million times—it was one of the most viewed doxes of all time. My dad's phone started to ring off the hook—we had to unplug it. Then the emails came in. "Roosh, you are a horrible, evil person. I'm not going to let you rape the world, and I know where you live, and I'm coming to your house to burn it down." I received a lot of emails like that. "I'm on my way. I'm going to burn it down." What do you do?

I didn't have a gun, but I could hire people who have guns. I hired a bodyguard service. There was an armed man outside my dad's house 24 hours a day for one week, but it was only one guy. How about if the mob comes in a big group? How about if they come in the back door? How about if it's a SWAT team type of deal where they descend from helicopters? Could this one guard really keep my family safe? I was starting to enter a state of genuine fear. I had lost all taste. I couldn't taste food anymore. Coffee, even, I couldn't taste it, and then my appetite went after that. I only ate food because I reminded myself, "Hey, Roosh, normally you eat this amount of food every day." It was the only time in my life I had experienced this.

How could I keep my family safe when this international mob was coming after me? People were driving by the house, taking photos. There was a media van outside. I called the cops, but they did not help. When you are in danger with the mob that you don't see, the cops can do nothing.

My stepmom is Muslim. During this crisis, she was praying over her holy books, and she seemed so calm. Doesn't she know that there is a mob trying to come and get us? She looked at me and said, "Don't worry, it's in God's hands now." Don't worry?! Are you joking? No, I had to do something to keep my family safe, but I was such a wreck that I think I made them more scared.

The thing that made me feel awful and guilty is that I had put my sister, who was in the most physically fragile state that she had ever been in, in danger. Because of my actions, she not only had to worry about the cancer, but she had to worry about the mob. You could say, "Well, Roosh, you didn't know that was going to happen." Well, I should have. I was just in Canada, not even six months prior, when a huge outrage came in only two cities. I should have known that for a 150-city happy hour, this result would have happened, but my ego blinded me. I just wanted to be able to say that I did 150 happy hours at the same time.

I received some advice to do a press conference with the media in Washington, DC, and I got to call them liars to their faces. Afterwards, I did a visible exit from the USA. "Okay, everyone, I'm leaving the country, goodbye!" This actually worked, the heat on me went down, and I'm glad to say that my stepmom was right, everything turned out fine, and my sister was not hurt.

One thing I have learned since then is that the US government has something called counter-insurgency predictive algorithms. They developed this in the Vietnam War when they wanted to know if a Vietnamese man would rise up and join the communists to fight against the USA. They started to profile the men, their age, where they're from, and who they're friends with to come up with a score that would predict if they would become an enemy of this country. If a man's score was too high, we'd have to neutralize him before he tried to neutralize us. Like a lot of things that the US military does, they first perfect their techniques on their enemies abroad before applying it to their own citizens. One thing I can tell you is that all of you here have a score that the Federal government has assigned to you that predicts your threat level, and the bad news is that by attending this talk, the score of everyone here doubles.

When your score gets a little too high, they start to apply Federal assets onto you to do soft interrogations to see if you're really a threat. One example is flying into the USA. When you arrive at the airport, you go through US Customs. You give your passport and the agent asks how long you've been away and then lets you go. I don't know if this has happened to you, but one option is for the agent to put your passport into a red box and say, "You need to go to the secondary screening area where all the Afghanis are." That happened to me the first time, and I asked the Customs officer why they did this to me. He said, "It was just your turn, it's like the lottery." I thought, "Uh huh." Then the very next time I flew back to the USA, the same thing happened. I got secondary screened twice in a row, which is unheard of.

What did they ask me, you are probably wondering. Well, they were so nice. They just wanted to get to know me and where I travel to and what I do. They were really concerned about my job. One question an officer asked me was, "Do you plan to do any live events?" Why would a Customs officer want to know that, unless another agency saw my high score and wanted to find out what my plans were?

The whole goal of this scoring system is to stop the revolutionary before he knows he is one. "Hey, guys, I'm just doing a happy hour with the most masculine men in the world in 150 cities." I looked at it as a genuine happy hour where men can bond, but the powers that be saw it as potentially the beginning of a movement that could threaten their power, so they got their media partners to apply so much heat and pressure onto me that that scared me straight. I have not attempted to do something like that again because of the pain it caused me.

The seventh thing I learned in life is that you're only free until you challenge those with power, and then you'll see how free you actually are. If, right now, I grab a gay flag and go into downtown Nashville and say "Gay pride," no one is going to bother me, though here in Nashville a couple of men may say "Get away, fag!" Maybe Nashville is not the safest place for that, because I hear that the tough men here are named C-Bass, and they are prone to anger. "We don't want you here in these parts!" Anywhere else, however, I can take the gay flag and shout about gay pride and a lot of people will cheer me on. "Yeah, gay pride! This bearded man is so open-minded!" But the second I take out a canister of gasoline and then I burn that flag—we have a hate crime here. We have to call the police, videotape all the men who are with him, and if you're with me when I burn the gay flag, you're going to have to answer to your boss come Monday morning. You were part of a hate crime that the police and SPLC are investigating.

A lot of people who think they are free, well, they haven't done anything that challenges those at the very top, and if all the behaviors you do in life are completely aligned with what the elites want you to do, what does that say? Those in power are obsessed with keeping their power, and we can see the extent they go to in order to hold onto that power.

As my sister's treatment was ending, I went back to Poland to reunite with my new girlfriend, who I had been Skype calling every week. We were deepening a relationship that started in a moment of passion, but I felt that it would go all the way, and things went pretty well for a while, but then something happened.

About three weeks after we decided to be exclusive, boyfriend and girlfriend, she was in my apartment shack on the phone, speaking in Polish. I couldn't understand everything she was saying. I had taken some Polish classes, but could only pick out a word here and there. After the conversation was over, she told me, "Tonight I'm going to meet a friend for pizza."

A few hours after that, I somehow had translated the words she had said in Polish in my mind. Turns out that she was going to pizza alright, but with her ex-boyfriend, the first guy she slept with because I was the second. She lied to me. I'm the godfather of the red pill—I don't take that crap! If any guy told me that his girlfriend lied to him, I would say, "Dude, she's doing some bad things. You should dump her." I was going to follow my own advice. I met up with her and said, "I break up with you. I… break up… with… you. It's over!"

Whenever you catch a girl in a lie, she has to respond very quickly, because the longer it takes her to come up with an excuse, the more she incriminates herself. What was the excuse my beautiful girlfriend said to me? "But he is a friend!"

"No, he's not a friend of yours, he's your ex. You left that out. It's over."

But I made a mistake: I let her meet face-to-face with me where she cried and cried. I had never seen so many tears in my life in such a short amount of time, and from personal experience I can't fake tears, so she must not be able to fake tears either. Those tears are real. They're genuine and they come from a place of pain. Why? Because her love for me is deepening.

I'm looking at her crying and thinking, "She must really like me. Look at all this pain she's in. Maybe I made a mistake. Maybe it was some kind of accident." Guys, it's not like she had sex with her ex-boyfriend after pizza, right? I began to doubt that I made the right call. A few days after that, she came to my apartment with my favorite cup of coffee from the café and gave it to me with the biggest puppy dog expression I had ever seen. I looked at her and thought, "There's no way she's capable of doing wrong of any sort." So what did I do? I took her back.

I must say that this was pretty close to the meetup outrage and when my sister's cancer treatment was coming to an end. I didn't want to be alone at that time, so I took her back and hoped that things would get better, but a month or two after that there was a new problem: she kept going to that same bar I picked her up in. I had stopped going there since I had a beautiful girlfriend. Why would I still go there? I said, "I don't like it that you go there." But it was her "favorite bar." Out of 50 bars in town, it was her favorite, and it happened to be a big meat market. All her friends go there and the drinks are so cool. She argued with me that she wants to keep going there.

One night around midnight, my friend sent me a text saying, "Your girl is here, hanging out." I got fed up with it and told her that she cannot go there anymore. She cried for hours. I couldn't believe that she was so attached to this stupid bar, but I held my stance. I said, "I forbid you from going there." Finally, she agreed. This is how things should be. The man lays down the law and the woman follows it. This will work now.

Things went well after that. She seemed red-pilled. She knew of my blog and videos and she agreed with them. She would join me in mocking cold women in the USA. She even liked Donald Trump. What are the odds that I was able to meet a 22-year-old Polish girl who liked Donald Trump? It was like a needle in a haystack. She liked him and thought me liking him was something cute, but she was a little bit hesitant when I brought home a mammoth photo of Donald Trump and put it on my wall. I thought she would be more excited. She said, "Do you really want Donald Trump watching us make love?"

"Yes! I do!"

My sister's cancer treatment was done. The doctors said, "We don't detect any cancer in your body. Go and live your life as you did before," as if the trauma from dealing with cancer would make that simple.

I started to bounce back from the meetup outrage. Things were looking up, so I planned a beautiful vacation for me and my girlfriend on the Mediterranean Sea. I took her there and remember we went to a restaurant by the water. We could feel the sea breeze and there was a man with long hair playing Spanish guitar. The moment was romantic. She leaned into my ear and for the first time she said, "I love you." I loved her too. I'm so glad I took her back. I'm so glad I put up with her resistance to doing the right things.

During the trip, I took so many beautiful pictures of her with my expensive DSLR camera, and I would frame them so that she would be in focus while the background had an artistic fuzz. We enjoyed the sea, town squares, and markets. I took photos of her and then after the trip was done, I organized them, cropped them, made them perfect. I spent hours on them, because it's easy to say "I love you"—it's very easy—but showing it takes a bit more. As a token of my love, I gave her the photos.

We went back to Poland, and now we're starting to talk about marriage and family. I guess I would move permanently to Poland. Then one Sunday afternoon we were lying in bed. She was on her laptop, using Facebook. I looked at her screen and there was a profile of some guy. "Who's that?" I asked.

She quickly replied, "No one." That was a bit weird. I made a mental note of it.

A couple of weeks after that, I was looking at the local news, and there was a picture of the graduating police officer class. One-third of the graduates was petite and thin women, and I said, "These little women cannot keep the peace on the mean Polish streets." I expected my red-pilled girlfriend to agree with me, but she looked at me with a frown and said, "You think there are things a man can do that a woman can't?"

"Yes! Actually I do!"

She started arguing with me, that if she was in great danger and two petite female officers came to save her, she'd be fine with that instead of two men who were big and strong. Something was going on. This wasn't what she had shown me in the previous year.

A week after, we got into a conversation about a craze that was sweeping the United States—twerking. Does everyone here know what twerking is, or do I need to show you? It was in all the music videos, girls jiggling their butts, and I'm supposed to like it, but I thought it was dumb. Anyway, we wondered if twerking had come to Poland. I did a YouTube search and we found a video. There was a Polish girl doing something like a belly dance. I said, "I'm an expert in twerking and this is a belly dance. This is not twerking." And then I looked at my girlfriend and she said, "That really hurts me."

"What?" I replied.

"It hurts me that you're watching that girl right now."

"It's on YouTube, what do you mean?"

"No, it's disrespectful that you're doing that."

I thought, "Hmm… that's weird. Does she have some guilt bottled up from doing something wrong, and now she's trying to project it onto me?" I didn't know what it was, but something was going on.

There were a couple of other things she did that were so unlike her. I didn't get it. I was thinking, "Is she going through a bad time? Is it her school exams?" I decided to be patient.

Then two weeks after that, or maybe it was one week after, because these hits were coming in quick, there were two shocks in one day. In the first one, she said, "I signed up for a new account on the internet."

"Oh yeah, which one?"

"Instagram."

"Don't I give you enough love and attention? Now you're going online and uploading filtered photos so thirsty beta males can compliment you and you can build a following? That's what you want to do?"

She gave me the excuse that she was using it to "keep in touch" with her friends. She was talking to a man who knows what Instagram is for. She was blowing smoke up my butt. I didn't like this one bit. I knew something was going on.

She said, "I'll make my profile private."

"So all the betas can follow you privately and still thirst after you?" I wasn't satisfied.

Then she said, "Me and my friend…" and she gave the name of a girl who was her best friend. Her reputation in town wasn't very good. She actually propositioned one of my friends for a sex act in a nightclub, and that was my girlfriend's best friend. Guys, that was just a yellow flag, not a red flag.

"Me and my friend are planning a vacation to Budapest, Hungary."

"What?" I replied.

If you've been to Eastern Europe, you know that Budapest is not a place where you go to visit the petting zoo to milk the goats—it was a party town. It's a place where you go in the town square, and you get drunk with the hopes that you can drag someone back to your Airbnb.

I looked at her and said, "You're not going on that trip."

She erupted! I was holding her back!

"My friend said that you were controlling!" she said. She was arguing with me about why she must go on this trip.

I asked, "Why didn't you ask me if I wanted to go with you?"

"Because you're always busy with your work!" Work that was trying to make the money to take trips with her. She pulled out the "you're not emotionally available" card on me.

I said, "Well, guess what? I'm free. I can go with you."

Her face turned. She said, "But I told my friend I would go with her." Now I was hurt.

What happened to my beautiful, red-pilled girlfriend who

likes Trump and who said all those soothing, pleasing things to me? It was just a couple of months ago she said, "I love you." That's huge, right? No one says "I love you" unless they mean it, right? I sure wouldn't. I thought that I was losing her totally, but what should I do?

She spent the night. Things were tense.

The next day she had to do a chore in town, and she left her laptop on my bed. Now I cannot violate the privacy of my girlfriend by going through all of her texts, her messages, her... yes I can. I opened the laptop and I had access to Facebook. I got a Google Translate window ready, side by side. I'm going to learn the truth about what's going on.

I started going through her chats. People from school, that looks fine. Her girlfriends, that's okay. Wait, who is that guy? I remember this face—it's "No One." I loaded up their chat and, whooo wheee, it was long! I'm going line by line using Google Translate, and what is this, kissy-face emoticons? I didn't like that one bit.

It turned out that every time she went to her village to visit mom and dad, the first person she would get in touch with was him. "Hey I'm in town now, do you want to hang out tonight?" This happened again and again. There was one exchange where it was him that told her, "Do you remember that late night on the playground?" I sure didn't. And just two weeks before, my girlfriend said she went to the club in her village with a group of people, but there in Polish text she made plans to go to the club with him and him alone. There was no sign of anyone else going. So she lied to me again. What do I do?

I called my sister. I said, "Hey, sis, I'm having some trouble with the girl. I caught her in a lie, again, and this and that. I think I have to break with her. What do you think?"

She said, "Brother, it doesn't sound like she's a good girl." Yes, that was true.

When my girlfriend came back, I guess she was a little surprised to see that I was not happy. I said, "I found your chat. I know you've been chatting with him and you lied to me again. You went to a club with him."

She had to come up with an excuse quickly. What is the excuse now? She said, "But you knew about it! You knew I had a friend in the village and…"

"Stop, stop. I didn't know about this. I didn't know you were meeting with him every time, with kissy faces, and with the lies."

"But other people came to hang out with us in the club. I called them, really!"

"No, stop…"

I had a big blue Ikea bag. I said, "Get your stuff, and get out." But before she came back into the apartment, because I'm from the USA where men go to jail when women call the police on them, I set up a tablet to record everything. My feminine girlfriend, when I was telling her to get out, got violent. She was pushing and getting in my way. I said, "Can you push me in front of here… yeah, do it again." I made sure all the action was captured by the tablet, because I didn't know what she was going to do. When a woman is scorned, she is capable of some bad things, but not the women in this audience, of course.

I put all of her stuff in the bag, and I noticed that half of it was stuff that I had bought her. Essentially, I had to physically take her out of my apartment. From the first break-up attempt, I learned not to meet her face-to-face after that. If she wanted to communicate with me, she could do it by phone, but I can tell you, she wasn't sorry. According to her, it was my fault. I misinterpreted things. I believed in a fantasy that something was going on with this guy she was extensively talking to and meeting with. Her girlfriends were right about me—I'm too jealous and controlling.

She wasn't sorry, but she was in pain. She tried to pull the same trick from last time. She got a cup of coffee and came to my apartment with an even bigger puppy dog face than before. She looked like a pug, almost, and said, "Can I get a hug?" It is moments like this that really determine which direction your life goes. I said to her, "No."

We did talk a bit on the phone after that, and I would see her in public because our town was so small, but the relationship was done. When she realized it was completely over, she got so angry at me that she said, "Don't ever play with my heart again!" I was the bad guy.

The eighth thing that I learned, and the women in the room can close their ears, is don't believe anything out of a woman's mouth. Much of it is manipulation. Instead, look at her actions. Do the actions match the words? Then it's fine. Look at how eager she is to be a woman who is good, a woman who doesn't want to party with her friends in this town or the next, but if she's saying "I love you, I love you, I love you," yet she's out in these honky-tonk bars getting drunk on Friday and Saturday, I've got some bad news.

Do you remember all those beautiful photos I took of her? What do you think happened to all of those? They went online, everywhere. The photos I took that make her look so beautiful, as a token of my love for her, she used them to get attention from other men after me. If I meet a woman right now and she becomes my wife and one summer we go on the beach and she says, "Rooshiepoo, can you take a picture of me please?" then my answer will be, "No, I can't."

Just one month after we broke up, she found a new guy, and I'm happy to announce that she is engaged to be married to him. Good for her. But if you're a guy and you break up with a girl, I got some bad news: there is not going to be a line of girls banging down your door. That was the case with me. What am I going to do now? The game teaching in the case of breaking up with a girlfriend is to go sleep with ten other girls, then you'll get over it. I tried it out.

I went to the bars and started to sleep with low-grade girls, but it had the opposite effect because they all reminded me of the love I thought I had but lost. I had to stop because it wasn't helping. Plus the thrill of the game wasn't anywhere near my peak—I wasn't getting a buzz anymore from sex with a new girl. I wasn't on cloud nine with this cool afterglow where I felt like a king. It was more like, "Is she still in my room? How do I get her out?" Something was definitely changing. I knew that I couldn't go back to what I was doing. I needed a break from girls, so I went to the seaside. Five long days without focusing on women.

I went to the Polish seaside up in the north near the Baltic Sea. There was a lot of sand, and usually in Europe the beaches don't have that. I went to the sandy beach and I looked around and saw a lot of birds. I thought, "Cool, I want to feed these birds bread." That's how you know you're getting old. I went to the supermarket, bought a loaf of bread, then came back to the beach, opened up the bag, and started tearing out little pieces of bread and throwing them to the birds. What happened next was I created a battle royale between four different species of birds.

The first species was the pigeon, dirty birds which I'm sure you know. They were bobbing their heads, persistently going after the food. The second kind of bird was the seagull. Those were the big birds, the alpha birds that had the highest bench press out of all of them. They were dominant; if they wanted a piece of bread, you better get out of their way. The third bird was the sparrow, tiny and weak birds. Do you even lift, bro? They couldn't compete, but they were very fast. I'd be throwing a piece of bread and a pigeon was about to get it, then out of nowhere a sparrow comes to pick up the bread and flies away to eat it in peace. Wow, they were smart. The fourth kind of bird was the crow. They were patient, sitting on the outskirts, calculating, thinking how they weren't going to get involved in this thunder-dome. They waited for a clear advantage, or just waited for me to throw the bread directly at them.

The seagulls were the strongest, but they couldn't monopolize the entire bread bounty. They weren't fast enough, and there wasn't enough of them to exclude the other birds that wanted the bread too, and I made sure that every bird on that beach had a tasty bread snack. It turned out that their fighting and jockeying was a waste. They didn't have to fight. They only had to line up and wait for me to give each one as much bread as they wanted.

One thing I could do was create battles based on where I threw the bread. If I threw a piece of bread right in between a seagull and a pigeon, I could cause the seagull to rip the feathers off of another bird. I felt like a god. Then I thought, "Aren't those birds not unlike us?" Here we are, competing and fighting, but for what? Fighting for food, money, girls, to live in this apartment or that one. We're always fighting. That leads to the ninth thing that I learned.

In the dinner of life, there is more than enough for everyone. Focus on your plate in front of you instead of worrying about what everyone else has. We have more than enough food that is coming to us, but we're obsessed about what Steve has or what Stacy has. We're obsessed about his money and cars without appreciating what we have in front of us, and almost always, we have more than enough, and the food in front of us is tailored for us. Your food is for you—me trying to take it is not going to make me happy, but it makes me think I will be happier.

The second thing I learned from this is that you don't need to do crazy, exotic things to understand how the world is. I thought I had to get myself in these really extreme situations, terrifying maybe, edge-of-your-seat excitement, exotic, this mountain or that mountain, but in 2017 when this happened, the biggest lesson of the year involved buying a dollar's worth of bread and feeding it to birds, and you can find birds anywhere. A wise man once said that he could understand the entire world just by watching his back garden, by looking at the interactions of the trees, plants, insects, and birds. You don't need to go as far as you think to get an understanding of what this life is really about. The answer for you could be much closer to home than you think.

After this trip to the beach, I had hit a critical crossroads. I had reached a dead end with hedonism, a dead end with chasing after girls. I was tired, exhausted. I was tired of being obsessed with genitals. Genitals, genitals, genitals—I was tired of it. I was tired of looking at a woman and thinking about how I could get her into bed and how to get her out of bed. The pleasure I was getting, the dopamine I was getting, was decreasing. I was no longer experiencing any joy out of it. I started to see the limits of what the material world could give me.

Now I'm not a super-famous guy, but I got a taste of what the super-famous guys have. I got a little bit of the girls, the money, the travel, the novelty, the fame online, the status, people stopping you, people saying that your work changed them—I got a taste of that. Even if all that doubled, I wouldn't be two times happier. In fact, my happiness would not change. Pursuing things of the world didn't make me feel better.

The second thing that was going on around this time is that I was watching the world get more evil. They were pushing the gay stuff everywhere. I remember in 2015 when I did a talk in New York City and held a happy hour after. On the television in the bar there was an interview: "Bruce Jenner is now Caitlyn Jenner." I thought, "This is not going to catch on." Boy, was I wrong. Not only that, but they started going after kids. Now we're supposed to celebrate that an eight-year-old boy is getting injected with hormones to block him from going through puberty, changing him into a her, or vice versa. Once I saw the children being impacted, where their free will was essentially being hijacked, I looked at that and thought, "That is objectively evil." Doing this to kids, brainwashing them to make them think changing their sex is okay, is the most evil thing I've ever seen, and as I looked around, this evil was growing.

The worst news that happened is that my sister's cancer came back, and it came back in her lungs. I was in Poland at the time when I got the call. I told her that we're going to fight it just like we did the first time. I didn't make the same mistake as before by going into a bar and finding the first girl who liked me.

I booked a flight back home, and I'm ready to go through whatever the oncologists have in store, some more rounds of chemo to stop the spread of it. I was pretty hopeful, but this time the cancer moved quickly. I remember she was already on nasal oxygen when I got back. I was in charge of changing her tanks, and even though the flow setting was very high, she still complained to me that she couldn't catch her breath.

When we went to the doctors, I noticed that their attitude changed. It wasn't so much that we're going to fight and beat this like before. They said things like, "We want you to be comfortable." I didn't understand it at the time, but they weren't honest about what was going on. It was a game to read between the lines of what the doctors were saying.

Unfortunately, my sister died. I can tell you that I didn't know what to do. Nothing in life had prepared me to deal with losing my sister. The only thing I did was that I started to wear her cross. We were baptized in the Armenian Church as kids. I had a belief in God, but I didn't have the faith. I didn't pray, I didn't think that things were operating according to God's will or plan. I was lost. I was lost even before this, but now I didn't even know how to live.

After a couple of months of being with my mom and dad, I went back to Europe to figure things out. I tried to read these secular books on grief, but they didn't help. I started to develop a daily drinking habit just to numb myself for one or two hours, but as soon as the alcohol wore off, the pain would come back. I hate to admit it to you all, but the only way I knew how to feel good was to sleep around, so even after she died, I tried it. I went to the bars, brought home some girls, but it became very clear that I couldn't do this anymore, and it's not something I even wanted to do. I would go to the clubs but feel disgusted with myself.

When your family is healthy and everything is fine at home, you can travel and have fun—it feels like a great thing. But when there is a missing piece in your heart, when a huge amount of meaning is lost, doing those things seem utterly pointless. Why am I even here in Europe?

The months carried on and I continued with live streams. When the camera was on, I could put on a show and make you laugh and provide entertainment, but once the live streams were over, I was back in that same pit, without any more knowledge of what to do or where to go.

Eleven months after she died, I was in Warsaw, just hanging out. I suddenly felt the urge to pray, an urge I had never experienced before. I didn't understand it. Up to that point, I thought praying was treating God like a genie in a bottle, where you make a wish for a million dollars, a Lamborghini, a hot girl, and you hope that the wish comes true. I made up a prayer that I thought sounded good—"Please God, help me endure this pain." I didn't do it in a formal, proper way, but when I would wake up in the morning, I would say the line and it was done.

Not long after that, something I had said on a live stream went viral. I said, "Obsession over butts is a gateway to homosexuality." Seven million people saw it. All the gays were writing to me saying, "No, Roosh, you're gay, you're in the closet." Because if you ever disagree with a gay, the reason is that you are gay. Then girls started to send me photos of their butts to prove me wrong.

One girl went above and beyond. She sent me a video of herself playing with sex toys. I thought it was custom porn for me, so what did I do... I masturbated. Then the urge to pray totally disappeared.

I moved to another Polish town a few hours away. The urge to pray came back and it was stronger than before. I thought that I had better take it seriously. I went online and Googled "how to pray" and found OrthodoxPrayer.org. I printed out the prayers. I must tell you where I was at the time: the same city as 2011 when

I had the highest notch count year, and actually the very same apartment. I couldn't pray by the bed because of all the filthy things I had done on it, so I prayed by the couch instead.

One night I got on my knees and started to read the prayers. I didn't fully understand what I was saying, but a short while into the prayer, tears started coming down my face, and they wouldn't stop. I wasn't sad, but now with the tears, I started to feel sad. I finished the prayer, and the next day I felt like a burden had been lifted. I wasn't as sad as before. I continued to pray.

Initially, I asked for advice on simple day-to-day things, and I was getting answers back. The first thing I asked is where I should live, because what was the point of living in Europe if I wasn't going to sleep with women? Was I going to stay there only for the coffee and the tasty croissants?

I asked God, "Where do I live? What do I do now?" The next day, the name of a city popped into my mind, and the city is only two hours to the west of where my parents live in Washington, DC. I had never been there before, but I had heard of it. I went online and learned about it, including how much it costs to live there and the political situation. Everything checked out. It was a conservative place, and after this tour is done, I plan to find a place to live that is close to it.

Other answers came from people. As the weather warmed in Poland, all the women began to dress in a sexy way, and I couldn't help but look at them with lust. I asked God to help me: "Please take these women away. Cover them up." Then the next day, my dad got into a conversation with me. He said that when he was young, a spiritual elder told him that even if a naked girl is in front of you, you do not see her. I thought, "Why is my dad talking to me about girls? He never does. Wait, isn't that what I asked God about?" There I learned that I have to use my willpower to control what I see. I have to maintain custody of my own eyes, because I can't change what every other girl is doing out there.

When I started to come out and tell people I was a Christian, many started getting angry. They accused me of lying, or trying to become a Joel Osteen with dreams of owning a private jet and yacht. Even some people who were close to me were doubting it. My mom, when she heard that I watched a documentary on being a monk, freaked out. She said, "You're going too far into this!" Maintaining her level of faith was fine, but anything past that was bad. I asked God, "What should I do about people who are not on the same spiritual path as me?" I wanted people closest to me to be somewhat on board. I asked this during prayer and hoped to get an answer in a day or so, since answers were coming back from other people. This time, the answer came back right away from the right side of the room. I could feel where the thought came into my mind, which I had never experienced before. The three words that came to me were, "Patience and love." Yes, this is what I have to do and what I have been doing, and I must say that when I pray, the icons are in front of me and Jesus Christ is on the right.

Nonstop coincidences were happening. One example is when I watched an old video online about spiritual warfare. It was a great video and the next day I met up with a friend and asked him, "What did you do last night?" It turned out that he watched the exact same video as me nearly at the same time, out of billions of videos on YouTube. What are the odds? So the tenth thing I learned is to humble yourself before God and ask Him for help, and He will help you.

One answer I didn't get from God is to the question of what happened to my sister. Why did she die? She was the good one while I was the bad one. I was the one hated by tens of thousands of people around the world. She lived with my mother and didn't even do 1% of the bad things that I did. Why was she taken away so young, at the age of 31, while her older brother is allowed to continue?

In Poland at this time I had a friend from the UK. His name is

Albert. He has done every drug known to man and survived to tell the tale. He was like a human experiment. He had been pushing me to try to magic mushrooms for a couple of years, but I don't do drugs. I tried pot a couple of times but didn't like it. I would do coffee and alcohol, but that's it. "No thanks, Albert, I don't want your drugs."

After my sister died, I went online and a few sites stated that mushrooms could help with grief, and so on. Two or three weeks after I had started to pray, Albert said it would be a good time to try it because the weather is warm, and he wanted me to take it outside. So on the first warm day of spring this year in Poland, in March, we went to a park and there we found a little encampment that was about 30 yards away from the main path, and he handed me 1.8 grams of the mushrooms soaking in lemon juice. I gobbled it down. I trusted Albert completely.

We sat and talked for a while. I noticed that the trees were starting to sway back and forth, unlike I had ever seen before, not in response to the wind or to birds landing on the branches.

I said, "Albert, is it just me or are the trees moving?"

And he said, "It's just you."

The trees started to move, but everything also started to have a movement to it. The ground, the forest floor, felt like a moon bounce. It was spongy. I looked at Albert and said, "Albert, I need to find solid ground." I walked to the asphalt path, and remembered asphalt as hard, but when I walked on it, it was as soft as this carpet. I thought, "Hmm... this is kind of weird. Well, let me sit on this bench and watch the people for a little while."

I told myself, "Alright, Roosh, act normal. Don't act high." But I didn't know how to act. Do I put my hands on my legs? Do I cross my legs? When people walk by, do I maintain eye contact with them? Do I smile at them? Do I wink? Do I say, "Hi! How are you doing?" Do I turn away from them? All the questions that I don't have to answer when I'm sober—suddenly knowing how to treat other people in a socially acceptable way was difficult. I didn't know how to sit in a way where I didn't look like a freak. Then I saw a kid pull up his mom's shirt and I thought it was the funniest thing ever. I started to laugh at it, and knew I couldn't be around other people.

I went back to the forest encampment and I said, "Albert, I can't find solid ground."

He laughed and said, "Isn't that a metaphor for life?"

I didn't get it at the time.

Then Albert offered me a second dose of the mushrooms, another 1.8 grams. I said, "Well, I'm tolerating this drug pretty well. Yeah, sure!" I didn't know it at the time, but the full effects of the first dose had yet to hit me.

I got hungry. I took out a roll of bread and bit into it. When you take a bite of bread, it expands back, and when it was expanding, I stared at it. The bread was creating a new world of nooks, crannies, stalactites, and little holes. "I made this—I created a world that has never existed before and will never exist again!" I had the bread right at my face, admiring the beauty that I had made.

I said, "Albert, I'm glad that no one is staring at me."

"Actually, they are."

People on the path were glancing at me. I turned away, so I couldn't see them, thinking that if I couldn't see them, then they couldn't see me, because I wanted to continue admiring the bread. It took me 15 minutes to eat it.

I took out other pieces of food and ate them slowly to examine their patterns. I had a pen and paper to take notes and watched the ink dry on the individual paper fibers. I thought, "Wow, this is so cool." Then I wiped my hands with a napkin and threw the napkin away, but it caught my eye. I held the crumpled napkin up in front of my face and thought, "This is a beautiful rose!" I examined it carefully. All the folds appeared to be perfectly made by a Japanese origami master. It was perfect! It was made in a deliberate way—that's how beautiful it was. I thought, "I'm going to save this napkin forever." I don't know where the napkin currently is.

I examined the trees some more. The branches moved quickly, but even if you stared at the tree trunk, that would move too. There was a movement in all things. If atoms move constantly, shouldn't there be movement in everything? Right now you can see the podium in front of me and think that it's solid, since it doesn't move, but if it's made of atoms that move constantly, the way we see it is filtered. The podium not moving is a filter, along with the chairs and so on, because if we saw the world for how it is, just taking a walk down the street would be difficult. "Whoa! Look at that and look at this!" Our brain filters out things for our own good so that we complete the mission we are tasked with in this life.

My friend Albert wanted to show me a video online. The video's name was "Jewish ASMR." I don't know if you've seen it before, but it's a video of a man dressed up as a rabbi. He takes out two coins and then rubs the coins against each other next to the microphone and says, "This is for the tired goyim to help them sleep." Then he took out a $100 bill and started rubbing that bill against itself. It created a soothing noise. Under the influence of the mushrooms, this was the funniest thing I had seen in my life. I laughed and laughed. I was crying with laughter.

I closed my eyes and that's when the trip took a different turn. I was staring at a tree, but when I closed my eyes I could still see the outline of the tree, and beside the tree was a skeletal framework. Was something holding the tree up? I opened my eyes and said, "Albert, there is no empty space!" Because how could there be with all the molecules and electromagnetic waves in the air. I told Albert that I think there is a lattice holding everything up.

Albert replied, "How can a lettuce hold everything up?"

I was talking, but my voice started to feel disconnected. It felt like it was being played back to me from a speaker. Do you remember the first time you heard your voice on the phone? You may have been thinking, "Do I sound like that?" This is how it was for me. I was talking, but my voice was not coming from me but outside of me. I was speaking gibberish, pure nonsense. I wasn't adding any value at all, so I stopped talking. Then I looked on the asphalt path and saw an African pimp in a red jumpsuit with four Asian girls. I told Albert.

He said, "You must be high." But when he looked at the path, he saw the same thing. "There really is a black guy with four Asian girls!"

The point is that I don't think I saw anything that wasn't there or that wasn't an amplification of what is there. I do think that matter—some scientists say it exists as a wave—has a movement to it.

Once the second dose hit me, that's when the trip completely changed. I closed my eyes, and for the first time, I could hear my breath. I could hear the air coming into my nose and going inside my lungs, and then coming back out again. This concerned me, because I had to focus on my breath. It took more energy to breathe than normal. I focused on the breath for a bit, but it made me feel uncomfortable. When I opened my eyes, the sound and difficulty stopped.

I thought to myself, "Well, Roosh, you've spent your life always analyzing things, trying to have outcomes go your way, scared of bad things happening, wanting to control the situations that you found yourself in, and always having a plan. How far has that gotten you? What do you have right now? You don't have much at all." I decided to go with it.

I closed my eyes again and the breathing got very hard. I almost chickened out a second time, but I decided to stay with it. I'm breathing, focusing, hearing the air go in and out of my lungs. That was happening for a while. Then the sound of the air stopped. I thought, "Hmm... that's not good." I tried to open my eyes, but I couldn't. Now I'm starting to get concerned. As if waking up from a bad dream, I tried to move my arms and kick my legs as fast as I could, but I couldn't move anything. I had no control over the body, and at that time I thought, "I'm not in my body anymore." But where was I?

Then I heard a *whoosh* sound and traveled somewhere else. I was in a different realm. I don't know how I could tell you, but I felt that I was in a place with no time or space. It wasn't in our solar system, but some place different. It was just a void, black totally. At this point, you would think that I would be freaking out, but I felt completely calm, serene. I had no concern over being back in the body. I didn't miss the earth. I didn't think of all the things that I have here. I just felt totally at peace.

Then a gray dome appeared before me. At the bottom of the dome was a white light. I looked at the light and instinctively felt, "This is home. This is where I'm from and where I'm going back to." I felt so at ease. I wanted to go towards the light. When I tried to do so, my eyes opened and I was on the forest floor, curled up into a ball. I took a deep breath and tried to speak to Albert about what I had just seen, but I couldn't talk. My chest felt heavy and tight.

I whispered, "Albert, I saw it!"

"You say what?"

"I saw the source!"

"You saw the sauce? What type of sauce? Ketchup?"

I remembered that Albert was still high, so I got up to get away from him. I found a tree trunk and sat down to understand what I had just seen. When was the first warm day of the year in Poland when we took these mushrooms? It was the exact one-year anniversary of when my sister died. I sat on the tree trunk and started to figure things out. I began crying.

Albert would often wear a Make America Great Again hat. He came up to me, and in an attempt to console me, he handed me the hat and said, "Would this hat make you feel better?"

"No, Albert, get away from me!"

Before I tell you what I think I saw, I have to say that anytime someone has a vision, you're going to apply your own biases, judgments, and experiences. Sometimes you just see what you want to see. What I believe I saw is that in some way God killed me to show me where my sister's soul went, and allowed me to be born again on the forest floor for a second chance at life. At the minimum, I can tell you that I saw that the soul is distinct and separate from the body.

I thought this experience I had was very common. Maybe everyone who took mushrooms saw this kind of thing, but I talked to people who did take it, in addition to going online and reading stories, but they didn't have the same experience I had. One experience that people have is the out-of-body experience where they kind of leave their body and can see themselves from above. The other experience people have is the ego death experience where their consciousness and being melds into the environment around them and they feel that they don't exist anymore, which seems terrifying. Maybe I had a little bit of that when I felt that my voice was being played back to me. The closest I can tell you to what I experienced was a near-death experience.

I went back to Albert and we moved locations to a more quiet area of the park. He offered a third hit of the drug. I declined. I already received the information I needed. He did take the third hit.

While he was doing his thing, I paced back and forth. I had so many questions. My mind wanted to understand this experience and how the world really was, and I'm lucky that a lot of men have since helped me answer a lot of questions I had, but there was one question that I needed an answer to at that time.

I walked up to Albert and I knew I was taking a chance, because by this time he had taken off his shirt and wrapped it around his head like a turban. He had a big stick and was bashing the trees with it, yelling at the trees for the crimes they had committed. I thought, "Man, Albert is gone, but I have to ask him this question anyway."

I looked at him and said, "Hey, Albert, why did God make this world? He didn't have to do it. He didn't have to give us all of this. Why did He?"

Then Albert stopped bashing on the trees. He looked at me and said, "And leave us hanging out there in space?" And he went back to bashing on the trees.

The last thing I learned in life is that this world is a gift from God, and when you are done here, you go back to Him.

One other thing I learned from this experience is that there is nothing to be afraid of in this world. Imagine this man in the front row right now comes up to me with a gun and says, "Roosh, I'm going to shoot you!" I would tell him, "You cannot hurt me. You can hurt my body, but you cannot hurt my soul. Only I can hurt my soul with the decisions that I make."

Since humbling myself before God and starting to pray, everything has changed. My whole mental orientation has changed. My moral compass has changed. It turns out that in the inverted world we live in, I was living a life that was inverted too. By turning to God, He lifted me up and inverted back to where I should be.

There are many ways to look at what happened to my sister, but based on the path of my life, I think my sister was a sort of sacrifice to save me, because my pride was so high that only losing the most important person in my life could humble me enough to seek out God.

One thing I can tell you is not to use drugs. Drugs are not a shortcut. In my case, it affirmed the path I was on but didn't create the path, so if you take this drug thinking you'll have the same experience, you will be disappointed, and some people take a drug like this and go down a more dangerous occult path. Be careful. I don't intend to ever use this drug again.

Last thing I want to share. While on this trip, I was asking

God what He wants me to do. What is my mission? Because now I will have a lot of free time, since I don't have to go to the bars or clubs to meet girls. I had a dream the day before my New York City talk in late June. In this dream, I was driving a yellow school bus. There were a couple of guys who were already on the bus. I was driving and then I see more guys on the side of the road that I have to pick up.

I stopped the bus and the guys got on. I wondered, "Where am I going?" I put the bus in park and walked outside. I looked at the front of the bus. There was one word: "Heaven." So I think I know a bit more about what I have to do.

Each day is hard. Things got easier in some ways and harder in other ways, but now I'm filled with a sense of purpose. I don't see things as hopeless as they were before, so I hope that the lessons and stories I shared with you today help you experience this gift of life, too. Thank you very much.

For more of my writing, visit my web site:

http://www.rooshv.com

Made in the USA
Columbia, SC
06 March 2021